Major Account Sales Strategy

Major Account Sales Strategy

Neil Rackham

McGraw-Hill, Inc.
New York   San Francisco   Washington, D.C.   Auckland   Bogotá
Caracas   Lisbon   London   Madrid   Mexico City   Milan
Montreal   New Delhi   San Juan   Singapore
Sydney   Tokyo   Toronto

Library of Congress Cataloging-in-Publication Data

Rackham, Neil.
  Major account sales strategy / Neil Rackham.
    p. cm.
  Includes index
  ISBN 0-07-051114-4
  1. Sales management. I. Title
HF5438.4.R33 1989
658.8'1—dc19   88-8038
                                           CIP

SPIN is a registered trademark of Huthwaite, Inc.

      19 20 DOC/DOC 0 9 8 7 6 5 4

ISBN 0-07-051114-4

*The editors for this book were Martha Jewett and Linda Mittiga, the designer
was Naomi Auerbach, and the production supervisor was Richard A. Ausburn.
This book was set in Baskerville. It was composed by the McGraw-Hill
Publishing Company Professional & Reference Division composition unit.*

Printed and bound by R. R. Donnelley & Sons Company.

This book is printed on recycled, acid-free paper containing a minimum of 50% recycled de-
inked fiber.

Contents

Box Titles

Preface

Some years ago I was working with the senior sales management team in a division of Xerox. Our task was to develop a sales strategy for an important new product. As the team assembled for our first meeting, one of the participants asked me, "Is there some strategy round here for getting a cup of coffee?" His use of the word "strategy" took me by surprise for a moment and reminded me of how easily a word can become abused. If a word had the right to sue for defamation of character, then "strategy" would be making its lawyers rich. My thoughts led me to put a question to the group. "What do we each mean by the word 'strategy'?" I asked. "Are we sure we mean the same thing?"

The first reply came from a member with an interest in military history. "Strategy," he explained, "is the big picture. It's what the general does. It's overall planning. It's setting out the grand design, unlike 'tactics,' which means putting the design into action—thinking on your feet." This view prompted another member of the group to ask, "Would you say, then, that we managers should set the strategy and our salespeople should be concerned with the tactics only?" "I'd go further than that," said the military historian. "Only the generals should set strategy. Middle-level officers should be concerned with tactics. The troops should execute the tactics, not decide them. Salespeople—and even junior sales managers—have no business meddling in strategy."

There was a murmuring of disagreement and then the most senior member of the group spoke. "I suppose you'd say I'm the general here," he began, "but I don't feel happy about unilaterally setting strategies. Selling doesn't work that way. It's the salesperson who's there in the account who should be in the driving seat. In fact, I believe that the role of a senior management group like ourselves has little to do with strategy. We set the *constraints*—things like pricing, availability, targets, and so forth. In terms of strategy we're just a support function. It's the account representative who should be responsible for forming and executing account strategies."

A third member of the group, trying to avoid potential conflict, offered a different perspective. "The military model is too restrictive a way to think about sales strategy," he suggested. "I'd define strategy in selling as working smarter, not harder. We've got to be smarter about our overall sales planning and support. That's what sales strategy means for senior managers like ourselves. But we've also got to be smarter about how we use our people and how we set account goals and plans—and I believe that's what strategy should mean for our sales supervisors." Seeing that the group was responding well to his point, he added, "But, above all, we've got to be smarter about how we handle individual major accounts. And that's strategy for salespeople—finding better ways to influence key customers."

There was a chorus of approval and the discussion moved on to other areas, leaving me well-satisfied with the answers to my question. In particular, I was pleased most of the group recognized that sales strategy wasn't the sole province of top sales management, but was a vital part of sales success at all levels. Unfortunately, that's not a universally accepted view among senior sales management, and I was glad to hear it.

Another thing which cheered me was the emphasis group members placed on strategy at the key-account level. Over the years I've sat through many discussions of grand overall strategic approaches to the marketplace. All too often, these discussions are very convincing and satisfying to the generals, but, when the elevated ideas get down into the trenches, they don't translate into actions which advance the sale. Everything I've seen in 20 years of studying selling has convinced me that unless strategy can be readily translated into specific actions within individual accounts, then it's just empty jargon. I've seen many a failed strategic sales plan, full of high-sounding phrases like "increase industry penetration by 20 percent through selling total systems, not individual boxes." When I've questioned the authors about exactly *how* a salesperson is supposed to act differently in order to execute such admirable intentions, I've generally received blank stares. Sales strategies rarely fail because of their noble grand intent. What usually brings them crashing is a dismal failure to think through their implementation at the account level. The success of a sales strategy lies in understanding how to relate it to individual accounts and individual customers.

In this book I'll be discussing strategy from an account perspective. I'll be down in the trenches with the troops, not up on the hill with the generals. For people like our military historian, who define strategy in strictly military terms, I'm probably not a true strategist. At best I would be a tactician. But if you take a less traditional view of strategy, if you believe that individual salespeople and their managers are the key to successful sales strategies, then you'll know that it's what happens in the trenches which decides whether strategy succeeds or fails. It was no less an expert than Napoleon who said, "Strategy is a simple art; it's just a matter of execution."

There's very little material, published or unpublished, to help you with the down-in-the-trenches approach to executing a sales strategy. In contrast, there's no shortage of grand strategic advice for the generals of the selling world. Admittedly, much of this advice is called marketing—which sounds more dignified than selling and is therefore more appealing to would-be generals. But as Jon Katzenbach of McKinsey puts it, many fine marketing plans sit on the shelf because nobody has answered the question, "How will this plan make our salespeople behave differently with their customers?" That's an excellent question. And coming up with an answer is one of the most pressing issues facing major sales forces today.

In this book I'll be sharing research findings with you and offering some models and methods that help to answer Katzenbach's question. I'll be looking at the customer's decision process and at how to form an account strategy which positively influences the decision. The various pieces of advice I'll be offering will have one common factor. Without exception, they will focus on the *account* and the customers within it. Too many sales strategies seem to forget the individual customer. They focus on the product or on the sales force. If the purpose of a sales strategy is to influence customers, then it seems logical that a good strategy must begin with a thorough understanding of the decision process from the customer's point of view.

My thanks to the talented team here at Huthwaite who made this book possible. In particular, thanks to Dick Ruff for helping me work through some of the difficult issues around competitive strategy, to John Wilson, who advised me on the negotiation chapter, and to Joan Costich, who suggested the book in the first place. But, as always, the greatest thanks must go to the many thousands of salespeople who, over the years, have generously allowed us to watch them in action. Through their willingness to share their sales calls with us we have evolved and validated the ideas in this book.

Neil Rackham

1

How Customers Make Decisions

Whether we're talking about an overall strategy for a market, or a specific strategy for an individual account, selling strategy is about customers. The measure of an effective selling strategy is how well it succeeds in influencing customer purchasing decisions. If we assess a strategy's success by its impact on customers, then it follows that the better we understand the customer decision process and how to influence it, the better our strategy will be. What counts is the customer. Selling strategies that ignore the customer, or that don't take sufficient account of customer behavior, will be likely to fail. That's why the central focus of this book is on understanding customer behavior. We'll be using research studies and cases to explore the customer decision process and to show you how it changes during the course of a major sale. As we'll see, different selling strategies succeed at different phases of the selling cycle. The strategy that works best during the early stages of the sale may become ineffective as the selling cycle progresses.

It's all too easy, in major sales, to let your selling strategy get weighed down by procedures and techniques. We've seen many account strategies collapse because they became so complex that they forgot the basic fact that decisions are made by *people*. All people, whether influencers, decision makers, purchasing agents, or evaluation committees, normally go through distinct psychological stages when they make decisions. By understanding these stages and how to influence them, you'll find it easier to form practical account strategies that have a positive effect on your customers. Effective strategy begins with an understanding of how people *buy*. The strategies you develop as a result of adopting the buyer's perspective are a powerful way to guide your actions through difficult competitive sales.

I've become very cautious about strategy models that focus exclusively on how to *sell*. Many of the clients who have come to us at Huthwaite for advice on increasing their sales productivity have shown us elaborate models of the selling process. These models are usually in the form of a series of *selling* steps they require their salespeople to take. A typical example might have selling stages like *prospecting, qualifying, fact-finding, presenting, proposing,* and *closing*. Each of these stages represents an activity that the *seller* is required to perform to execute the strategy. Generally each stage is also associated with paperwork the seller or sales manager must complete.

We usually find ourselves giving two pieces of advice. The first, simply, is to reduce the paperwork. In some organizations salespeople spend up to 10 hours a week completing paperwork in the name of selling strategy. Much of this time is unproductive; much of the information is faked to a point where it's an unreliable guide for management action. A measure of the health of a sales organization is the amount of time it spends relating to *customers* compared with the time it takes relating to the internal needs of the company. By this measure many organizations are sick, and we've seen some that border on the terminally ill. So our first piece of advice is usually to cut the paperwork.

Our second piece of advice is to build a selling strategy that focuses on the steps the customer takes in making a decision, not on the steps the salesperson takes in making a sale. The two are not the same. As we'll see in future chapters, strategies based on the selling process are usually far less effective than strategies based on the buying process. Our problem, as salespeople, is that it's far easier to understand the steps of selling than those of buying. And it's far more dangerous, because we tend to base strategy on what we understand, rather than on what's effective.

The Research Base

Before we examine each of the stages of a buying decision, let's briefly consider the origin of the ideas covered in this book. I wish I were writing as a sales genius who had decided to share with you my unique insights on selling strategy. Unfortunately, I'm not. Let me confess: I'm not a sales strategist, I'm a voyeur. I've spent many years watching other people sell. I've directed research teams that have studied more than 35,000 sales calls in 27 countries. With my colleagues here at Huthwaite, I've watched the behavior of over 10,000 salespeople. We've studied many markets where strategy is paramount. In the computer markets we've worked with IBM and Digital, in telecommunications with AT&T and GTE, in banking with Citicorp and Chase Manhattan, and in the business equipment markets with Kodak and Xerox. From the mass of data we've collected from these and many other corporations that Huthwaite has worked with, we've been able to draw conclusions about customer behavior and how it changes during the sale. These conclusions, we believe, can have profound implications for account strategy.

Our research uses a method called behavior analysis. At its most basic, it involves watching sales calls and counting how often sellers or customers use certain key behaviors. This allows us to build statistical models that show how particular behaviors are associated with sales success. The behavior-analysis method has allowed us to bring sound research principles of experimental psychology to the complex and subtle art of selling—an art that has stubbornly resisted objective analysis. As far as I know, our team at Huthwaite is the first group of researchers to use these behavior-analysis methods as a tool for understanding selling and learning how to make it more effective.

The Customer Decision Process

We said earlier that the customer decision process in a major sale normally progresses through distinct stages. Three of these stages take place before the decision, and a fourth stage happens after the decision has been made. These stages are usually visible even in simple sales. Think about your own purchasing decisions—buying a car, for example. How does your decision process begin? If you're completely satisfied with your present car, then there's no decision to be made. The decision process begins when you no longer feel totally satisfied. You begin to perceive problems with your car. Perhaps it's getting old, or it's less reliable, or it doesn't look as good as newer models—for whatever reason, you feel dissatisfaction. You're now in the first of the three phases of the buying decision, which we call *Recognition of Needs*. During this stage, you move from minor irritation to real dissatisfaction, and then finally to a point where you decide you're going to do something about it. Once you've made the decision to act, you leave the first stage of the buying process and move into the second, *Evaluation of Options*. In the Recognition of Needs stage, your chief concern is, "Do I need to do something about my present car?" Now, in the Evaluation of Options stage, your concern becomes, "What are my choices? Do I fix my existing car? Do I lease or buy? If I buy, then which one? How do I choose between the competing models?" This stage normally begins with a confusing array of choices and options. As it continues, you become increasingly clear about the option that suits you best. Finally, you settle on the option that you feel fits your needs better than any other option. Let's imagine you decide to buy a good quality used car that you've seen in the showroom of a local dealer.

Once you've arrived at this clear preference, you're moving into the final psychological stage of the purchasing decision. We call it the *Resolution of Concerns* phase, and, as we'll see, it can be one of the most significant and complex stages of any decision. During this stage, although you've decided you need to change and this car is the best of the options you've considered, you may nevertheless feel reluctant about going ahead. You think about things like "What if there's some hidden defect I haven't discovered?" "How will I tell the family I've decided to spend all this money?" or "Is their after-sales service really as good as they say?" Until you've overcome these fears you won't be ready to move ahead to make the final decision.

The process I've described in buying a car would probably apply equally to any purchasing decision where (1) the decision is made over a relatively long time period, rather than in a single meeting or sales call; (2) there are competing alternatives to choose from; and (3) there are penalties or risks if you make a bad decision. So buying a can of beans in a supermarket isn't a decision that goes through the three stages because, even though there are competing alternative brands, the decision is usually made immediately and has negligible penalties if you've made the wrong choice. However, most of the major purchasing decisions we make as individuals *do* go through the sequence of Recognition of Needs, followed by Evaluation of Options, and finally Resolution of Concerns. The whole customer decision process, including these phases, is illustrated in Figure 1.1. Think about the last time you made any large buying decision, such as the purchase of a house. You can probably remember each stage, how it felt, and how, as a buyer, you had different preoccupations at each point.

The same stages are present when one of your key accounts is making a major buying decision. First, people in the account become dissatisfied with the existing situation and begin to recognize a need to change. During this Recognition of Needs phase, the most effective selling strategy, as we'll see in Chapter 3, is to uncover the source of dissatisfaction and to increase the customers' perception of its intensity and urgency.

Once people in the account are agreed on the need to change, the sale moves into the second stage, the Evaluation of Options. During this phase the account is weighing the various options and their merits. Sometimes this involves a formal procedure with written specifications,

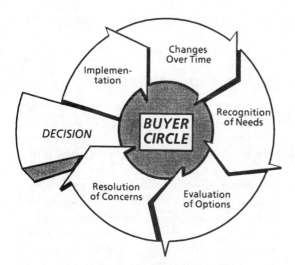

Figure 1-1. The customer decision process.

a proposal process, and an evaluation committee. At other times the procedure may be loose and relatively informal so that only one person needs to be convinced of which option is best. In either case, your optimum selling strategy during this stage of the sale is to influence in your favor the criteria the buyer or buyers are using to evaluate available options. We'll be looking more closely at how to do this in Chapters 4 and 5. Finally, when there's a consensus in the account on which options adequately meet their criteria, the third and final decision phase, the Resolution of Concerns, begins.

In this final phase the buyer may show great anxiety about the risks of going ahead with you and your product. As we'll see in Chapter 6, sometimes these concerns are expressed openly to you. However, that isn't always the case. Often the issues that arise during the Resolution of Concerns stage may stay hidden or may be expressed in the "respectable" form of price issues. A good selling strategy at this point in the sale must find a way to uncover and resolve fears and concerns of this kind. It's here, in the final stage of the sale, that you are likely to be pressured to negotiate special terms or to make some additional concessions to get the business. In Chapter 7 we'll examine strategies for effective sales negotiation.

Next comes the decision. In smaller sales, once the decision is made your selling ends. That's not normally true in major sales. There's usually a stage of *Implementation* when you continue to support and help the account after the sale has been made. During this stage there are some interesting sales opportunities that many people miss. We'll see in

Chapter 8 how to take account of these opportunities in forming an effective post-sale strategy.

Phases of the Purchasing Decision

Early in our research, I asked Fred Mostyn, of British Petroleum, Central Purchasing, to describe the stages of a typical purchasing decision he would handle. At the time we had not worked out the three-stage model of purchasing decisions, so neither Fred nor I knew how closely his answer would compare with our findings. Here, with our stages in italics, is his description of a typical purchasing decision.

"There's not exactly a standard procedure, but I suppose that most new purchases—where we don't have a routine order with a supplier—begin because someone in the organization has a problem which he or she can't solve with existing equipment or supplies. Either that or there is dissatisfaction with something like quality or delivery. (*Recognition of Needs*)

Next we get a phone call or a request from a department. We discuss things and try to form a specification with them. We find out a list of 'musts' and 'nice-to's.' We help people think objectively about how to make a cost-effective decision. Then we go to look at various vendors. (*Evaluation of Options*)

If it's a big decision, we send out a formal request for proposals. For smaller decisions the method varies quite a lot. Anyway, when we've found our short list—which might be one, two, or possibly three potential suppliers—we look at each one carefully to check their references, their financial stability, their ability to deliver, and so forth. We don't want to take unnecessary risks, and so this checking out process can be important, especially if we feel concerned about the supplier." (*Resolution of Concerns*)

Why the Stages Matter

The research project that first gave us hard statistical evidence that sales fall into the stages I've just described was carried out across 13 of the Xerox operating companies in Europe. For the first time we had the evidence we needed for a customer-based model of account strategy. It was an important discovery because we knew in theory that a good strategy model had to be customer-based, not seller-based. Unfortunately, until the Xerox results were available, we didn't have enough information on the psychology of the customer decision process to enable us to build a valid customer-based model.

Like most other people who worked in sales, the researchers at Huthwaite knew a lot more about selling than we did about buying. We could produce strategy models of how to sell; in fact, we had produced several of them. Each of these models had been based on the relatively conventional steps of the sale as described from the selling point of view. First you prospect, then you refine your prospects into suspects. Next you make approach calls to collect data and find facts. You then make sales presentations. Then you propose. Then you follow up your proposal, and finally you close.

There's nothing intrinsically wrong with this kind of strategy model based on selling steps. But increasingly we felt uncomfortable with our own selling-step models because we didn't think they helped answer important questions about customer buying behavior and how to influence it. For us, the Xerox research was a breakthrough. Since then we've worked to develop those germinal findings into practical methods and strategies for increasing the probability of sales success at each of the decision phases.

Account Strategy in the Recognition of Needs Phase

We said that during the first phase of a purchasing decision, people in the account are recognizing a need for change. This need usually begins as dissatisfaction with existing methods, systems, products, or suppliers. During this phase customer dissatisfaction grows until it reaches a critical mass. When dissatisfaction reaches a sufficient level of intensity or urgency, the account makes a decision to change.

The most effective selling strategy during this phase is to uncover dissatisfaction in the account and to develop that dissatisfaction until it reaches the critical mass. Few people would quarrel with developing dissatisfaction as the main strategic objective in the early stages of a major sale. It doesn't need a massive research project to show that dissatisfaction is necessary for change and that the vendor who can effectively uncover and focus dissatisfaction has a strategic advantage over competitors. The objective of our research was to discover exactly *how* successful salespeople create and develop customer dissatisfaction. Our first finding was simple but crucial. Successful people ask a lot more questions during sales calls than do their less successful colleagues. We found that these less successful people tend to do most of the talking. They become involved in product discussion very early in the sale. Frequently, they give presentations as a means of generating customer interest.

What does this mean for account strategy? As we'll see in Chapter 3, effective strategy requires that in the early part of the Recognition of Needs phase you hold back on product discussions and presentations. Instead, an effective strategy concentrates on developing dissatisfaction. Our research found that successful salespeople have some very powerful methods for developing dissatisfaction. In particular, they use questioning sequences that not only help the customer discover and articulate dissatisfaction but also intensify any dissatisfaction which the customer already feels.

Account Strategy in the Evaluation of Options Phase

Once the customer's dissatisfaction has intensified to a point where the account takes a decision to act, we enter the second phase, the Evaluation of Options. During this phase, the customer's attention turns to making choices. Successful account strategy during this, the most competitive part of the selling cycle, centers on understanding, influencing, and responding to customer decision criteria. As we'll see later, effective salespeople are able to change the way in which customers evaluate their products or services. It's particularly important in this phase of the sale for your selling strategy to differentiate you clearly from your competitors.

A common fault in selling strategy during this phase is failure to recognize that a shift has taken place in customer concerns. As a result, salespeople continue to behave as if they were still in the Recognition of Needs phase, uncovering customer dissatisfaction and developing needs. I had a clear personal illustration of this the first time I bought a computer system for one of my companies. We had decided we needed a comprehensive system to handle a number of specialist data processing needs. We were using cumbersome semiautomated methods that were so expensive that it was clear that a new system would pay for itself in less than a year. We therefore decided to move ahead urgently, so we agreed on an outline specification that the new system would have to meet, and we invited several vendors to visit us to find out whether any of their systems was what we were looking for. In other words, we were no longer in the Recognition of Needs phase—we'd already decided our need was urgent enough to justify changing our system. We were firmly in the Evaluation of Options phase. Our main interest in meeting the vendors was to make a *choice* through getting a better understanding of how well each vendor met the tentative specification we'd set.

The first seller we met spent a couple of hours trying to convince us that our present system had many costly disadvantages and that a new system would give us all kinds of benefits. If we'd been in the Recognition of Needs phase it would have been a very effective piece of selling. She certainly uncovered our dissatisfaction with the present system. If she'd called on us a couple of months earlier I would have been deeply impressed. Unfortunately for her, I was no longer in the Recognition of Needs phase. I *knew* the existing system was unsatisfactory. What I wanted to know was how to choose between her system and the three others that we were considering. At the end of our meeting, all I had on my notepad was her name, the name of her company, and half a dozen very elaborate doodles. The same story was repeated with the next two salespeople.

The following day we met the final salesperson, who was from IBM. He began by saying, "It's very confusing choosing between different systems. So I'd like to begin by looking at some of the factors you should consider to help you make the right choice." He had our attention. This was what we'd been waiting to hear. Unlike his competitors, he'd understood that we were in the Evaluation of Options phase. Our concern was with making choices, and we were attentive and impressed when we met someone who understood what we were going through. Needless to say, we bought the IBM system, even though we suspected that it was underfeatured and overpriced.

What's the moral of this story? Three of the four salespeople lost a potential sale because they made the elementary strategic mistake of not recognizing which phase of the customer decision process we were in. Yet each of them sold in the correct textbook manner. They each worked to uncover our needs and to make benefits. But, like untold thousands of unsuccessful salespeople, their failure to match their selling strategy to the buyer's decision process cost them business. In contrast, the IBM representative adapted his selling strategy to take into account where we were in the decision process, and, consequently, made the sale.

Of course, it's not always that simple. In our case we didn't have clear or fixed criteria for differentiating between the alternative systems. Consequently, until the seller helped us, we lacked an adequate basis for making a decision. We were typical of the less sophisticated customer who is a first-time buyer. When customers frequently buy in a particular market, the opposite problem can exist. Instead of lacking purchasing guidelines, or criteria, the buyer may have criteria that are all too clear and fixed. The purchasing agent who buys repetitively in a market and for whom price is criterion number one, number two, and number three, would be an example. As we'll see in Chapter 4, even in cases like this there *are* selling strategies for influencing, and even radically changing, criteria that are apparently rigid and inflexible. But you can't set about influencing or changing a buyer's criteria unless you know what those criteria are.

Failing to Uncover Decision Criteria

John C. sold industrial control systems. One of his key products was about 5 percent more expensive than an equivalent product sold by his main competitor. However, John had learned to justify his slightly higher price by showing that his product had certain desirable technical features which his competition lacked. When he and his competitor each made a bid for equipping a new factory, John was told that the purchasing committee had been impressed by the technical features of his product. He therefore confidently expected to get the order because he felt able to justify the price difference. He wrote a proposal showing that his technical superiority more than compensated for his modest price premium, and he made a presentation to the purchasing committee which focused on the same message. He was astonished, a few weeks later, to hear that his competitor had been given the order.

Several months afterward he was having lunch with a member of the committee, who told him, "We were sorry not to give you the order, but your competitor could deliver the system in six weeks and you said it would take twelve. Delivery was our number one criterion, even though we liked your product better." "But," John protested, "I could have delivered the system in *five* weeks if I'd known it was that important to you. I only suggested twelve weeks because I thought it would take you at least that long to get the site ready for installation."

John's mistake was that he assumed he understood the committee's decision criteria. Like so many salespeople in the Evaluation of Options phase, he lost because he acted on the decision criteria he incorrectly believed were the most important ones. In contrast, his competition won because they had found the crucial criterion and used it to their advantage.

The most common strategic error that salespeople make in this phase of the sale is that they don't try to uncover the customer's guidelines, or criteria, for making the decision. In consequence, they don't know how to differentiate themselves from their competition or how to emphasize those things that will have greatest impact on the customer. This is clearly illustrated in the above case, where failure to uncover the customer's criteria for making the decision resulted in a lost sale. What's worse, as both seller and customer realized afterward, the seller's failure to uncover customer decision criteria resulted in a suboptimal decision for the buyer. When we examine the Evaluation of Options phase more closely, we'll look at a range of useful techniques for uncovering and influencing decision criteria that are an essential part of effective selling strategy in this crucial and competitive phase of the sale.

Account Strategy in the Resolution of Concerns Phase

Once the account has assessed competing alternatives, the sale moves into its final phase, the Resolution of Concerns. In this phase, last-minute fears and concerns arise that can block the decision or cause customers to reopen discussions with competitors. Sometimes this phase is a nonevent. For example, you might be a long-term supplier with an excellent reputation in the account. Because the customer knows that your product meets needs well, you've gone through the Recognition of Needs phase without difficulty. During the Evaluation of Options phase, people in the account remain convinced that your product is better than alternatives. In circumstances like these it's quite possible that your customer has no concerns to resolve. You may be able to move straight from Evaluation of Options to the final purchasing decision.

Unfortunately, these ideal circumstances are rare. In a complex sale it's unusual for any vendor to meet all needs perfectly. During the Evaluation of Options phase it's uncommon for one vendor to stand out so clearly from all others that the choice is a foregone conclusion. A more usual outcome, at the end of the Evaluation of Options phase, is for the customer to feel that, in making a choice between imperfect solutions, one vendor is *on balance* preferable to others. In these circumstances it's not surprising that customers feel uncertain about whether they are making the right decision. If a customer feels that a decision is risky, then selling strategy must take this into account. An effective strategy, as we'll see in Chapter 6, must uncover and help resolve perceived risks. A dangerous strategic error, as the next case study illustrates, is to hope that perceived risks will somehow resolve themselves. They don't. People who are successful during this phase of the selling cycle are the ones who work to uncover and resolve issues that are troubling the customer—even if these issues are uncomfortable and difficult to discuss.

Ignoring Customer Concerns

I was told this story by Ann Rivers, a partner in a local accounting firm. For a year she'd been in discussions with a manufacturing company that wanted help in overhauling some of its financial control systems. She knew that the company had also been talking to one of the large big eight accounting firms, but she felt confident that she would win the business.

Just before the final decision she had a meeting with her prospective client. The client was less friendly than in earlier meetings and raised a number of minor issues about her proposal. She dealt with each issue well, but she was left with an uncomfortable feeling that the client was still unhappy about something. "Shall I try to find out what's wrong," she thought, "or would that be dangerous? Perhaps it would be better to ignore his behavior and just hope it goes away." Sure enough, after bringing up another couple of insignificant issues, the client stopped raising objections. Ann was relieved. "I did the right thing," she told herself. "If I'd tried to find what was troubling him I might have opened up a whole can of worms."

When Ann heard that she'd lost the business and that the company had decided to go with the big eight firm, she went back to see the client. "We very nearly chose your firm," he told her, "but we were concerned that a small firm like yours might not have the level of experience we needed. We discussed it for hours, but, in the end, we felt it was safer to go with a larger firm." Ann was stunned. Her firm was especially well qualified in this area and would have been ideal for the client. "Why didn't you tell me you were concerned?" she asked. "I nearly did," the client replied, "but I felt awkward about raising issues over professional qualifications."

Ann lost the sale because she didn't understand one of the basic strategic rules for handling the Resolution of Concerns phase of the sale: it's more dangerous to ignore signals of customer concern than it is to explore potential concerns and get them out into the open.

Later chapters will explain several strategies you can use to uncover concerns and to assist the customer in resolving them. Sometimes, at this stage of the sale, negotiation becomes an important selling tool. The customer may wish to negotiate special terms as a condition of going ahead, particularly over issues of price or delivery. There are some clear rules about successful sales negotiation, as we'll see in Chapter 7.

Most people make the mistake of negotiating too early in the selling cycle. And, frequently, negotiation turns out to be an unexpectedly costly strategy for getting the business. Nevertheless, sales negotiation can be a powerful tool if it's carefully used.

Account Strategy in the Implementation Phase

It's easy to take a naive view of selling that suggests that once the decision is made, the selling job is over. That's a dangerously limited way to think about selling or account strategy. Very few major sales stop when the customer signs the contract. The majority of sales involve implementation, installation, after-sales support, or some other continuing contact with the customer. The period *after* the decision is one of the most fertile areas of sales opportunity. In Chapter 8 we'll discuss some strategies for using the post-sales period effectively.

A Summary and a Look Forward

In this chapter we've covered some basic points that we'll be looking at in more depth throughout the book. We've said the following:

- Sales strategy should be about customers and how to influence them. It therefore follows that the better you understand customer behavior, the easier it will be to form an effective selling strategy.

- Customer behavior goes through three distinct phases in making a major purchasing decision. These phases are summarized in Figure 1.2.

- After the decision, there's usually a fourth phase of Implementation, which is a neglected area of selling strategy but one which, if it's well handled, can generate significant additional sales opportunities.

- Each of the four phases requires a different set of strategies and skills. A seller can be very effective in handling one of these phases, but may not be skilled at another.

In the chapters which follow, we'll examine in turn each phase of the customer's decision process. We'll put forward strategies that we've seen

Decision Phase	Typical customer concerns during phase.	Sign that this phase is over and the next one starting.	Common strategic errors in this phase.
Recognition of Needs	• Have we a problem? • How big is it? • Does it justify action?	Customer accepts that the problem is severe enough to justify change and therefore decides to take action.	• Failure to investigate / develop customer needs. • Making product presentations too early.
Evaluation of Options	• What criteria should we use in making a decision? • Which competitor best meets our criteria?	Customer has a clear decision mechanism in place and has used it to select 1 or more final contenders.	• Failure to uncover customer's criteria. • Little attempt to influence/change stated criteria.
Resolution of Concerns	• What are the risks of going ahead? • What if it goes wrong? • Can we trust these people?	Customer makes the purchasing decision.	• Ignoring concerns in the hope they'll go away. • Pressuring the customer to make a decision.
Implementation	• Are we getting value from this decision? • How quickly will we see results?	New needs and dissatisfactions arise.	• Failure to treat implementation as a sales opportunity. • Failing to anticipate vulnerable implementation points.

Figure 1-2. Phases of the purchasing decision.

successful salespeople use to positively influence each phase of the decision. If there's one theme throughout the book, it's this: Effective selling strategy isn't about grand design, and it isn't about clever tricks. It's about thoroughly understanding your customers—knowing the concerns your customers will have at different phases of the sale and understanding how to respond to those concerns effectively.

2
Account Entry Strategy: Getting to Where It Counts

I was discussing strategies for selling professional services with a group of tax partners in one of the big eight accounting firms. We were talking about the first part of the customer decision cycle—the Recognition of Needs phase. "When you're selling tax-related services," I asked them, "what's the hardest part of this phase?" I confidently expected that the partners would offer replies such as "getting a consensus of needs when several different people are involved in the decision" or "getting customers to see that the need is urgent enough to justify action." We had found that people generally have real difficulty handling issues such as these. I was surprised when the group agreed that, for them, the hardest part of the phase was getting in the door in the first place. "It's not so bad once you're talking," one of them said, "but the problem is how do you get face-to-face with a potential customer?"

Back at the office I talked this over with my colleague Dick Ruff. "Perhaps professionals like accountants are reluctant to get the sale started," I suggested, "because they don't like to knock on doors." Dick had been working with major-account sales groups in the capital goods area, and he had a different perspective. "It can be a problem in any major sale where one of your strategic objectives is to get new accounts," he said, "and it's a severe problem if there's no established purchasing function for the thing you're selling." I wasn't clear what he meant. "Explain that bit about 'established purchasing function,' " I asked. "Sure," said Dick. "Suppose you manufacture a product which you want to sell to retail stores. It's not too difficult to get into face-to-face selling because every store, or every chain, has a purchasing function and has buyers whose job is to talk to people like you." "Yes," I agreed, "the strategic selling issue there is how you *persuade* buyers, not how you get in to see them." "But," Dick continued, "suppose you're trying to sell something for which there's no purchasing function. For example, suppose your company has invented a machine which recognizes people's voices. You decide to sell it to banks because, if a customer phones the bank wanting to make a transaction, your machine could be used to check the authenticity of the customer's voice, which would prevent fraud. Now, who would you go to in the bank to sell your machine?" "If it prevents fraud," I suggested, "you'd go to the head of security." "And what do you do," asked Dick, "if the assistant to the head of security says, 'We can't help you. Dealing over the phone with customers is the responsibility of Customer Service; we don't have a budget for things like that'?" "Then you go to customer service," I replied. "And when you get there," said Dick, "they say, 'Oh no. Customer Service doesn't have any capital budget for security equipment. Sorry.' That's what I mean by 'no established purchasing function.' Nobody in the account is responsible—or has any budget—for buying the thing you want to sell."

The Purchasing Channel

I had to admit that Dick had an excellent point. How do you begin the sales cycle when there isn't a defined purchasing channel for the things you're trying to sell? The classic answer to getting started in a new account is that you would normally first meet *gatekeepers*—people whose job is to filter potential vendors and to allow entry only if the vendor has something to offer which the account might want. Gatekeepers, as the name suggests, are strictly people who are able to impede your access or make it difficult for you to gain entry. They influence the access decision, but they don't positively influence the purchasing decision. Suppose you're successful in getting past gatekeepers; then, traditional theory suggests, you are next likely to meet *influencers*—people like assistants, technicians, users, and advisers. Influencers don't have the power to make decisions, but, as the name implies, they exert a significant influence. Finally there are *decision makers*—individuals, or groups of individuals, who have the power to place an order for your product.

The *gatekeeper, influencer,* and *decision maker* models, and their more sophisticated variants such as those developed by Webster and

Wind (*Organizational Buying Behavior*, Prentice-Hall, 1972), are useful when there's an established purchasing channel. But models based on well established acquisition channels are less useful when your product or service is innovative or new to the customer. As Dick Ruff's voice-recognition machine example illustrates, the model breaks down when the customer doesn't have a purchasing process ready and waiting for your product. Without a purchasing channel, getting into the account does, indeed, become one of the hardest tasks in the selling cycle. The one crumb of good news is that you meet fewer gatekeepers because the account isn't being pestered by salespeople offering similar goods and services.

Where's the Decision Maker?

Although gatekeepers can present a real difficulty for the inexperienced salesperson, they are a minor impediment for reputable and tenured salespeople. Consequently, it's not strategically important that there are generally fewer gatekeepers involved in the purchase of innovative products and services. What *is* important on a strategic level is the absence of decision makers. "My problem," said the vice president of a consulting firm, "is knowing who can make the decision out of the dozens of people I talk to in a potential account. What selling strategy means to me is a systematic way to search the haystack until I uncover a needle."

We've tracked sales of innovative products where as many as 15 sales calls have been made to a single account in order to uncover the decision maker. Worse, we've seen cases where—after months of frustrating effort—the seller has legitimately concluded that *nobody* in the account is a decision maker for the new product.

Entry strategy is further complicated by the irritating habit of some customers of pretending that they have decision-making authority when they don't. Their numbers seem almost exactly counterbalanced by people who probably *could* make the decision, but find all sorts of ways to disclaim any decision-making responsibility. I remember an Australian communication-systems sales manager in Melbourne who expressed the frustration of many salespeople in language too poetically explicit for me to repeat exactly. "It doesn't seem fair," he protested, "when you've worked your tail off to get to the decision maker and the first thing the bastard does is say that he isn't able to make the decision. It's even worse when, in order to get there, you've wasted months in the account sweating blood, selling to stinking crooks who swore blind that they had the authority to sign the order, and then you find they've no more power than a mosquito's hindquarters."

The Elusive Decision Maker

Neil R. (you may be able to guess his identity) had invented a computer-tracked method for sales managers to coach their people during sales calls. Tests showed that the method brought significant productivity gains so Neil was hopeful that his better mousetrap would not only meet with a positive reception but would also create substantial sales for his company.

First he called on sales-training managers, because they seemed the obvious purchasers for the new system. But while the sales trainers were generally impressed, they explained that they had no control over field sales management. "This system would alter the work patterns and priorities of our sales supervisors," one of the trainers explained, "and sales training can't make that decision. You'd better talk to line sales management."

When he'd heard this story enough times, Neil changed his strategy and began to approach senior sales management. They too were generally receptive on a theoretical level. "But," the typical sales manager would explain, "you're talking to the wrong people. This is a coaching program. It's a *training* decision. We don't have a budget for something like that."

Finally Neil decided he should be talking to a higher level in the organization where training and sales came together under one individual—usually the V.P. of Marketing. It was harder to gain access to these elevated individuals, but Neil succeeded in getting to meet a number of them. Their story was much the same. "Great idea," said one, "but don't bother *me* with it. I'm too far removed from the sales supervisor position to assess whether it's practical for this company. You should be talking to sales management or training."

This wasn't the easy sale Neil had hoped for. Like many other optimists who devise new products and services, he hadn't realized what a terrible disadvantage it can be when there isn't an established purchasing channel for your product.

Entry Strategy

So how *do* successful people create an entry strategy which gets them economically and efficiently to the real decision maker even when there isn't a defined purchasing channel? We questioned successful salespeople from a variety of innovative market sectors such as consulting, state-of-the-art technical systems, and specialized financial services. These people had all demonstrated their ability to track down the elusive decision maker. We were looking for a pattern. How did they get to the decision maker? Were there some rules which would help other salespeople who were still struggling to find the right entry strategy?

We found considerable variation in the approaches adopted by these successful people. But one pattern did emerge with some consistency. Successful people tended to seek a *sponsor*—an individual within the account who helped them, advised them, and, if necessary, represented them in places where they couldn't gain access. This was hardly a new discovery. For years writers on selling have been emphasizing how much easier it is to penetrate both new and existing accounts if you have political support on the inside. So it wasn't surprising that a common factor in successful entry strategies was the identification, cultivation, and utilization of a sponsor. Often, rather than rely on an individual person to act as sponsor, successful salespeople would try to find a particular function or area of an account to sponsor them. They would find a *focus* within the account—a person, a committee, or a department—who would help them move toward a point from which they could begin developing needs. For example, they might go to the personnel department to obtain sponsorship which would give them access to the training department. Or they might ask a scientist to sponsor them in order to get in front of the Engineering Evaluation Committee. In really complex sales, it was common to find successful people using several different sponsors, or focus points, to help them penetrate the account.

The Three Focus Points of an Entry Strategy

From our observations and discussions, it was clear that an account had three different focus points where successful people could find sponsors. As Figure 2.1 illustrates, these points were:

- *The focus of receptivity*—the point in an account where there were receptive people who were prepared to listen sympathetically
- *The focus of dissatisfaction*—the point in an account where there were people unhappy with the present system or supplier
- *The focus of power*—the elusive point in an account where there were people able to make the decision

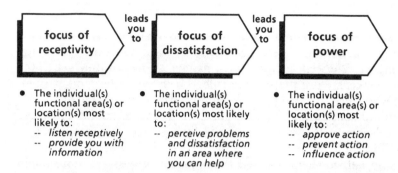

Figure 2-1. Entry strategy. Sometimes one individual may hold more than one of these sponsor roles.

Although we initially developed this model specifically for entry strategy to accounts where no purchasing channel existed, we found—as we'll see later—that its ideas can also be helpful in gaining entry to a wide range of major accounts.

In simpler sales, it's common to find that one individual customer can cover all three focus areas. In such cases, where a single individual is receptive, has a problem you can solve, and has power to make a decision, then entry is relatively easy. In more complex accounts, the three focus areas tend to involve different people and functions—the most receptive person may not have a problem, or the person with the problem may not have authority to make the decision.

The Focus of Receptivity

If you're trying to penetrate a new account, the easiest starting point is usually to find a receptive individual or function—somebody who's prepared to listen. It's here, at the focus of receptivity, that you'll be most likely to discover your first sponsor. People may be receptive for a whole variety of reasons. They may, for example, be interested in the technology which your product uses. They may have had previous good experiences with your products or services. Or they may just like to keep up-to-date with what's available.

It's important to be clear about your objectives when you approach people at the focus of receptivity. Calls to people who are purely receptive—which is a way of saying that they are not dissatisfied and they don't have decision power—tend to be most successful if your strategic aims are to **find out information** about the account and the people in it and to **gain access** to others in the account who are located at the focus of dissatisfaction.

Entry Strategy Made Easy

A neighbor of mine, Mary J., is in the desktop publishing business. One day, on a plane, the man next to her noticed that she was reading a brochure on laser printers. "I've not seen that printer before," he remarked, "and I'm very interested in laser printers." Mary found that her traveling companion was office manager of an industry association located in her territory. "We're sending out newsletters every week," he told her. "They're expensive and time-consuming to produce—and they look awful." Further questioning revealed that he was returning from an industry meeting which had just voted him a six-figure budget to improve his newsletters. By the end of the flight, Mary had set up a demonstration. Three weeks later she had the order.

She was lucky. She happened to meet a single individual who combined the three prerequisites for a successful entry strategy—*receptivity, dissatisfaction,* and *power.* Her traveling companion was interested in new developments—so he was *receptive.* He was also unhappy about his newsletters—which meant that he had *dissatisfaction* which prompted him to look for a change. Finally, he'd just had a budget approved so he had the *power* to make a purchasing decision. It's rare, in major sales, for all three characteristics to be found in a single person.

The Dangers of Receptivity

A receptive person is ready to listen—and that's sometimes dangerous. When you're talking with someone who's a willing listener, a show of interest can easily be misinterpreted as progress. You feel you're moving forward in the account, even when you're actually standing still. There are three common dangers to watch out for when you're selling at the focus of receptivity: danger of distraction, danger of misinterpretation, and danger of presentation.

- *Danger of distraction.* Above all, receptive people can distract you from other more profitable activity. It's comfortable to talk with someone who's prepared to listen, which means that you're likely to continue calling on a receptive source, even if the sale isn't getting anywhere. That's why it's so important to set yourself clear objectives which will help you make progress in penetrating the account. In calling on a receptive person, your strategic objectives are *information* and *access.* If you're not getting either, don't let yourself become distracted. It's easy to make too many calls to the focus of receptivity because of the comfortable reception offered you.

- *Danger of misinterpretation.* Don't confuse the individual with the account. Because you're meeting with receptivity from one person, it doesn't mean that you'll get an equally positive reception in other areas of the account. In general, those at the focus of receptivity are more likely to welcome you than those at the focus of dissatisfaction or the focus of power. Many salespeople get inflated expectations from talking with those at the focus of receptivity. This can make their sales strategy unrealistic and lead to disappointment when they finally move to the focus of dissatisfaction or power.

- *Danger of presentation.* If someone's prepared to listen, then you'll be prepared to talk. A common mistake at the focus of receptivity is for the seller to do all the talking—in effect, to turn the discussion into a presentation. This is particularly true if the receptive person is interested for technical or professional reasons. He or she may have many detailed questions to ask you. It's easy to fall into the trap of spending the whole meeting presenting or answering questions, only to discover at the end that the customer's found out all about you and you've found out nothing about the customer. If you let that happen, you've wasted an opportunity. One of your strategic objectives for making a call to the focus of receptivity is to find out information which will help you to sell. If you've allowed yourself to become a presenter, not a seeker, then you've not met an important call objective.

The willingness of receptive people to listen and to make positive noises of approval can seduce even the most experienced salespeople. Most of those we questioned admitted to at least one potential customer whom they called on again and again just because they were given a warm reception. Lulled by receptivity, they often thought they were making progress. I've a client like that in New York. He's always delighted to see me, always tells me how wonderful my work is, always writes me a note afterward saying what a good meeting we had, and, yes, he even buys the lunch. It's taken me several years to realize that I'll never sell one single cent of business to him because he doesn't have any problems which I can solve.

Moving from Receptivity to Dissatisfaction

We found that salespeople who had a successful entry strategy frequently started their penetration of an account by finding a receptive person or function. Their objective was to use this focus of receptivity to gain them access to a person or function where there was a probable cause of dissatisfaction. They would ask the receptive person questions like "Do you know anybody in your company who's experiencing problems in this area?" "Would you introduce me to them?" or "You've agreed that this is a useful product—which departments in your company could benefit from it?" In this way, they used the focus of receptivity as a stepping stone to get to the next level—the focus of dissatisfaction.

Salespeople with less successful entry strategies concentrated on impressing the receptive person. They behaved as if the individual they were talking with could make the decision. Sometimes they were lucky—they found they were talking with someone who was not only receptive but who also had *dissatisfaction* with existing suppliers or systems and had the *power* to do something about it. But, as we've seen, these three roles are rarely combined in a single individual. More often than not, their selling effort stopped at the focus of receptivity.

The Dangers of Receptivity

An engineer whom we'll call John C. left his employer to start his own company. His first task was to build business, so his initial strategy was to call on customers he'd known in his previous job. Because John was an excellent engineer with a very good reputation in the industry, these customers were generally delighted to see him. John couldn't have asked for better receptivity. Many of the customers he called on even invited him to lunch—which he took as a real sign of interest. What's more, they asked his advice on all sorts of technical and engineering issues, so that John felt he was building credibility which, ultimately, must lead to business.

Six months later, John was still calling on the same people. They were still receptive and they still bought him lunches, but nobody was giving him business. John was talking with the wrong people. Receptivity—in isolation—doesn't lead to business. You must also have *dissatisfaction* and *power*. The people John sold to weren't dissatisfied. They didn't have any problems in areas where he could help. John's mistake was to believe that receptivity alone is enough to gain entry. If he'd been more experienced he would have used the focus of receptivity to lead him to the focus of dissatisfaction—he would have questioned the receptive people to find out who in the account had dissatisfaction in areas where he could help. But, like so many technical specialists, John was happiest talking to those who were interested in the technology—that's where he started and that's where he stayed.

It's worth asking why it's so important to find the focus of dissatisfaction. Put simply, without dissatisfaction, there's no basis for a sale. A customer who genuinely feels totally satisfied doesn't need you. Needs begin with dissatisfaction. Looked at another way, you could define a product or service as a solution to a customer's problem. If you sell telephones, you are solving communications problems. If you sell cars, then you obviously solve problems of transportation—but you may also be solving more subtle problems of image, status, and ego gratification. By solving problems you remove the source of dissatisfaction. Thinking of products in problem-solving terms is an important mind-set for successful selling. It's one of the most visible differences between successful and less successful salespeople.

The Acapulco Product Launch

I had a clear example of how successful people think differently when I was invited to a product launch in Acapulco a couple of years ago. The company was a major financial services corporation, and it was introducing some important new product offerings to its sales force. I remember that after the product launch there was a big dinner to give out awards to the company's top salespeople. The top performers were all sitting together at a table near the stage, and I'd been placed with them. I listened with great interest as they discussed the new products. Everything they talked about was in terms of the problems these products could solve for customers. They said things like "One of my customers has a cash flow problem and I think this product could help" or "I've a customer who's very dissatisfied in this area and up to now we've not had a product. This could give me something positive to offer."

Later in the evening I circulated to other tables and sat with a group of inexperienced salespeople. They too were discussing the products. However, their talk was very different. As far as they were concerned, customer problems hardly entered into the conversation. Most of their discussion was about product details like "How will the 30-day credit process work?" or "What's the refund procedure?" It was clear that the inexperienced people were focused on the product, while the superstars focused on customer problems and dissatisfactions.

Identifying the Focus of Dissatisfaction

In terms of entry strategy, thinking about products in problem-solving terms is a useful mind-set because it automatically leads you toward the second of our three types of sponsors—the focus of dissatisfaction. If you're going to be successful in penetrating the account, there must be some person, group, or function with dissatisfaction in an area where you can offer a solution. As we've said, successful people use receptive contacts in the account to lead them to these sources of dissatisfaction. Because they think of their products in problem-solving terms, they are always on the lookout for dissatisfactions they can resolve.

Searching for Dissatisfaction

The facsimile market is competitively tough, and more salespeople fail in it than succeed. One success we know is Wayne Davis. His company introduced a mid-priced fax machine aimed at the mail rooms of small- to medium-sized companies. Unfortunately, partly because of strong competitors in this sector, overall company sales were disappointing. However, Wayne was very successful. His sales were so far ahead of anyone else's in the sales force that his management decided to find out what he was doing differently.

When questioned, Wayne explained, "You told us to sell this product to mail rooms, but I found I wasn't getting anywhere because most mail rooms were happy with equipment they already had. So I asked myself, 'Who else might have a problem which this new machine could solve?' I figured out that most sales organizations of small companies had branch offices with just a couple of salespeople, a secretary, and a telephone. They didn't have fax machines. So I asked them questions about things like whether they were satisfied with how long it was taking at the moment to get an urgent proposal in front of one of their customers, through the mail. Most of them hadn't thought about using fax as a sales tool, so it was an easy sell. The more they thought about it, the more dissatisfied they felt about not having a fax machine."

Wayne's success was the result of uncovering new sources of dissatisfaction. He realized that his organization's marketing strategy, aimed at mail rooms, didn't bring him into contact with the focus of dissatisfaction. Unlike most of his colleagues, who continued their unproductive visits to mail room customers who weren't dissatisfied, Wayne went to areas where he could find and use dissatisfaction.

Successful people's orientation toward dissatisfaction will often lead them to look at an account in a different way. During our research, I often asked salespeople to identify the individuals in an account who were most important to sales success and to tell me why those people were so important. Less successful people would usually pick out either those who were receptive or those who had power. They would say, for example, "Ms. Anderson's important because she's always willing to listen" or "The key person is Dr. Martin because he's the one who can make the decision." Top salespeople would also pick out receptive individuals and decision makers—customers who, in other words, were the focus of receptivity or the focus of power. However, their descriptions were more likely also to include customers who were at the focus of dissatisfaction. They would say, typically, "Kurt Johannsen is crucial because he's the one that the problem is hurting most" or "Joan is upset with the existing supplier, so she'll be important in this sale."

Influencing the Focus of Dissatisfaction

It's no coincidence that successful people pay so much attention to the focus of dissatisfaction as the cornerstone of their entry strategy. Our studies of sales success have consistently demonstrated that the ability to uncover and develop dissatisfaction is the most important of all selling skills. In the next chapter we'll look more closely at exactly how successful salespeople develop dissatisfaction. For now, let's just observe that it's here, at the focus of dissatisfaction, that the real selling begins.

Essentially, there are two strategic objectives for sales calls to individuals or departments at the focus of dissatisfaction. These objectives are to:

1. Uncover dissatisfaction and develop it to a point where the customer wants to take action, and
2. Use the dissatisfaction you've developed to gain access to the decision maker, either directly or by using your sponsor to sell on your behalf

Notice how these objectives differ from those for sales calls to people at the focus of receptivity. Remember from our previous discussions that calls to individuals who are purely receptive are likely to be more successful if they concentrate on finding out information about the account and the people in it (rather than developing dissatisfaction) and gaining access to the focus of dissatisfaction (rather than the focus of power).

Developing dissatisfaction is particularly important if you're selling innovative products or if there isn't a defined purchasing channel. But, even where there's a tightly structured purchasing process, it can be very helpful to find and use the focus of dissatisfaction. I recall traveling with a very successful salesperson from a division of Exxon. He was

A Premature Power Play

Pat M. was a bright, brash, and aggressive young capital goods sales rep. He'd been taught in business school that you should always start at the top. Because he was well educated—and very well connected—he found it relatively easy to set up appointments with decision makers in his customer's organizations. He congratulated himself on his ability to get to the focus of power. "Why waste time in the gutter when you can go straight to the palace" was his way of describing his entry strategy.

Despite the fact that Pat had a level of access which most salespeople would envy, his sales record was mediocre. Although he could get in front of decision makers, he didn't know enough about an organization and its problems to make a compelling impact once he'd gotten there. Consequently, he didn't know how to relate his products to needs which the decision maker was experiencing. Because of this, he was frequently turned down, until finally he realized that he was running out of contacts so he'd better use them more carefully.

He changed his strategy. Instead of trying to *convince* decision makers, he would briefly describe his products and then ask if the decision maker would introduce him to someone lower down in the organization who might have problems which the products could solve. Pat would then promise to find out all he could from the people with the problems and then come back to the decision maker with a recommendation. At first Pat had high hopes that this would be successful. He had gained access to people at the focus of dissatisfaction—the people with the problems—plus the promise of a return meeting with the decision maker. Unfortunately for Pat, he found that when he came back with his recommendations, many decision makers were no longer willing to see him. A typical response from the decision maker's secretary when he phoned for the return appointment was, "Mr. Smith says he's too busy to meet with you right now—please put your thoughts in writing, and he'll pass them on to the appropriate people."

Pat's mistake was that he went straight to the focus of power without adequately preparing himself in advance by talking to people at the focus of dissatisfaction. As a result, in his first meeting he didn't have any powerful ammunition to impress the decision maker. Remembering that the first meeting had been such a nonevent, most decision makers didn't want to see Pat a second time.

selling commodity chemicals to the purchasing agent of a manufacturing company. On the call I observed, he was trying to persuade the buyer to specify Exxon as a supplier. The buyer was using a competitor who was generally cheaper, and consequently he felt no pressure to change. The Exxon salesman, being a good strategist, had understood that his only chance of entry was the focus of dissatisfaction. So the previous week he'd visited chemists in the plant and uncovered considerable dissatisfaction with the competitor's product due to inconsistent specification and delivery. During the meeting he was able to persuade the purchasing agent to call one of the chemists to check that there were delivery problems. Because of that conversation, Exxon became listed as a supplier. As the Exxon seller said afterward, "Unless you've an unusually good price, you've got to have a friend in the account if you want to influence a purchasing agent. And the best friend is the person who's having the most problems with your competitor."

Moving to the Focus of Power

We've said that there are two strategic objectives in making sales calls to the focus of dissatisfaction. The first of these is to intensify the dissatisfaction—and in the next chapter we'll see how this is done. The second objective is to use the focus of dissatisfaction to help you identify and reach the focus of power. As we saw earlier, identification of the decision maker can be a serious problem. It's difficult, if not impossible, for a person outside the account to tell who has, and who doesn't have, decision power. At the focus of dissatisfaction you'll find the people in the account who have the most incentive to change things. And, if you've done a good job of developing their dissatisfaction, they will be your strongest allies in finding who can—and who can't—make the decision to acquire your products and services. This can be invaluable for the efficiency of your selling effort.

We were once involved in selling to Citicorp a massive project which affected the operation of more than 20 of their major business units. It would have taken us years to find all the people who needed to be involved in the decision, and, because Citicorp has such a decentralized decision-making structure, we couldn't have moved ahead without the decision approval of upwards of 40 different people. If we'd been left to ourselves we'd still be stumbling around trying to find the focus of power. Fortunately for us, we had sponsors at the focus of dissatisfaction. They were three people who were so determined to change things that they brought their decision-making colleagues together in groups so that we could quickly and efficiently get the message to them. The decision was made in a matter of weeks. Without the active intervention of these people from the focus of dissatisfaction, the selling cost of such a project would have been astronomical and the selling cycle never-ending.

Selling at the Focus of Power

Life would be simple if, once you'd reached the focus of power, all you had to do was convince the decision maker and take the order. In major sales, as we've seen, that's rarely going to be the case. The decision maker may be in the Recognition of Needs phase, the Evaluation of Options phase, or even the Resolution of Concerns phase. And, as we've also seen, each phase represents different psychological orientations and each of them therefore requires a different selling strategy. The rest of the book deals in detail with these phases and how to handle them. For now, I'd like to make just one general point about selling at the focus of power. It's difficult to gain access to decision makers—so don't waste it. Why am I offering such obvious advice? Because, from our studies of many thousands of salespeople and their customers, we found that one of the most frequent of all selling faults is wasted access to decision makers. Among the common ways in which salespeople waste their access, we found the following to be the most prominent.

- *Failure to do homework.* Sellers often waste most of the call collecting facts which could have been obtained from company reports or from those lower in the organization. If decision makers are asked routine questions like "How many people do you employ?" they become bored and then impatient.

- *Failure to take control.* Many sellers, when they come face-to-face with a decision maker, behave as if they expect that the decision maker will take full control of the conversation. It's true that decision makers are usually busy, so they may appear impatient and anxious to move the conversation along. It's also true that they are generally senior people who are used to taking control. But that doesn't mean that you can afford to sit back and hope the decision maker will control the conversation and channel it into the most appropriate areas. It's smart for you to have a plan about how you intend to use your time—and to share that plan with the decision maker at the start of the conversation. You might, for example, say, "I know how busy you are, Dr. Frankenstein, so I'd like to be sure I use your time efficiently. If you agree, I'd like to cover three areas during the next 15 minutes. These areas are..." Alas, I've sat through literally hundreds of conversations where, instead of taking control in this way, the seller waited for the decision maker to structure the meeting. As a result, 18 minutes of a 20-minute conversation would be spent on pleasantries and trivia, while the closing 2 minutes became a frenetic outpouring of product features. Don't ever let that happen to you. Once you reach the focus of power, give careful and explicit attention to planning and structuring each meeting efficiently.

- *Premature meetings.* There's a superstition in selling that the sooner you can get to the decision maker the better. Effective selling, so it's said, is going straight to the focus of power. That's a questionable belief. There's plenty of evidence that the people who have most impact on decision makers are those who have prepared a case by conversations at the focus of dissatisfaction. I was once taught a valuable lesson in this area. I was flying from Stockholm to London with my colleague Bill Allen. Bad weather delayed the flight for several hours, and we found ourselves in conversation with another passenger who turned out to be the chief executive officer of a large conglomerate. As we talked, it was clear that there was an opportunity to sell the CEO a significant consulting study. "This is a very urgent issue for us," the CEO told us. "Come and have lunch with me in London tomorrow so we can talk more about this." What luck! Here was a chance meeting taking us straight to the focus of power. I confidently expected that Bill would leap at the chance. Instead he asked, "Could we make it the day *after* tomorrow?" On the flight back I asked him why he'd put the meeting off for 24 hours. "Because," he explained, "I don't yet know enough about their problem. Consequently, you and I will spend every minute of tomorrow talking to his people and getting an understanding of the issues. *Then* we'll be ready to talk with him." Bill was a fine salesman. I wish more salespeople would realize how powerfully they could influence the decision maker by holding preparatory meetings with people at the focus of dissatisfaction.

- *Inappropriate expectations.* Meetings with people at the focus of power are often wasted because the seller has an inflated expectation of the decision maker's ability to make a unilateral decision. Twenty years ago most corporate cultures allowed senior people to make decisions, including purchasing decisions, with little or no consultation. The present management climate of most organizations has changed. Consultation is now the rule, not the exception. Although the decision maker may have the authority *on paper* to make a decision without involving others, in practice it's usually wiser to consult. I've seen many salespeople—including those who are experienced enough to know better—acting as if the decision maker should be expected to sign on the spot. I've cringed as I've watched these sellers pressure the customer for a decision and treat the decision maker's need to consult with an open skepticism. For a major purchasing decision, the focus of power is rarely exclusively located in one individual. The traditional distinction between *influencers* and *decision makers* is breaking down. In my own organization, I'm the president and—you'd think from the organization charts—I'm the decision maker. A few weeks ago my company bought a number of desktop publishing systems. I was very interested in this decision because I was going to be using one of the systems myself, so I worked hard to influence the outcome. However, my voice was just one out of 10 who were involved in placing the order. I begged, I pleaded, and I whined and wept in order to get the system I liked best. But Elaine, our production coordinator, and Sandy, one of our graphic artists, were the ones who had the most impact on the decision, and they kept me firmly in my place. Now, judging from job descriptions and the organization charts, they were just influencers. In reality, roles were largely reversed. It's not clear, even to us, who *really* made the final choice, and I suspect our decision making isn't very different from that of most other organizations in this respect. So, when you're meeting with people at the focus of power, don't let your selling become distorted by unrealistic expectations of immediate unilateral decision making.

When the Focus of Power Changes

The main message of this chapter has been that there are three different focus areas which successful people take into account in preparing an effective entry strategy. For the sake of simplicity, I've talked as if each focus area resides in separate functions or individuals. I've written as if, for example, there will be different individuals at the focus of power than there were at the focus of dissatisfaction. That's not always true. It's frequent to see two roles—or sometimes all three—combined in one person. For instance, a person with dissatisfaction will often be receptive, and sometimes the person with the problem also has decision power.

The three focus roles are not static. Sometimes shifts in the account or the marketplace cause the roles to change with devastating results. The Health Sciences Division of Eastman Kodak provides a classic example of what can happen when the focus of power shifts. For years the division's sales force had been very successful selling x-ray film to radiologists, and Kodak's product excellence and outstanding technical support had allowed the company to build a dominant market position. The radiologists usually combined all three of the focus roles. They were *receptive* because they were strongly technically oriented, and Kodak salespeople were usually well informed about developments and changes in the technology. The radiologists were also at the *focus of dissatisfaction,* because they were the people whose problems Kodak's product development had set out to solve. Finally, and most important, the radiologists were at the *focus of power,* because purchasing decisions came directly out of their budgets. However, during the early 1980s the market began to change. Hospital administrators took over the budgets and displaced radiologists as the focus of power. The Kodak sales force, which had previously experienced the rare luxury of a single customer combining all three roles, was suddenly faced with radiologists who couldn't decide and administrators who had no interest in the technology. It took traumatic changes at all levels of the sales organization to realign selling strategies to cope with the shift in the focus of power.

Developing Entry Strategies

When we first investigated the three focus points of receptivity, dissatisfaction, and power, we did so to help people devise better entry strategies for innovative products where no defined purchasing channel existed. Since then, we've found that the concept has proved useful even to those who sell existing products through well defined purchasing channels. How can you use the idea of the three focus points to help you develop better entry strategies to gain selling access to key accounts?

Here's a typical sequence of steps you might go through, using the concepts we've discussed in this chapter to help you get to the focus of power.

- First, decide who is likely to be most receptive to products or services like yours. You may, for example, be selling a product with a new technology which would be likely to interest engineers, or maybe you've found in your other accounts that production people tend to be receptive to the ideas you're offering. Remember that the issue is *receptivity.* The person you're seeking will listen and will provide you with information. At this point you're not asking yourself the usual seller questions about who will buy. That will come later.

- Approach the individual or department that you suspect will be receptive and ask for a meeting. Be careful how you make your approach. Many receptive people, because they lack power and there-

When the Focus of Power Shifts

Dan E. sold for IBM's GSD Division. He'd had a successful career selling mainframe computers, and he was now hoping to be equally successful selling smaller minicomputers. In the past he'd been very effective working with data processing managers because he was technically knowledgeable. During the first year in his new job, Dan did well selling minis to DP departments.

Then the market changed. User departments no longer relied on DP departments to make data processing decisions on their behalf. The focus of power shifted. Individual departments now bought minicomputers from their own budgets, and DP departments had no more than an advisory role. Like many gradual changes, the shift wasn't obvious. Dan didn't notice it in time, so he continued to direct his selling efforts to his old friends, the DP managers. His sales began to fall. By the time he realized what was happening, competitors had approached most of his potential users and eroded his sales base.

Dan's mistake, from which he never recovered, was to rely on old purchasing patterns and not to look for shifts in the focus of power. When such shifts happen they can take place across a whole industry with remarkable speed—2 or 3 years in this case. And within an individual account the change can happen overnight. The reason why Dan's competitors beat him was, ironically, because Dan had too *good* a relationship with one focus area in the account. He was therefore able to sell by relying on just one customer—the DP manager. In contrast, his competitors, who lacked the strong existing relationship, were forced to look more widely for support. They talked with individual departments and found that these departments became the focus of dissatisfaction. When the user departments were given budgets so that they also were the focus of power, the competitors were suddenly in a strong position.

The case has two lessons. First, always be on the lookout for shifts in the focus of power. Second, if such shifts are likely, spread your contacts across several areas of the account—don't just rely on one individual at the existing focus of power.

fore can't make a decision, are reluctant to talk with salespeople. They fear that the seller will pressure them and try to sell them something which they have no authority to purchase. So a good approach will set this potential fear at rest. You might, for example, say something like,

"Ms. Fitt, I know that as a food technologist you don't have anything to do with buying food processing equipment. However, we're launching a new product in your industry, and I'm trying to get the reaction of some qualified food technologists. I wonder if I could come to see you for a few minutes to explain our new product and to ask you some questions about how a food technologist would judge some its features."

- At the meeting do exactly as you've promised. Don't try to sell anything. Explain things about the product which you think might interest the receptive person. Ask a lot of questions to find out what the person thinks. In particular, ask questions to find out information about the account. Who are the players? What competitive products do they use? Finally, and most important, you must try to find out where the *focus of dissatisfaction* lies. Who, in the account, has a problem which your product could solve? Will the receptive person help you to set up a meeting with them?

- When you've located the focus of dissatisfaction and, ideally, set up a meeting, you should prepare a list of questions which you'll ask to uncover potential dissatisfaction. We'll talk more about how to do this in the next chapter.

- The meeting with your contact at the focus of dissatisfaction may well be the first of several. Often you'll need to meet other individuals in order to understand the problem and to develop sufficient dissatisfaction to justify involving people at the *focus of power*. Remember that your first objective in these meetings is to develop dissatisfaction—to intensify perceptions of the severity of the problem and the value which your product could bring by solving it.

- Your second objective from meetings at the focus of dissatisfaction is to find a sponsor who will either introduce you to or represent you at the focus of power. Don't feel defeated if your sponsor will not let you meet directly with the decision maker. As we'll see in the next chapter, it's more important that your key *ideas* get to the decision maker than that you should present them in person.

Once you've gotten this far into the account, you could reasonably say that entry has been completed and your selling is already well underway. You've started round the buyer circle we discussed in the first chapter, and you're now firmly in the Recognition of Needs phase. In Chapter 3 we'll look more closely at this phase, and we'll introduce you to some techniques for developing needs which are the cornerstone of effective account strategy during this all-important phase of the sale.

3

How to Make Your Customers Need You: Strategies for the Recognition of Needs Phase

Whenever I speak at a sales conference, I know that, when question time comes, somebody will inevitably ask me, "Which phase of the buying process is the most important one to influence when you are selling—is it the Recognition of Needs phase, the Evaluation of Options phase, or the Resolution of Concerns phase?" You can tell I've a background in research because my standard answer to this question is to say, unhelpfully, "It all depends on the particular sale." If I'm pressed further, as sometimes I am, then I confess that if I had to put my money somewhere, it would be on the Recognition of Needs phase, shown in Figure 3.1. My reasoning is simple. If this first phase of the cycle is handled well, then all subsequent phases become easier. Conversely, if you make serious mistakes in this early part of the sale, then you may never survive long enough to see any of the other phases.

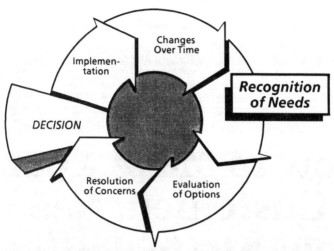

Figure 3-1. The Recognition of Needs phase. The account recognizes that a need exists which justifies a purchasing action. Strategic objectives: uncover dissatisfaction, develop dissatisfaction, and selectively channel dissatisfaction.

Objectives for the Recognition of Needs Phase

Let's imagine you're about to begin selling to a new account at the start of the Recognition of Needs phase. I choose a new account for simplicity because there's no prior selling history to consider, but the same principles would apply to making additional sales to an existing account. We'll assume, using the ideas we discussed in Chapter 2, that you've progressed beyond the focus of receptivity and you're now about to meet your first potential customer at the focus of dissatisfaction. What strategic objectives should you set?

Remember that during this phase of the decision, people in the account are trying to decide whether a need exists and, if so, whether it's serious enough to justify attention. Your selling in this phase should ensure that the process of needs recognition proceeds smoothly, efficiently, and in a way that predisposes the account to want the kinds of solutions that your products and services can provide. Specifically, this means that you'll have three strategic objectives during the Recognition of Needs phase. You must aim to:

1. *uncover dissatisfaction,* because without dissatisfaction there's no reason for the account to buy

2. *develop dissatisfaction,* so that, as a result of your sales discussions, the dissatisfaction you uncover will increase to a level of severity that causes the account to make a decision to act

3. *selectively channel dissatisfaction,* so that people in the account selectively feel dissatisfaction in those areas where your products and services provide them with the best solutions

In order to achieve these objectives, you must be interacting with individuals at the focus of dissatisfaction or at the focus of power. Of course, as we saw in the previous chapter, it makes life much easier if you are fortunate enough to be talking to a single individual who combines both dissatisfaction and power.

Uncovering Dissatisfaction

How do you achieve your first strategic objective—to uncover a customer's dissatisfaction with the existing product, method, or procedure? The answer is simple enough. You ask questions. But there are two other steps you should go through before you start asking a customer questions to uncover problems. The first of these is such an obvious point that it gets overlooked by most salespeople. You must begin by deciding what problems your products can solve for customers.

This first step sounds so self-evident that you wouldn't think it needed much thought. However, its importance was made very clear to me early in my selling career when I was traveling with an experienced seller from Xerox. You can tell how long ago this event happened, because Xerox had just invented a new machine which was the first commercial copier in the world able to make double-sided copies. What problems did the new machine solve for customers? Obviously, it let them copy on both sides of the paper, not just on one side. But, for the experienced seller I was with, the answer wasn't that obvious at all. "The really important problems this machine solves," he told me, "aren't directly copying issues. For example, I've many customers who are facing cost problems created by last year's sudden increase in postage rates." I didn't immediately see the connection, so he explained: "At the moment I've a customer who mails out about 5000 bulky documents a week, so the recent increase in postal charges is costing thousands extra each month. By copying on both sides of the paper you could get a document onto half as many pages, which reduces weight and therefore cuts mailing costs. So a double-sided copier could offset the postal increases, and it would pay for itself within two months."

What Problems Does Your Product Solve?

While studying commodity petrochemical sales, we interviewed Bill
S. His principal product line was solvents. He represented a major
multinational company which, at the time, was hurting because its
smaller competitors could use the volatility of the petrochemical market to offer lower prices. Bill's products were true *commodities*—that
is, his solvents were chemically exactly the same as those of his
cheaper competitors. But while others in the sales force were losing
business, Bill was gaining extra business despite his price disadvantage.

When we talked to Bill he told us, "Every competitor's chemicals
solve exactly the same manufacturing and technical problems. So I
realized that if I wanted to sell at a price differential, then I'd have to
find some unique problems I could solve. At first I couldn't think of
any because, after all, our solvents were just the same as their solvents. Then an idea struck me. I approached buyers who had single
supply contracts with a competitor which were coming up for re-
newal. I knew that most buyers were very jittery about price increases
and were afraid that they would get taken for a ride during any contract renegotiations. I offered to solve that problem for them. 'Look,'
I told them, 'at present you're taking 100 percent of your supply
from one vendor. How good is your negotiating position? Wouldn't it
be easier for you to get maximum price leverage in the renegotiation
by giving 25 percent of your business to us? That way your existing
supplier would almost certainly feel vulnerable and would be frightened into giving you a better price.' I was offering them an insurance
policy. It worked like a charm."

Bill's success came from a simple piece of selling strategy. He
thought about what problems he could solve for customers. And he
didn't stop at the most obvious problems. He continued thinking until he hit upon problems where he had an advantage over his competition.

So, the starting point for your strategy should be to think carefully
about the problems your products and services can solve for customers.
Go beyond the obvious. Look for examples like double-sided copying
solving postage cost problems. The best examples may be unique to a
particular customer. I recall when facsimile machines were a new concept and were very expensive. A particularly smart seller realized that
offshore oil rigs had a problem. Every day they had to send seismo-
graphic readings back to the mainland. Because these readings were in

the form of complex graphs, they couldn't be called in verbally over the standard rig-to-shore telephone line. Consequently, every day the oil company would send out a helicopter to pick up the graphs. The cost of getting the information back to shore was several thousand a day. By installing fax machines, the readings could be transmitted over the telephone line. The fax system solved a unique problem and paid for itself in a matter of minutes. Now *that's* problem solving. Of course, such elegant solutions aren't always possible. But, even if you can only think of relatively ordinary problem-solving capabilities for your products, ask yourself whether there are any problems that you can solve and that your competitors can't.

Setting Your Objectives

Understanding the range of problems your products can solve is the first step toward setting effective sales call objectives—an important but neglected part of successful selling. It's astonishing how rarely salespeople set themselves call objectives of *any* kind—let alone effective ones. Although most books on selling emphasize the importance of clear call objectives, it's rare to see these exhortations turned into practice. One reason, I suspect, is that many people don't know what objectives to set for the Recognition of Needs phase of the sale. It's too early in the sale to expect an order, so that's not an objective. And if you can't take an order, what should your objective be? When pressed, the first answer people offer is that their objective should be to "build relationships." I've come to mistrust general relationship-building objectives because they are vague and they lack the kind of specificity that can be turned into measurable action. In my experience it's the less successful salespeople who set broad objectives of this type. More successful people tend to set objectives that measurably advance the sale. Rather than "to build relationships" they are likely to set call objectives such as "to get an introduction to the Planning Department" or "to agree to the steps we must go through to get on the vendor list." Their objectives specify some action that moves the sale forward.

If relationship building is the first questionable objective, then the second must be "to collect information." It's not that information gathering is an invalid objective. Far from it. It's an essential part of *every* sales call. However, with the exception of initial sales calls to the focus of receptivity, information gathering isn't likely to be effective unless it has some very specific aims that support an overall call objective. So, while less successful salespeople tend to set very broad information gathering objectives such as "to find out things about the account," more successful people typically set specific objectives such as "to find out which individuals have a problem with machine reliability" or "to discover whether John King is the only person in the account who makes technical assessments."

I've picked out two general characteristics of effective call objectives. Good objectives must be *specific*—so that they state clearly identified purposes, not global intentions like "collect information" or "build relationships"—and *forward-moving*—so that they advance the sale in some clearly identifiable way.

How do you make sure that your objectives—at this Recognition of Needs phase of the sale—are specific and forward-moving? The easiest way to assess this is to ask yourself how well your call objectives move you toward the overall strategic objectives of this phase. You'll remember that your overall strategic aims during the Recognition of Needs phase are to uncover, develop, and selectively channel the customer's dissatisfaction. Early in the phase, for example in your first call to a customer at the focus of dissatisfaction, your primary objective may be to *uncover* dissatisfaction. Ask yourself what dissatisfaction you're hoping to uncover and how, by uncovering it, you can move the sale forward. Later calls may have objectives primarily concerned with *developing* or *selectively channeling* dissatisfaction. Again, the question you must answer in order to establish whether your specific objectives are useful is, "How will developing or channeling dissatisfaction help me move the sale forward?"

Planning Your Questions

Once you've decided on your call objectives, you must next plan some questions that you can ask. These questions should encourage the customer to talk about the problem you're hoping to uncover. It will help your planning, and your actual questioning, if you divide the questions you intend to ask into two classes:

- *Situation Questions*—questions that collect facts about the account and the individuals within it. Typical Situation Questions would be, "How many people do you employ here?" "What sort of equipment do you use?" "Do you own it or lease it?" and "Who will be responsible for setting the purchasing specification?" Situation Questions provide the basic factual data you need in order to form a sales strategy.

- *Problem Questions*—questions that probe for problems, difficulties, or dissatisfaction. Typical Problem Questions would be, "Are you satisfied with your present rate of return?" "What sort of reliability problems are you having with this older equipment?" "Is it cumbersome to perform this operation with the existing system?" and "What parts of this operation give you the most difficulty?" Problem Questions uncover customer dissatisfaction.

Why is it so important to divide your questions into these two types? It's important because each has a different psychological effect on the buyer. Look at the examples of Situation Questions and ask yourself, "Who benefits most from these questions, the seller or the buyer?" Clearly it's the seller who needs the information, so the seller is the obvious beneficiary. The buyer doesn't have much to gain from giving the seller background facts. As a buyer, I groan inwardly whenever I'm asked Situation Questions like "How long has your company been in business?" or "What type of system are you using?" Like most other buyers, I feel I'm spending precious time educating the person who's selling to me. My hope is that once I've given all these facts, then the conversation will go somewhere useful. But my experience warns me that this won't always be the case. I'll frequently spend a long time answering Situation Questions, only to find that the seller's product doesn't meet any of my needs. Most buyers have learned the hard way that answering a long series of Situation Questions can be both time-consuming and, ultimately, unrewarding.

In contrast, Problem Questions have a more positive psychological effect on the buyer. For one thing, Problem Questions, by definition, ask about areas where the buyer may have concerns, or dissatisfactions. It's reasonable to suppose that the buyer will feel more motivated to answer questions in these psychologically more important areas. We've carried out extensive research to demonstrate the link between Problem Questions and sales success. Those research studies, and several other studies relating to the four types of questions discussed in this chapter, are described in detail in another book I've written, *SPIN® Selling.** Any reader interested in the research justification for what I'm saying here, or wanting additional material on this phase of the sale, might find those studies worth reading.

As a general observation, less experienced salespeople tend to ask too many Situation Questions—and even experienced people may ask more Situation Questions than they realize. One of the reasons why it's useful to plan your questions in advance under the two headings of Situation and Problem Questions is that the length of your lists can alert you, before the call, that you're planning to give too much attention to de-

---

*Neil Rackham, *SPIN® Selling* (New York: McGraw-Hill, 1988). SPIN® is a registered trademark of Huthwaite Inc.

tails of the situation and you're not putting enough emphasis on the customer's problems. If, for example, your list of intended questions has more than three times as many Situation Questions as it has Problem Questions, you might want to reconsider your strategy. You might want to give increased attention to Problem Questions or find ways to reduce the number of Situation Questions so that you have less risk of boring the buyer.

Asking Situation Questions

From our research we were able to come up with some general rules about Situation Questions and how to ask them. In complex sales you *must* ask a lot of Situation Questions because there's so much information you need to obtain. However, effective people don't ask unnecessary Situation Questions. Here are some ways you can prevent your level of Situation Questions from becoming excessive:

- *Do your homework.*   Use sources such as annual reports, trade journals, and periodicals to find out basic facts in advance.

- *Use the focus of receptivity.*   Ask Situation Questions of people at the focus of receptivity so that you don't have to waste time asking basic fact-finding questions of people at the focus of dissatisfaction or at the focus of power. As a general rule, a receptive person in the account is likely to be tolerant of Situation Questions.

- *Spread your questions.*   Don't try to ask all your Situation Questions during a single meeting. Instead, spread your questions over several meetings, using each meeting as an opportunity to gather more facts. Don't make the mistake of expecting to find everything you need from one long conversation.

- *Earn the right to ask Situation Questions.*   Customers will be prepared to answer your Situation Questions providing you've made it clear to them that the only reason you want to find facts is to help the customer solve a problem. So make it clear that your questions are motivated by an interest in the buyer's problems and out of a desire to help solve them.

Asking Problem Questions

We've said that most inexperienced salespeople are reluctant to ask Problem Questions. That's a pity because Problem Questions form an essential part of an effective account strategy during the Recognition of Needs phase of the sale. Remember that your first strategic objective during this phase is to uncover dissatisfaction that your products or services could help solve. You can't uncover dissatisfaction efficiently unless you ask customers about their problems. Alas, we've seen many salespeople who don't seem to believe this. In particular, it's common during the Recognition of Needs phase to find salespeople who try to uncover customer problems not through their questions but through use of the "spray-and-pray" style of presentation. These people try to generate interest through exhaustive (and exhausting) descriptions of their products. They are the reason why so many professional buyers— and others who make frequent purchasing decisions—have developed a deep hatred of sales presentations.

There's a curious difference between the effectiveness of Problem Questions in small sales and in large sales. In small sales—and here I mean the kind of sale that can normally be completed in a single call— the more Problem Questions you ask, the more likely the sale is to be successful. That's not true in larger sales, where the number of Problem Questions you ask has a relatively low correlation with sales success. We interpret this as evidence that strategic objectives are different in large sales. In the small sale, the primary strategic objective is likely to be *uncovering* problems. If you uncover problems and demonstrate that you can solve them, then you've probably made the sale. Not so in the larger sale. It's still important to uncover problems. But success rests much more on how problems are *developed* after you've uncovered them—on how you come to an agreement with the customer about the problem's extent and its urgency.

How Problems Are Developed

Let's imagine that you are selling to a new major account and that you've followed the advice we've given up to this point. By now you're talking to the focus of dissatisfaction. You've asked Situation and Problem Questions, and, as a result, you've uncovered customer dissatisfaction in an area where your product can help. Where do you go from here? Most people, asked that question, would suggest that once you've identified the problem, your next step should be to show the customer that your product has benefits that can solve or alleviate the problem you've uncovered.

However, our studies of successful salespeople showed that before they offered benefits, capabilities, or solutions they tended first to ask additional questions that *developed* the customer's needs in a way that made these needs clearer and more urgent. Let's take an example showing some of the questions a successful salesperson might ask that could make a customer feel the need more strongly. Assume that the seller's product is a new and faster system. The customer begins with a weak perception of need:

> CUSTOMER: I'm not entirely satisfied with the speed of the present system, but I'm not too worried because we've learned to live with it.

What's the customer telling the seller here? The essential message is that the need is small and the customer doesn't feel any urgency to act. What would be the impact of describing benefits of the seller's faster system? Very slight, because the customer doesn't yet feel a need to change, so showing that the new system would be faster isn't going to have much impact. Even so, less successful salespeople can't resist jumping in at this point with glowing testimonials about the speed of their machine.

In contrast, here's how a more successful salesperson might have handled the customer's statement.

> SELLER: You say you're "not entirely satisfied" with the speed of your present system. Is that because its slower speed is losing you production?
>
> CUSTOMER: No. We've been able to maintain production by planning the work load around the system. For example, by scheduling a week in advance we can balance the load so that the system doesn't create a bottleneck.
>
> SELLER: I see. But don't you lose flexibility if you're trying to schedule that far in advance?
>
> CUSTOMER: To some extent. I know it isn't ideal.
>
> SELLER: What impact would it have on you if one of your major customers wanted more flexible production—which would cut down on your scheduling lead time?
>
> CUSTOMER: That's happening more often nowadays, as I'm sure you know. So far we've been able to cope by subcontracting some work outside.
>
> SELLER: And if you're forced to send work out to subcontractors, how does that affect quality control?
>
> CUSTOMER: That's one of our big worries. You can't maintain the same standard in a subcontractor that you can with your own people.
>
> SELLER: Sure. And does sending out unscheduled work at short notice make it even harder to get a good subcontractor?

CUSTOMER: You're certainly right about that. Why, just yesterday the Production Committee agreed that we needed an urgent review of our subcontractors' quality standards. But, like I told them, you can't expect to get the best subcontractors if you can only give them a day's notice.

SELLER: So it sounds like the slowness of your present system is creating some real problems with rigidity of scheduling, which is leading to quality control difficulties with your subcontractors.

CUSTOMER: I'd not thought of it in terms of system speed, but you're right, we've a serious problem.

The example, of course, is artificial. In order to make the point I'm condensing a conversation which in real life might have taken 10 minutes into less than 1 minute. But notice the kinds of questions that the seller is asking. Each is an example of an *Implication Question*. Implication Questions develop a problem by asking about its effects or consequences. In major sales, Implication Questions are very strongly linked to success during the Recognition of Needs phase.

Selling to the Focus of Dissatisfaction

Implication Questions are particularly powerful in helping you sell most effectively to the focus of dissatisfaction. In the last chapter we specified two strategic objectives for making sales calls to people at the focus of dissatisfaction. The first of these objectives was to uncover dissatisfaction and to develop it to the point where the customer wants to take action. Problem Questions, as we've seen, are an effective way to uncover dissatisfaction. Implication Questions allow you to develop the dissatisfaction that you've uncovered. When we've been training salespeople in account strategy, helping them plan better Problem and Implication Questions has proved a powerful tool for increasing their impact at the focus of dissatisfaction.

Gaining Access to the Decision Maker

The second objective for making sales calls to the focus of dissatisfaction is to use the dissatisfaction you've developed as a means for gaining access to the decision maker—to get to the focus of power. Obviously, the

Asking Implication Questions

Implication Questions can have a profound impact on sales success, as this next case shows. Brian Palmer sold scientific instruments. He was bright—"too bright for his own good" his manager told us—self-confident, motivated, and energetic. Despite this, his sales record was poor, and there was a question about his future in the sales force.

We made calls with Brian and discovered he had a fault common to many bright people. As soon as he saw a problem, he assumed that the customer saw it too. If the customer said, "I agree that the instrument I'm using lacks resolution, but I've used it successfully for years, so I'm not too concerned," the first assumption which Brian would make was that the customer clearly understood all the implications of poor resolution which could make the problem more severe. So, instead of asking questions to explore each implication, Brian would launch into a description of how the technology of his product gave it superior resolution. Not surprisingly, customers who didn't see the problem didn't see much value in what Brian was offering.

We encouraged Brian to plan his calls by making a list of problems the customer might have which his instrument could solve. When his list contained a problem such as "poor resolution," we asked Brian to write down the implications of poor resolution which could make this problem more severe for the customer. We then asked him to rephrase each implication statement in the form of a question which he could ask during the call. At first Brian found this very difficult. Asking questions from a list felt artificial and awkward—and it didn't always bring a positive response from the customer. However, he persevered, and, as time went on, his Implication Questions became more spontaneous. Three months later his performance had improved to a point where his future was no longer in question. A year later he was in the top 5 percent of sales performers. Brian believes his success came from changing his questioning strategy. "There's no doubt," he says, "that the effort of asking Implication Questions has paid off. It's helped me communicate more effectively with customers."

better you develop dissatisfaction, the more willing a customer will be to introduce you to people at the focus of power. And getting to the focus of power, most of us have been taught, is what selling is all about. Books on selling, for example, constantly emphasize how vital it is for you to get face-to-face with the decision maker. They make it sound as if the sale is inevitably doomed unless you're able to gain entry to the focus of power.

While it's certainly true that direct access to the focus of power is a great asset and increases your chance of sales success, it's *not* true that failure to gain direct access to the decision maker means defeat. In some major sales, vendors don't ever come face-to-face with the decision maker. And in many more sales, where several individuals at the focus of power are involved in a decision, a vendor may meet only one or two of the people responsible. I recall how taken aback I was a couple of years ago when I was consulting to AT&T. I'd succeeded in selling them a research project, and I thought that I'd been talking with the sole decision maker. After the contract was signed I learned that there were *six* people involved in making the decision. I'd met only one and I didn't even recognize the names of the other five.

With the increasing trend toward shared decision making and committee purchasing, access to the full range of individuals at the focus of power is likely to become increasingly difficult. Salespeople must learn more effective *indirect* methods to influence these unseen but powerful people.

Selling Indirectly to Decision Makers

What do you do if you can't gain access to the decision makers? It's an interesting strategic question and one that is becoming more important because, judging from the general consensus of the salespeople we talk to, gaining access is getting harder in most marketplaces. If you can't get in front of the decision maker, then what *should* you do? The answer is that you should use your sponsors at the focus of dissatisfaction to sell to the decision maker on your behalf. That's easily said, but it's far from easy to do successfully. A common tale of woe that salespeople tell is about how the sponsor insisted on presenting on their behalf and screwed up the presentation. Perhaps that's why the textbook approach insists that you *must* get in front of the decision maker yourself, because your sponsor can't be trusted to make an adequate presentation on your behalf. In reality, however, in many situations you'll be forced to rely on your sponsor—somebody from the focus of dissatisfaction who has a problem and a vested interest in getting it solved.

Preparing Your Sponsor

When you're forced to sell indirectly through a sponsor, the issue becomes one of how you can best prepare your sponsor to make a convincing presentation on your behalf. Most salespeople make a funda-

Rehearsing the Customer

In some parts of the printing industry it's notoriously difficult to get in to see the decision maker. Because of this, many successful sales forces consist of older, experienced people from the industry, who gain access because they have built a network of contacts over many years. It's difficult for newer people to enter a sales force and compete because, without contacts, they can't get the same level of access to decision makers.

When Susan T. joined the sales force of a small company in this industry, few of her colleagues or competitors thought that she'd last a year. "For a start," one of these skeptics told us, "she doesn't have the contacts, so she'll never get in to see decision makers—and in this business, if you can't get face-to-face with decision makers, you're dead."

But these gloomy forecasts were wrong. Susan's sales record turned out to be above average. However, there was something unusual about her selling. Unlike most other successful people in her industry, she very rarely came face-to-face with decision makers—she didn't meet customers at the focus of power. Instead, she mainly sold to people at the focus of dissatisfaction—which the seasoned professionals in the industry had told us was a difficult if not impossible selling strategy.

How did she succeed at a contact level where most others had failed? When we watched her sell we found that, unlike the less successful people in the industry, she spent a good deal of time *rehearsing* people at the focus of dissatisfaction to prepare them to represent her at the focus of power. Realizing that she couldn't gain direct access, she coached those who could. In particular, we found that she coached through the use of questions. Instead of saying, "Tell your boss that this will be a benefit," she would ask, "Why might your boss find this a benefit? How would you explain it to him?" Her questions helped customers to express benefits in their own words and to prepare them for a successful meeting with the decision maker.

mental mistake here. They try to prepare a sponsor by telling and suggesting points that the sponsor should explain to the decision maker. "Be sure you mention how the impeller increases efficiency," the salesperson typically says, "and tell her about the quantity discount. And, don't forget that we offer a year's free maintenance." What's wrong with preparing your sponsor in this way? Two things:

1. People don't remember all they've been told. Much of what you tell your sponsor will be omitted or filtered by the time it's repeated to the decision maker.

2. People never give somebody else's message as convincingly as they would give their own. So if you put words in your sponsor's mouth, that's exactly how it's going to sound to the decision maker—second-hand and lacking in conviction.

Need-payoff Questions

So, if you shouldn't tell your sponsors what to say, how can you prepare them to sell on your behalf? Successful people *rehearse* their sponsors. They encourage sponsors to find their own ways to express the key ideas that they'll be trying to communicate. They then coach sponsors so that the ideas come across clearly and powerfully. Fine though that may sound in theory, most people find it a difficult concept to put into practice.

We found that one of the most effective ways to rehearse a sponsor was by asking *Need-payoff Questions*. These are questions that ask the customer about the value or usefulness of a particular solution, product, or approach. Typical examples would include, "How would that help you?" "Why would this be useful?" or "If we could cut your costs in this area by 5 percent, would that be a worthwhile saving?" Our research found that Need-payoff Questions are strongly associated with sales success throughout the selling cycle. In other words, we found that sales calls are more likely to be successful if the seller asks a lot of Need-payoff Questions during the call. The strength of Need-payoff Questions is that they get the *customer* to explain the benefits. Consequently, they are a particularly powerful way to rehearse a customer to sell on your behalf. When you can't get direct access to people at the focus of power, your fallback strategy should be to ask Need-payoff Questions of people at the focus of dissatisfaction so that they practice explaining the benefits that your product offers.

The SPIN® Questioning Strategy

At the start of this chapter we said that the three strategic objectives for the Recognition of Needs phase of the sale are to *uncover dissatisfaction* with the existing situation, to *develop dissatisfaction* so that problems are perceived by the customer as serious enough to justify action, and to *selectively channel dissatisfaction* so that you develop those areas of dissatisfaction where your product or solution best fits the customer's needs.

We've also considered four types of questions that provide a probing sequence which you can use in planning and executing calls to help you meet these objectives. The types were:

Situation Questions—questions that gather data and background facts. We said that Situation Questions should be used sparingly because buyers may become bored, impatient, or even antagonistic if these questions are overused. Our evidence suggests that, if possible, you should ask most of your basic Situation Questions at the focus of receptivity so that you find as much factual information as you can before you talk to other parts of the account. Notice we're not suggesting that you should completely avoid Situation Questions with people at the focus of dissatisfaction or power. That wouldn't be realistic—Situation Questions provide you with essential information, and you couldn't sell without asking them. However, you should keep in mind that because Situation Questions are easily overused, you should try to ask them efficiently.

Problem Questions—questions that uncover problems, difficulties, and dissatisfactions. Problem Questions are particularly useful at the focus of dissatisfaction. By understanding what problems your products can solve and by asking the appropriate Problem Questions, you can begin to achieve the first of your three strategic objectives for this phase of the sale—uncovering dissatisfaction.

Implication Questions—questions that explore the consequences or implications of a customer's problems. Implication Questions are particularly useful for achieving the second and third of your strategic objectives—developing dissatisfaction and selectively channeling dissatisfaction into areas where you can provide the most effective solution. Our research studies found that Implication Questions are very strongly associated with sales success during the Recognition of Needs phase of the sale. They are valuable in *any* of the three focus areas, although we found that they are particularly associated with success when selling to decision makers at the focus of power.

Need-payoff Questions—questions that explore the value or usefulness of solving a problem. Need-payoff Questions are strongly associated with success when asked at the focus of dissatisfaction or the focus of power. One specific function of Need-payoff Questions is to

Situation Questions	• Achieve fact-finding objectives. • Have low selling impact. • Useful at focus of receptivity.
Problem Questions	• Achieve uncovering dissatisfaction objectives. • Have moderate selling impact. • Useful at focus of dissatisfaction.
Implication Questions	• Achieve objectives of developing and channeling dissatisfaction. • Have high selling impact. • Useful at focus of dissatisfaction and focus of power.
Need-payoff Questions	• Achieve objectives of rehearsing and selectively channeling customer attention. • Have high selling impact. • Useful at focus of dissatisfaction and focus of power.

Figure 3-2. The SPIN® questioning strategy.

help you rehearse sponsors who will be selling on your behalf to people at the focus of power.

The initials of each type of question give the acronym "SPIN," and it's by this name that the questioning model has become widely known. Many of the world's leading sales forces now use this model as a central part of their skills training. In this chapter I've covered just the basics of the model. If you'd like to know more, then I'd urge you to read *SPIN® Selling,* in which I've devoted a whole book to the SPIN® model and some of its intricacies.

The SPIN® questions can be useful in any phase of the selling cycle, but they are particularly powerful here in the Recognition of Needs phase. As Figure 3.2 shows, the component questions of the SPIN® model are tools that enable you to move toward your strategic objectives for this phase of the sale. And, as we said earlier, if you can make a strong impact on your customers during this early phase of the selling cycle, then you'll be well placed to face the strategic challenge of the next phase—the Evaluation of Options—where competition rears its ugly head.

4

Influencing the Customer's Choice: Strategies for the Evaluation of Options Phase

It was on the fifth call to a promising new account that the breakthrough came. The sale had started with a chance meeting at a social event where the seller, Mary Morales, had been talking with a technologist from a potential major customer. From this initial contact with a person at the focus of receptivity it had been a textbook case. Mary had progressed to the focus of dissatisfaction and had been able to uncover some significant problems which she could solve. Through discussions with people at the focus of dissatisfaction she had found a sponsor and convinced him that the problems were urgent and serious enough to need immediate attention. Mary wasn't able to get face-to-face with the decision maker, but she felt she'd done a good job of rehearsing her sponsor, so she was confident of success. Now I was sitting with her in her sponsor's outer office, waiting to hear the result of the sponsor's meeting with his boss—the person at the focus of power.

Mary's sponsor returned from his meeting with a broad smile. "We've done it," he said. "The boss has agreed that the problem's serious and the system's got to be replaced." We shook hands and left cheerfully. "It's been hard work," Mary told me, as we went down in the elevator, "but worth it because it's likely to be a seven-figure sale, and all I've got to do now is wait for the order."

When I met her 3 months later in the branch office, I asked Mary how big the order had turned out to be. "I don't know," she confessed, "we haven't gotten it yet." "What happened?" I asked her. "They set up a committee," she told me, "and if that wasn't bad enough, then they produced specifications and sent them out inviting bids from our main competitors. We still have a good chance of getting the sale because we influenced the specification. But I spoke too soon when I told you I just had to wait for the order. I've had to work even harder—and I'm not there yet."

Like so many salespeople before her, she was facing the difficult selling issues which arise during the Evaluation of Options phase of the sale. By pure coincidence I'd been with her at the very moment the phase started. The transition from the Recognition of Needs phase to the Evaluation of Options phase had, in this case, been clear and visible. The moment her sponsor had told her that his boss had agreed to replace the system, then the issue was no longer "do we need it?"—the account was no longer concerned with the Recognition of Needs. In its place was a whole new set of buyer issues. For a period of 3 months the purchasing energy of the account was channeled into setting up an evaluation committee, deciding on a purchasing specification, locating other vendors and inviting bids from them, screening the incoming bids, and hearing presentations from vendors. What's the common factor in this great flurry of account activity? Each one of these actions was motivated by a single question, "How do we make the best choice?" That's the central psychological factor in this phase of the sale, the Evaluation of Options phase illustrated in Figure 4.1.

People in the account know that they have a need—that's no longer the issue. Now their concerns are about choices—about the Evaluation of Options.

Recognizing the Evaluation of Options Phase

Before you can begin to execute an effective selling strategy for the Evaluation of Options phase, you must first be sure that you've correctly identified the phase which the sale has entered. In the case I've just quoted, recognition was no problem. The customer told us that his boss had decided to act—had, in other words, recognized the need. It's not always that simple.

In many sales the account has already entered the Evaluation of Options phase before you make your first face-to-face contact. That would almost

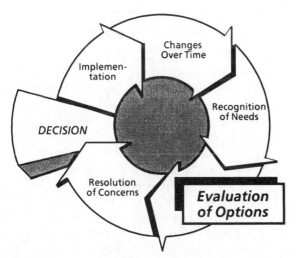

Figure 4-1. The Evaluation of Options phase. The account makes choices between competing alternatives. Strategic objectives: uncover decision criteria, influence decision criteria, and maximize perceived fit.

certainly be the case when the sale begins with a Request for Proposal, or a bid specification, sent out by the customer. The need has been defined before you arrive. Of course, that doesn't mean that you shouldn't ask about needs. It may be appropriate at a first meeting—even when the customer is in the Evaluation of Options phase—to explore needs or even try to redefine them. But it's important to understand that the customer's psychological attention will be directed to making choices. A competitor who helps a customer understand how to make choices is likely to have more impact than one who wants to reopen discussion of needs.

Another complicating factor in deciding whether you've entered the Evaluation of Options phase is the problem of multiple decision makers and decision influencers. Sometimes one person in the account is already convinced of the need to act and is now looking around at alternative options. Simultaneously, in the same account, there may be people who are not yet convinced that there's any need for change. Consequently, within the same account, you must sometimes face customers who are in different phases of the decision. However, despite this it's usually relatively easy to tell when the critical mass of people in an account has moved from the Recognition of Needs phase to the Evaluation of Options phase. Watch for signs such as:

- *Published specifications.* When you receive a specification or a Request for Proposal in writing, then it's fair to assume that the critical

Choosing the Wrong Selling Strategy

The materials purchasing specialist of a company which was a large user of industrial abrasives called a potential supplier and suggested a meeting to discuss a supply contract. This was an opportunity for Willard F., the territory sales representative. The customer who was asking for the meeting was the largest in Willard's territory, although currently only a small user of Willard's products. Willard was anxious to increase his penetration.

During the meeting, which lasted for 3 hours, Willard tried to uncover and develop needs. He asked lots of questions to convince the customer that the existing loose abrasives were a health and safety hazard. His objective was to develop a need for one of his company's products—a resin-embedded abrasive which gave off fewer sparks or dust particles. At the end of the meeting the customer told him, "I completely agree with you that we need to change to matrix-embedded abrasives." Willard felt pleased with himself. He'd had a very successful meeting. Consequently, he was taken aback when, 6 weeks later, he heard that the customer had bought a resin-embedded abrasive from another supplier.

What went wrong? We talked with Willard's customer, who told us, "It was a good meeting with Willard. He was very professional and he impressed me. I'd like to do more business with him some day. Unfortunately, he spent the whole meeting convincing me that we needed to change to embedded abrasives. But I didn't need to be convinced. I'd already decided we should change. What I needed to know was how Willard's abrasives were different from his competitors'. I was trying to decide which embedded abrasive to choose—not whether embedded abrasives were the right way to go. So, the following week I talked to one of his competitors, who showed me some of the things I needed to consider in choosing between the different resin-based products. I was impressed and I went with the competitor."

Willard's mistake was that he believed his customer was still in the Recognition of Needs phase of the sale. As a result, he concentrated on developing a need to change. If he'd realized that the customer had already decided to change, then he could have adopted the strategy used by his successful competitor—he could have influenced the customer's decision criteria and greatly increased his chances of success.

numbers of people at the focus of power and the focus of dissatisfaction are in the Evaluation of Options phase of the sale. If the specification is very broad (if, for example, it just says, "We're interested in acquiring a new telephone system, and we should like you to send details of your systems"), then you're likely to be right at the start of the phase. The need has been recognized, but the customer hasn't yet developed specific purchasing criteria. In contrast, if the specification is very detailed (if it were to say something like "the chosen system must have a capacity of 700 units, must have software-driven programmability, and must have a time-based unit usage record"), then the account has progressed further into the Evaluation of Options phase.

- *Purchasing committees.*   When the account sets up a purchasing or evaluation committee, or delegates purchasing decisions or recommendations to a named group of individuals, it's a sign that the Evaluation of Options phase is under way. I've met many salespeople who have a dislike of purchasing committees which borders on hatred. They believe that such committees must inevitably slow a sale down and tangle it in time-wasting bureaucracy. Objective evidence suggests that the opposite is true. The reason for the purchasing committee is that there is no individual at the focus of power who is willing or able to make a decision. The committee is a mechanism to overcome this—to spread the decision risk so that the account can move forward. The bad reputation of purchasing committees comes mainly because an organization tends to set them up when it doesn't have the experience needed to make a decision. So an evaluation committee is typically formed when the account has never purchased this kind of product or service before. Consequently, committees *do* move slowly. But think how much slower the decision would be *without* the committee. That's why very experienced salespeople—if they see that an unsophisticated account is entering the Evaluation of Options phase—will actually suggest to the account that it should set up a purchasing committee. I once witnessed a heated conversation between an IBM sales manager and one of his people. "You did *what?*" exploded the sales manager, when he heard that the seller had suggested to a sponsor that he should set up an evaluation committee. "Now it's going to be six months before we get a decision." "You're probably right," replied the seller. "It could take six months—but unless they set up a committee it will take them a year." So don't feel discouraged or negative about committee mechanisms. Just take them as a sign that the account has firmly entered the Evaluation of Options phase of the sale.

- *Vendor presentations.*   Another sure sign that you're in the Evaluation of Options phase is when the account is inviting presentations from several vendors. Sometimes, if the account sets up a "vendor fair," several vendors will come to make presentations on the same day or in the same week. In these cases the committee sits through a series of presentations. I must confess that I dislike any arrangement where more than three vendors make presentations in succession. From sitting on purchasing committees myself, I've noticed how, in a long series of vendors, one presentation blurs into another; how committee members become bored; and how an entertaining and lively presentation can sometimes be given much more credit than it deserves because the committee is so grateful for some light relief. But a concentrated series of presentations can have two clear advantages for the seller—a faster decision process and a clear indication of who the competitors are. And knowing your competition is essential. It's rarely possible to do an effective job in the Evaluation of Options phase unless you know whom you're competing against.

Objectives for the Evaluation of Options Phase

What are your overall strategic objectives for this phase of the sale? Obviously, you want to emerge as the leading competitor—you want to ensure that the customer evaluates the options you offer as superior to those available from the competition. Incidentally, as we'll see in the next chapter, when we're considering how the customer evaluates options, competition shouldn't be narrowly defined as other vendors selling comparable products. Alternative demands on the customer's budget, for example, can be just as important a competitor as another vendor.

But, beyond your broad strategic aim of emerging as the leading contender, what specific objectives should you set for this phase which will help you plan and execute effective sales calls? Our research suggests that you should have three specific strategic objectives in mind when making sales calls during the Evaluation of Options phase. You should aim to:

- *Uncover decision criteria.* Find out which factors or criteria the customer intends to use to make choices between vendors. Is price, for example, more important than quality? Is delivery a factor in deciding between competitors?

- *Influence decision criteria.* Introduce criteria or factors which should be important in making the decision but which the customer may not have considered. And influence the relative importance of the customer's existing criteria so that your product or service will be judged favorably against competitors.

- *Maximize perceived fit with decision criteria.* Demonstrate to the customer that your product or service adequately fits those criteria which will be used to make the decision.

In order to see how you can meet these strategic objectives, let's look more closely at the psychology of how decisions are made—at how people and organizations make choices.

How People Make Choices

How does an account set about the task of making a choice between vendors? Are there any general rules which could influence selling strategy? To answer these questions we must have an understanding of decision psychology. When a customer is choosing between competing alternatives, the decision process normally goes through three clear stages, which are as follows:

1. *Identifying differentiators*
2. *Establishing the relative importance of differentiators*
3. *Judging alternatives using differentiators*

These are shown in Figure 4.2. Let's look at each in turn.

Identifying Differentiators

At the start of the process the customer may have no idea at all about how to begin making a choice. This isn't so improbable as it may seem.

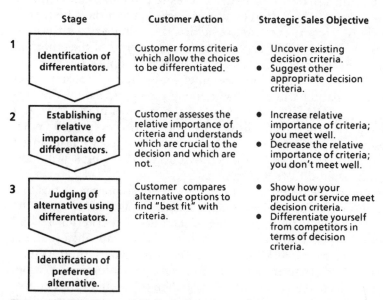

Stage	Customer Action	Strategic Sales Objective
1 Identification of differentiators.	Customer forms criteria which allow the choices to be differentiated.	• Uncover existing decision criteria. • Suggest other appropriate decision criteria.
2 Establishing relative importance of differentiators.	Customer assesses the relative importance of criteria and understands which are crucial to the decision and which are not.	• Increase relative importance of criteria; you meet well. • Decrease the relative importance of criteria; you don't meet well.
3 Judging of alternatives using differentiators.	Customer compares alternative options to find "best fit" with criteria.	• Show how your product or service meet decision criteria. • Differentiate yourself from competitors in terms of decision criteria.
Identification of preferred alternative.		

Figure 4-2. The three psychological stages in the assessment of alternative choices.

There are many everyday examples of potential purchasers whose decisions are paralyzed because they have no choice mechanism. Take a typical case. A person who knows nothing about photography decides to buy a camera. This person visits a photography store. The seller demonstrates a bewildering array of cameras, ranging from sophisticated 35mm systems to simple point-and-shoot options. Prices vary from cameras costing little more than a roll of film to those which would require the customer to take out a mortgage. Formats vary, automation varies. Out of the cameras the customer has been shown so far, no two are alike. And plainly visible around the store are another 50 models. If the unfortunate customer knows *nothing* about cameras, then there's no way to make a valid choice. The first decision task for this customer is to establish *differentiators*—to identify what it is that makes one camera different from another. Price is an obvious differentiator and it's easy to measure. Even a totally naive customer can tell the relative cost of each camera, just from looking at the price tag. Other important differentiators may become apparent as the customer thinks about them, such as quality, durability, ease of use, or versatility. Some of these differentiators will be harder than others for the customer to assess.

Differentiators are criteria which the customer can use to judge between alternatives. We'll generally use the term *decision criteria* when we're talking about differentiators, although other terms such as *decision guidelines, selection parameters, assessment criteria,* or *differentiating factors* could also be appropriate. There are two important elements which make an effective differentiator or decision criterion. The first of these, obviously, is that the criterion allows the customer to differentiate—so some options will be superior to others in terms of the criterion. It would *not* be an effective decision criterion if all options performed equally well. To take our camera example, an ineffective decision criterion might be that the camera is light enough to be carried by one person. It's not a good criterion because all the cameras in the store will pass; the criterion therefore fails to differentiate. However, in the nineteenth century, when some plate cameras could weigh several hundred pounds, the criterion "can be carried by one person" might well have been an important differentiator.

The second element necessary to an effective decision criterion is that it relates in some way to the customer's needs. Going back again to the camera example, it would be possible to set a decision criterion related to the noise level of a camera's shutter. It would certainly differentiate. Different cameras have different noise levels—mechanical shutters tend to be noisier than electronic shutters, for example. If, for some reason, the customer needed a very quiet camera, then this would be an appropriate decision criterion—it differentiates and it relates to needs. But it wouldn't be a very effective criterion if, as in most camera purchases, shutter noise level doesn't matter to the customer. As we'll see in the next chapter, helping the customer to develop and use effective differentiators is vitally important to success in the competitive sale.

Establishing Relative Importance of Differentiators

Once the customer has identified some differentiators—or decision criteria—which are related to needs and which allow differentiation between alternative options, the next psychological step in the decision process is for the customer to decide which of these potential differentiators is most important in making the decision. Is quality more important than price? Is extra speed crucial? Do we really care if we can't get delivery for 3 months? As a result of asking themselves questions like these, customers turn unstructured "wish lists" into coherent weighted scales. Put in diagrammatic form, as Figure 4.3 illustrates, what customers are doing is ranking potential decision criteria on a scale of importance which ranges between crucial and incidental.

That makes it sound like a very formal and structured procedure. Sometimes that's just what it is. In many committee decisions the first task on the agenda of the committee is to establish decision criteria and to decide on their relative importance. In many other cases, however, all

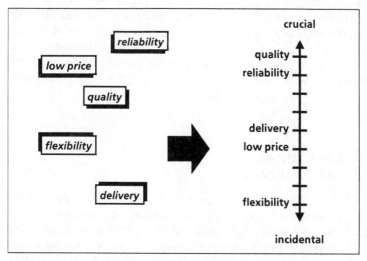

Figure 4-3. Establishing relative importance of differentiators. Customer thinks about needs and criteria, then decides which are most important.

that happens is an informal sorting-out process which goes on in an individual's head. When you're selling you can often tell how far the customer has come in this step of establishing the relative importance of differentiators. At the start of the Evaluation of Options phase, the customer often unrealistically perceives all criteria as equally crucial. So you'll meet customers who honestly believe that they should be able to find the highest quality, the most versatility, the greatest reliability, and the lowest price all in one competitor's product. Later in this step customers tend to be more realistic. When they come to understand that no product can give them everything, then they trade one criterion off against another. So they realize that if they want to ensure quality they may have to sacrifice price, or that to get increased speed may mean accepting lower reliability. As a result, some of their decision criteria which were earlier rated as crucial, may be downgraded to become less important.

Judging Alternatives Using Differentiators

Finally, once the customer has a list of criteria ranked in order of importance, the judgment process itself can begin. The customer assesses competing alternatives to see how well each one matches the ranked list. Put simply, the customer compares the strengths and weaknesses of competing products in terms of the decision criteria. Once again, it's important to emphasize that, expressed in this simple way, the process sounds very much more mechanical than it tends to be in real life. Often, particularly where it's just one individual making the decision, there are no visible signs of the process I've just described—not even scribbled notes on the back of an envelope. But a very similar *informal* sequence of events is almost certainly taking place in the customer's mind.

How Decision Criteria Influence Sales Success

When I'm helping salespeople to improve their account strategies, I always encourage them to give close attention to how the customer forms and uses decision criteria. At first, many of the sellers I work with will say, "That's interesting, but it's very theoretical. How will understanding the psychology of decision making help us make more sales?" If people say this loudly enough I usually pause to try a little exercise which helps demonstrate why it's so important to understand decision criteria. If you're uncertain about the relevance of these concepts to your sales success, then I invite you to try this exercise for yourself. Think of a sale which you *won* and draw up the criteria which you think the customer used to make the purchasing decision. Rank these criteria from "crucial" to "incidental" on a scale. Next to it, rank the strengths and weaknesses of your product *as you think the customer assessed them,* using a scale which goes from "strong" to "weak." Your result should look something like the example in Figure 4.4.

You'll see that in the example there's a fairly close fit between the two scales. The product was perceived by the customer as strong on the dimensions or criteria which were crucial. Where the product was seen as weak, then the criterion was unimportant, or incidental, to this customer. It's generally true, in successful sales, that there's a good fit between both scales. It's likely that the two scales in your own example will also match fairly closely. It's rare, however, to find a perfect match, so don't be surprised to find minor differences.

Now try exactly the same procedure with one of your *unsuccessful* sales. How closely do the two scales match? The fit is likely to be much less close, as in the example in Figure 4.5. In this case, there are two major mismatches. The product is strong in terms of quality, but that's not an important criterion to this customer. An even more serious mismatch is in the area of compatibility, which is crucial to the customer

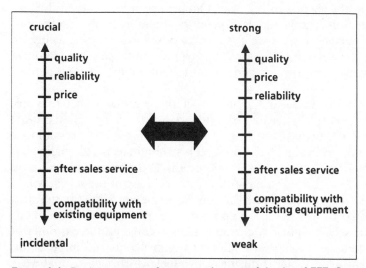

Figure 4-4. Decision criteria for a typical successful sale. LEFT: Customer's decision criteria. RIGHT: How *customer* assessed the successful product.

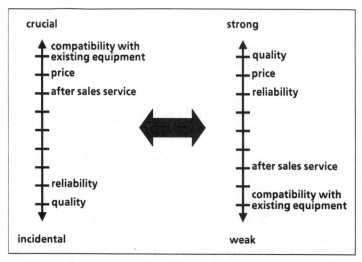

Figure 4-5. Decision criteria for a typical unsuccessful sale. LEFT: Customer's decision criteria. RIGHT: How *customer* assessed the unsuccessful product.

and where this product is clearly weak. It's easy to see why the sale was lost. Look at your own case. What were the mismatches which cost you the sale?

I like this little exercise because it shows how customers' decision criteria link to the success of the sale. The better the fit between the customer's decision criteria and your product, the more likely that the customer will choose you. As we'll see in the next chapter, by drawing up scales like these when you plan a call, you can anticipate how strongly placed you are competitively and, as a result, develop better competitive strategies.

An even more important point about these scales is that they are rarely fixed and unchangeable. Skillful sellers *influence* decision criteria to bring about a better fit with their products. In the unsuccessful case in Figure 4.5, for example, the product is strong in terms of quality, but the customer feels quality to be unimportant. If the seller had drawn up these scales during the Evaluation of Options phase of the sale, it would immediately be evident that an urgent strategic objective for the next call would be to increase the importance of quality in the customer's eyes. So the seller might, for example, plan to convince the customer of the importance of quality by exploring the problems and implications which might arise from acquiring a product which lacked quality. A more difficult—but equally vital—strategic selling objective in this example would be to reduce the importance of compatibility as a crucial criterion. The customer sees compatibility as crucial, and the seller's product is weak. In cases like these, as we'll see in the remainder of this chapter, there are some techniques which successful salespeople use to reduce the importance of crucial decision criteria they can't meet.

The judgment sequence of *identify differentiators, establish relative importance of differentiators,* and *judge alternatives using differentiators* generally happens in the three steps we've described. However, if customers meet difficulties at any step, they may need to go back and revisit an earlier step in the sequence. If, for example, during the judgment step it appears that none of the competing products adequately meets a crucial decision criterion, the customer may go back to an earlier step and revise the importance of the criterion or change it in some way.

By understanding the customer's decision process during the Evaluation of Options phase of the sale, you'll find it easier to set effective call objectives. You'll see that the three overall strategic selling objectives for this phase, *uncover decision criteria, influence decision criteria,* and *maximize perceived fit with decision criteria,* each relates to influencing the steps of the customer decision process we've described.

Some Points about Decision Criteria

If we're talking about the sale of a new product to a new customer, then it's very probable that the first time the customer will think seriously about decision criteria is during the Evaluation of Options phase. But that doesn't mean that customers are unaware of decision criteria, or uninvolved in evaluation issues, during other phases of the buying cycle. For example:

- *The account may set criteria before needs are fully established.* Many organizations set screening criteria even before they have identified specific needs. These criteria constitute some minimum "musts" that a vendor will be required to meet before being placed on a vendor list. Then, if a need arises, the organization's purchasing function consults the vendor list to decide who should be invited to bid. On the whole, the decision criteria developed at this screening stage are very general and will be relatively easy for a serious vendor to meet. There are exceptions. Sometimes political criteria are set—especially in government procurement. The message comes down from on high saying, for example, that we must give more business to small companies. So larger organizations, which may be better equipped to deliver value, may in this case be unable to bid because they fail to meet the screening criterion of size. Most of the experienced salespeople we talked with drew a distinction between "one-off" screening criteria and "constant" criteria. When the criterion is a "one-off," the account has set it for one purchase only. Most experienced people feel that, unless it's a strategically important piece of business, it's best not to try to challenge one-off criteria—even if they exclude you from the sale. They reason that it's not necessarily bad to be excluded once in a while, provided that the exclusion involves a minor piece of business and doesn't help a strategic competitor to gain an account foothold. This is particularly true where the buyer feels uncomfortable about having a single supplier.

In contrast, where screening criteria exclude you from an account on a continuing basis—what we'd call constant screening criteria—then you've no choice but to challenge the criterion on which you've been excluded. Some salespeople are reluctant to raise a challenge, even if the existing screening criteria totally prevent them from doing business. I once knew a consultant who was an expert in training design. Her office was less than a mile away from a large airline I was working with. "Why don't you do business with the airline?" I asked. "They use a lot of consulting services in the training area." "There's no chance of getting in," she replied. "Just look at this bid specification." She handed me a list of screening criteria which the airline had developed for consultants. About halfway down the list was the criterion "must have previous experience in the airline industry." "I've never worked with airlines before," she told me, "so there's no way I could bid on a contract." The following week I was talking with the airline's head of training. "It's sad," I remarked, "that your screening criteria keep out some very good people." "Frankly," he replied, "half the consultants working for us don't meet the criteria. If somebody's good, we'll always make an exception." Even after I passed this information on to the consultant, she was still reluctant to make an approach—because, I suppose, nobody likes to risk failure. It took considerable persuasion from me, and from her other associates, before she overcame her reluctance and put in a winning bid. The airline ultimately became her second biggest customer. The moral of this story is that you shouldn't take screening criteria at their face value. It's usually worth making at least an exploratory challenge if you feel you can meet the customer's needs but you can't meet the screening criteria.

- *Customers may have preexisting criteria.* To keep the concept simple, I've made it sound as if customers don't have any decision criteria until the Evaluation of Options phase of the sale. Then, through thinking about differentiators, customers start to develop criteria. This can be true if the customer—or the account—has never before bought products like yours. But clearly it *won't* be true if the customer already has experience of purchasing products like the ones you're offering. Through research, previous purchasing, or contact with similar products, customers may have a preexisting set of decision criteria before the Evaluation of Options phase begins. Most of us, for example, have decision criteria for buying a car. In my own case I can tell you that reliability is important, and so is safety. I'm not concerned about size—it doesn't matter to me whether a car I buy is large or small—but I *do* care about resale value. However, although I can give you some of the decision criteria I'd use to select a car, that doesn't mean I need to buy one. The fact that I have criteria tells you that I have previous buying experience in this area; it doesn't tell you whether I have needs.

Preexisting decision criteria can sometimes make selling difficult. That's particularly true when you're selling to "experts." By definition, an expert is a person with experience in an area, and, inevitably, that experience means the expert will already have some decision criteria for making purchasing decisions even before the sale begins. If your product doesn't meet these criteria, you may find that the expert is resistant to discussion of needs. Because of that, it's often necessary, if you're selling to technical experts, to influence their criteria *before* you try to uncover and develop needs.

- *By developing needs you influence decision criteria.*   During the first phase of the sale, the Recognition of Needs, your strategic objective is to uncover and develop customer needs in areas where your products or services can provide the best solution. In doing this you also begin the process of influencing the customer's decision criteria. Suppose, for example, that your product is the fastest on the market. It's likely that during the Recognition of Needs phase you'll ask Problem and Implication Questions to uncover and develop customer dissatisfaction with the speed of the existing equipment. If your questions succeed, the customer will feel a need for a faster machine. So, when thinking about decision criteria, the customer is likely to include speed. You'll remember that we said that an effective decision criterion must have two components: it must allow differentiation between alternatives, and it must reflect customer needs. By developing the need for speed, you've ensured one of the components for a decision criterion—that it should reflect customer need. And because speed objectively differentiates you from your competitors, you also have the basis for the other component—differentiation between alternatives. So, when the customer enters the Evaluation of Options phase, speed becomes a ready-made decision criterion. The seller, in this case, has turned a need into a decision criterion and, in the process, knocked out some key competitors.

- *Decision criteria live on after the sale.* We've emphasized the importance of decision criteria during the Evaluation of Options phase. However, they have an influence which extends beyond this phase and even beyond the present sale. One interesting difference between a need and a decision criterion is that a need disappears after it has been satisfied. In contrast, a decision criterion lives on to influence future sales. When you've just bought a new car, for example, you don't usually feel a need to go out to buy another. The purchase has satisfied your need, and the need no longer exists. In contrast, the decision criteria you developed to help you choose which car to buy remain with you after the decision. If, in thinking about which car to buy, you'd decided that reliability or carrying capacity were crucial to you, then it's likely that they will remain equally crucial after you've made the decision. Unlike needs, decision criteria don't go away once the decision is made.

    Perhaps it's because decision criteria remain to influence future decisions that successful salespeople give considerable attention to them when they sell. The durability of decision criteria makes them particularly important in the development of long-term business in major accounts. If you can convince the customer of a key criterion in an area where your products are strong, then you'll have a continuing competitive advantage.

Influencing Decision Criteria

Obviously, if you can positively influence decision criteria, then the customer is likely to judge your product in a way which favorably differentiates it from the competition. That's why the influencing of decision criteria is your primary strategic selling task during the Evaluation of Options phase. Unfortunately, it's also the primary strategic task for your competitors. Every skilled seller who talks to the customer during this phase will be trying to influence decision criteria in some way. What do we know about how to influence decision criteria successfully? What can you do to create the best fit between your products and services and the decision criteria which the customer will use to judge you and your competitors? First, before you even begin to influence decision criteria, it's important to free yourself from any assumptions you might have about how customers make judgments. It's fatally easy to imagine that because *you* think a particular decision criterion is important, the customer will too.

Selling to Technical Experts

In the complex field of telecommunications, many customers use technical experts—either internal specialists or external consultants—to screen vendors and to make purchasing recommendations. Carol L. was very successful in selling to these "experts," even though she wasn't an electronics engineer. Most of the other salespeople in her company—many of whom *were* engineers—began discussions with the technical expert by trying to uncover and understand needs. Carol, in contrast, didn't start with needs. She began with *decision criteria*. "How do you judge a telecommunications system?" she would ask. "What sorts of data emulation options are important in a flexible system? How much of a cost saving would a system need to have for it to be worth sacrificing transmission speeds?" Through rather abstract questions like these she uncovered the criteria which experts used to judge telecommunications systems. As a result, she was able to position her products in terms which met the experts' criteria. By establishing that she was "on their wavelength," as she put it, experts were generally more willing to open up and talk about needs.

Carol's success came from realizing that experts' overall decision criteria are often more important to them than the specific customer needs they are supposed to be representing. By understanding their criteria, she was able to appeal to their fundamental expert judgments. "I wouldn't have put it in quite such fancy terms," she said. "I just try to talk about the things which matter to people. And experts really like to explain to you how they set about making their decisions.".

The more you know about your products and marketplace, the easier it is to fall into the trap of knowing what the decision criteria "should" be and assuming that's also how the customer is making judgments. *Don't* assume. Whether the customer's decision criteria are accurate or inaccurate, well-thought-out or ill-conceived, they are the mechanism by which the decision will be made, and it's important that you understand them. There are four major strategies for influencing decision criteria. Some strategies are easier to use than others. In order of difficulty, starting with the easiest, they are:

- Develop decision criteria from needs you've uncovered during the Recognition of Needs phase of the sale.
- Reinforce crucial decision criteria you can meet.
- Build up incidental decision criteria in areas where you are strong.

- Reduce the importance of crucial decision criteria which you can't meet.

As with other effective approaches to selling, flexibility is important in influencing decision criteria, and there's no rigid sequence in which you should use the four strategies listed here. But, as a general rule, it's better to use the easy ones first.

Let's consider each of the four in more detail.

Developing Criteria from Needs Uncovered Earlier in the Sale

The most basic method for influencing decision criteria is to develop needs where your product or service is strongest and then get the customer to agree that these needs will be used as criteria for making the purchasing decision. It's particularly effective to do this with needs which you can meet better than your competition. If you can gain the customer's agreement to a decision criterion your competitors can't meet, then you've obviously put yourself in a very strong strategic position.

Making Wrong Assumptions about Decision Criteria

Paul T. had been asked to bid on a contract to supply floor covering for an industrial laboratory. He visited the laboratory and found that they worked with corrosive materials which were likely to damage conventional floorings. Consequently, he proposed an expensive covering which was acid-resistant and which, even with spills of corrosive liquids, should last for at least 20 years. It seemed self-evident to Paul that corrosion resistance *must* be the number one decision criterion, so he wasn't worried that the specification asked for a cheaper vinyl surface. "They haven't thought about it," he reasoned, "so if I emphasize in my proposal that my surface is corrosion-resistant, they're *bound* to be convinced."

Paul didn't get the business. "I can't believe they could be so stupid," he complained to his friends. "They bought cheap vinyl which won't last them two years." A year later, when the laboratory closed its existing site and moved to its new building, Paul realized his mistake. Because the move was being planned, long-term corrosion resistance wasn't a crucial decision criterion.

Reinforcing Crucial Decision
Criteria You Can Meet

The next strategy for influencing decision criteria is to strengthen and reinforce any crucial decision criteria that the customer already holds in areas where your product or service is strong. Throughout the Evaluation of Options phase of the sale, successful people listen carefully for customer statements which suggest decision criteria in areas where their products perform well. They ask questions to encourage the customer to talk about each criterion, and, if they can do a good job of meeting it, they will reinforce its importance.

Building Up Incidental Criteria
Where You Are Strong

Many sellers make the mistake of focusing all their attention on decision criteria that the buyer says are crucial. Obviously, if you're in the happy position of being able to meet these crucial decision criteria better than your competitors, then there's no problem in giving them 100 percent of your attention. But that doesn't happen often. It's more common for the customer to express decision criteria that you can only partially meet.

Crucial decision criteria are important to the customer, which may make them difficult to influence. Don't give all your attention to crucial decision criteria you can't meet. Attempts to reduce the importance of crucial decision criteria often fail and may antagonize the buyer. It's a better strategy to capitalize on the areas where you are strongest. Reinforce crucial decision criteria you can meet, but then turn your attention to building up less important decision criteria in areas where your product is strong.

When a buyer considers a decision criterion to be unimportant or incidental, it can be for one of two reasons. Either:

- *The buyer hasn't thought about the criterion* and therefore hasn't even considered that it might be important, or

- *The buyer* has *thought about the criterion and discarded it,* so that it is judged as unimportant or incidental as a result of careful and conscious consideration. The more the account has thought about a decision criterion, the harder it may be for you to change it.

But if a decision criterion is seen as unimportant because the customer hasn't given it much thought, and if it's in an area where your product is strong, then it will be relatively easy to change. Developing the importance of these decision criteria is the easiest way to improve the fit between your product and the criteria the customer will use to judge it. What skills do you need to develop the importance of a decision criterion which the customer sees as incidental or noncrucial? Exactly the same ones which you would use to develop the importance of a problem during the Recognition of Needs phase. The SPIN® questions, particularly Implication Questions, can be used to develop incidental decision criteria in just the same way that they develop needs.

Reducing the Importance of Crucial Decision Criteria

So far, we've discussed three strategies for influencing a customer's decision criteria. We've said that you can develop decision criteria from needs you uncovered earlier, during the Recognition of Needs phase; reinforce crucial decision criteria you can meet; and build up incidental decision criteria where your product is strong. Each of these strategies is relatively easy to put into practice, because in each of them the buyer is likely to be responsive and not especially resistant to change. But the fourth strategy—reducing the importance of crucial decision criteria which you can't meet—is more difficult to execute.

Why is it so difficult to change a crucial criterion? Because:

- The customer has *thought about* any issue which is perceived as crucial—and people don't easily change opinions which they've thought about.

- The issue is *important* to the customer—and people are most resistant to change in the areas they see as important.

Although it's difficult to change crucial decision criteria, it's certainly not impossible. Successful salespeople frequently cause customers to re-evaluate the importance of the criteria by which decisions will be made. There are four methods which have a good track record in helping to reduce the importance of crucial decision criteria. These are:

- Overtaking
- Redefining
- Trading-off
- Creating Alternative Solutions

Let's look at each of these methods more closely.

Overtaking. The first method for handling a crucial criterion (price, e.g.) you can't meet is to take a criterion which *can* be met—preferably one which

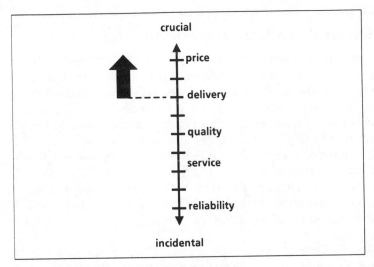

Figure 4-6. Overtaking a crucial decision criterion. Building the importance of a lesser criterion so that it becomes more important than the crucial criterion you can't meet.

is already quite important to the customer—and increase its importance so that it *overtakes* price and replaces it as the most crucial criterion. In the example in Figure 4.6, the seller's product is more expensive than the competitors', but it is available for immediate installation. The cheaper competition, however, requires a longer lead time on all deliveries—making delivery an area where the seller is strong.

Overtaking can often be used even earlier in the selling cycle, during the Recognition of Needs phase. As we saw earlier, by developing customer needs in areas where you are strongest, you can increase the importance of these needs and influence the customer to use them as decision criteria during the Evaluation of Options phase. Overtaking doesn't directly address crucial decision criteria which you can't meet. It leaves crucial decision criteria alone and, instead, builds up the importance of other areas. The next method, in contrast, *does* deal directly with crucial decision criteria and how to reduce their importance.

Redefining. When customers tell you that a criterion is "important," they are letting you know that it matters to them—and that it will be hard to change. So if you're unable to meet the criterion well, don't make the mistake of trying to persuade a customer that it's *unimportant*. Attempts to talk people out of crucial decision criteria usually fail and often only make the criterion even stronger. This isn't something which happens just in selling. Put any two people together who have opposite

Overtaking a Crucial Decision Criterion

A certain desktop publishing system was relatively inexpensive, but its output quality was less good than output from the machines of more costly competitors. Krishna Y. was was trying to sell this system to a consulting organization for whom output quality was the crucial decision criterion. "I'd rather pay a lot more," his customer told him, "if it means that I can get better quality." Krishna knew that the customer was talking to a competitor who was very expensive but who provided excellent output quality—considerably superior to anything Krishna could offer. He knew that the competitor had impressed the customer, so he was afraid that he might lose the sale. "I don't think I've more than a one percent chance of getting this one," he told his manager.

But, contrary to everyone's expectations, Krishna *did* make the sale. "How did you do it?" his manager asked. "I got the customer's agreement that desktop technology is changing rapidly," Krishna explained to her, "and that within a year there would be even better quality available than there is now. So, if the customer *really* wanted quality, it would be better to wait a few months. The customer certainly wanted quality but couldn't wait. So I suggested he install a temporary system to tide him over until the new technology was available which could offer him the top quality he wanted. He liked the idea. However, if the system was to be temporary, he didn't want to pay too much for it. So price suddenly became a more important criterion. Consequently, because we had reasonable quality at a low price, we met his criteria better than the competitor." Krishna's success came from using Overtaking to change a customer's crucial decision criterion.

beliefs about what's important—in areas such as politics, religion, or education—and what happens? The more they talk, the stronger each one's existing beliefs become. Challenge only serves to *increase* the importance of strongly held beliefs.

So how can you address a crucial criterion without challenging it and increasing its importance still further? One of the most powerful methods is through *Redefining*. Redefining doesn't challenge the importance of the criterion; instead, it redefines it so that the criterion changes its meaning. Naturally, in selling, Redefining is used to change meaning in a way which allows the seller to meet a crucial criterion better.

For example, a customer may be thinking of buying information processing equipment and may be using ease of keyboard operation as a crucial criterion. A seller whose machine has a cumbersome keyboard will be in trouble unless the criterion can be redefined in some way. In this illustration, the customer equates ease of use with having a simple keyboard. The seller doesn't challenge the importance of the customer's criterion, but instead redefines it to include areas where the seller is strong—user-friendly software and training support—both of which contribute to easy use. As a result, the customer still judges "ease of use" as the most crucial criterion, but, because new elements have been introduced into the definition, now sees "ease of use" in a way which the seller is better able to meet. So, Redefining doesn't challenge the importance of a criterion, but allows the seller to interpret its meaning in a more favorable way. Figure 4.7 illustrates the Redefining that takes place in this keyboard example.

Redefining is such a versatile and important method for handling crucial decision criteria that almost every complex sale gives opportunities for its use. Many "war stories" of how a difficult selling situation was turned around involve Redefining of decision criteria.

Almost every experienced salesperson can remember times when a sale hinged on the ability to redefine a crucial decision criterion and to reexpress it in ways the salesperson could meet. I recall selling a supervisory development program. The customer, a large European conglomerate, was concerned that the training should be "effective." Unfortunately for me, the customer measured effectiveness mainly in terms of the enthusiasm with which supervisors who had been sent on various vendors' programs reported back on their experiences. Because of this criterion, the customer was near to purchasing a competitor's

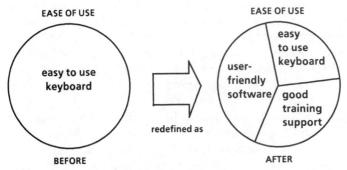

Figure 4-7. Redefining a crucial decision criterion. BEFORE: "Ease of use" means easy-to-use keyboard. AFTER: "Ease of use" also means good training support and software, so "easy-to-use keyboard" becomes a less important component.

program which was highly enjoyable and entertaining, but did little to help supervisors perform more effectively. The program I was selling was hard work. It received only an average level of enthusiasm from participating supervisors. However, my program had an excellent learning design and a good record of achieving on-the-job productivity. Fortunately, by encouraging the customer to modify the definition of *effective* to include factors like these, I was was able to meet the "effectiveness" criterion and take the business.

In the cases we've examined here, Redefining has involved adding new elements. Although the introduction of new elements is the most common form of Redefining, it also is possible to redefine a criterion without increasing the number of elements which the customer is considering. So, for example, a customer might define the "quality" of a product in terms of its durability, its appearance, and the use of expensive materials in its manufacture. A seller whose product is strong in terms of durability may try to alter the balance of these three components by Redefining "quality" to put greater emphasis on durability.

Redefining is an essential tool to help you achieve your key strategic objective during the Evaluation of Options phase of the sale—influencing decision criteria so that there is maximum perceived fit with your product. All four of the techniques we discuss here are useful in influencing a customer's perception of decision criteria. But, for my money, Redefining comes out the clear winner in terms of the number of otherwise hopeless sales which have been turned into successes because of it.

Trading-off. In an ideal world it might be possible for your product to be strong in every area—so that it's the most versatile, the highest quality, the fastest, and the cheapest on the market. But real life, inevitably, is a series of trade-offs. The more quality that's built into a product or service, the less cheap it's likely to be; technical sophistication often means a sacrifice of reliability.

Product design involves a series of compromises for you and for your competitors. When customers set their decision criteria they usually create a specification based on what they would ideally like from a product or service. So, for example, as we saw earlier in this chapter, it's common for customers initially to give equally high importance to price *and* to quality. But when they begin to look at vendors, they discover that cheaper competitors don't meet their quality criterion, while the vendors who are best in terms of quality have the problem of high price.

It's rare for any product to meet a customer's criteria *exactly*. By making your customers aware that meeting one of their criteria may mean making a sacrifice in other areas, you can often demonstrate that a cru-

---

Redefining a Crucial Decision Criterion

Wendy F.'s customer wanted a machine which would increase output and, therefore, was using operating speed as the crucial criterion for judging a number of competitors. Wendy had a relatively slow machine and, consequently, was being judged in a poor light. However she was able to redefine "high output" in terms of total number of units produced per week. As a result, the customer was persuaded to take into account additional factors such as downtime and setting-up time—two areas where Wendy's product was particularly strong. Because she was able to prove to the customer that her machine had less downtime and was quicker to set up, the customer was convinced that Wendy's machine would produce the most units per hour, even though it was slower than some of its competitors.

Wendy had succeeded in Redefining machine speed from the customer's original meaning of operating speed to a new and expanded meaning of total output per unit time. This allowed her to introduce new ways in which she could meet the redefined criterion.

---

cial decision criterion has penalties which will reduce its perceived importance. *Trading-off* is the identification of limitations, penalties, or disadvantages which result from meeting the crucial criterion. Most of us can remember times when trading-off has been used to change our decision criteria as buyers. I recall, many years ago, that I'd convinced myself I needed a car which would be a luxurious piece of *fun*. It needed, I'd decided, to be very quiet. I'd never liked noisy cars, and so a low noise level was a crucial decision criterion for me. But I also wanted the car to be fun, so I decided that another criterion was that the car should be a convertible. Alas, it didn't take me more than a couple of test drives to find out that convertibles were noisy. I couldn't meet both criteria—I was forced to trade off one of them. Quietness won, and I no longer looked for a convertible. Most sales involve some trading-off between decision criteria. In the simple examples we've given, the trade-off has been between different product capabilities such as quality versus price, or availability versus experience. Sometimes in complex sales, the trade-offs are between the needs of different people or functions, not just between product capabilities.

Trading-off is a useful method for handling any decision criteria which can be met only if the customer is prepared to make sacrifices in other important areas. It's especially helpful in dealing with price issues.

If your product or service costs more than the competition's, it's generally because it has extra strengths in other areas—like quality, reliability, or after-sales support. You can use these strengths as a trade-off to compensate for your higher price.

Trading-off a Crucial Decision Criterion

A firm of marketing consultants was negotiating a major consulting contract with one of their clients. The customer told them, "We've decided that our two crucial criteria for awarding this contract are that the consultants used on the project should be very experienced and—because it's urgent—that you can begin right away." The consulting firm was very busy at the time, and there was no way consultation could begin in less than 3 months. It was clear that they would fail on a crucial selection criterion.

A director of the firm, Victor D., met with the client in an attempt to influence the decision criteria. "Would you agree," he asked, "that the more experienced a consultant is, the more demand there will be for his services?" "Yes," said the client, "that sounds reasonable." "That," Victor continued, "is why our most experienced consultants are going to be the least available. If you want experience, you can't have an immediate start. And any firm which offers you an immediate start isn't likely to be staffing the project with its most experienced people." His client understood that it was unreasonable to expect to meet both the decision criteria. "If it's one or the other," he said, "then I'd rather wait and get the most experienced people." Victor got the business because he used trading-off—showing that in order to meet one crucial criterion the customer must make sacrifices in other important areas.

Creating Alternative Solutions.   The final method for handling crucial criteria which you can't meet is one which requires imagination and creativity. It's not always appropriate or possible to use this method, but when you can use it, it's probably the most effective way to handle difficult decision criterion issues. *Creating Alternative Solutions* involves probing a decision criterion to discover what lies beneath it, and then finding a creative alternative way to satisfy the customer. Creating Alternative Solutions has elements in common with Redefining. Like Redefining, it changes the meaning of a crucial decision criterion. But there's an important additional element to Creating Alternative Solutions, and that element involves *action*—finding an active way to provide the customer with an acceptable alternative.

Creating Alternative Solutions

An electronics manufacturer sold commodity components which its customers used in the assembly of consumer electronics products. One day it received a bid specification from a major potential customer. Among the "musts"—which was how this customer described crucial decision criteria—was the requirement that the chosen vendor would guarantee the delivery of any component within 12 hours. The manufacturer couldn't offer a better delivery promise than 48 hours, so it looked as if it would be excluded.

At a meeting with the customer's component buyer, the manufacturer's people probed to find out *why* 12-hour delivery was so important. "It's absolutely essential," the buyer explained, "because if we run out of a component we're forced to shut down a whole production line—and that costs us thousands. We'd insist on a four-hour delivery if we thought that any vendors could provide it." The electronics manufacturer realized that any delivery time of less than 48 hours would be impossible to achieve, so it offered to set up a buffer store on the customer's site, which it would undertake to keep stocked with all components. "That's even better than a four-hour delivery," the manufacturer's salespeople explained to the customer, "because you'll have additional stocks available instantly." They won the business. They were successful because they creatively found a way to get behind the customer's stated requirement and suggested an alternative method for achieving the customer's real needs.

Creating Alternative Solutions requires ingenuity and an in-depth knowledge of your business. By observing the different and creative ways in which customers use products like yours to solve their problems, you can often learn methods and alternative approaches that will help you sell. The more you know about imaginative ways in which your products or services can solve problems, the more you can become a consultant to your customers, not just a vendor.

The Psychology of Handling Crucial Decision Criteria

The four methods we've discussed for handling crucial decision criteria all start from the same psychological principle. Never try directly to diminish or minimize something which is important to another person. By making a direct challenge to a crucial criterion you are more likely to strengthen it than to diminish it. Your best strategy is to begin by accepting that the criterion is legitimately important.

- *Overtaking* recognizes that it's dangerous to challenge a crucial criterion and concentrates instead on building up the importance of other criteria.

- *Redefining* allows the crucial criterion to remain important to the customer, but alters its definition so that the seller can meet it more easily.

- *Trading-off* accepts the importance of a criterion, but shows that there are other factors which must be balanced against it.

- *Creating Alternative Solutions* recognizes that the criterion is important and therefore searches out new and creative ways to meet it.

Each of these four methods starts from the recognition that you should never directly challenge the importance of a crucial decision criterion or try to lessen it by confrontation. Yet, of all the strategic errors I've seen in this phase of the sale, the most common must be the sellers who challenge the importance of crucial criteria they can't meet. By trying to "talk the customer out of it," they actually strengthen the very criteria which they are trying so hard to change. When you're involved in this phase of the sale, don't try to argue the importance of crucial criteria with the customer. Instead, use the four methods we've described here, either singly or in combination. They will help you influence crucial decision criteria and improve the fit between your product and how the customer judges it.

Some Final Words on Decision Criteria

In this chapter we've been considering the Evaluation of Options phase of the sale, when the account is assessing the competing alternatives open to them. In the next chapter we'll look more closely at competition and how to handle it during this phase. We've not said much about competitive strategy so far; instead we've concentrated on the basic strategic objectives of the Evaluation of Options phase and how to achieve them. At the start of the chapter we suggested three overall strategic objectives which help you gain a competitive advantage during this phase. These objectives are:

- To uncover decision criteria
- To influence decision criteria
- To maximize perceived fit with decision criteria

The behavioral skills involved in uncovering and influencing decision criteria are essential to success in achieving these objectives. Through the effective influencing of criteria, you not only increase your chances of making the sale, but you also have a continuing positive effect on future purchasing decisions. Add to that the powerful impact which skillful handling of decision criteria has in strengthening your position against competitors, and it's easy to see why so many people rate the ability to influence customer decision criteria as the most important of all selling skills.

However, even with the most experienced salespeople, the skills of influencing decision criteria don't come naturally. They require careful thought and planning. If you're making a sales call to a customer during the Evaluation of Options phase, you should always spend some planning time thinking about how the call will help you meet the three strategic objectives for this phase of the sale. What's your present understanding of the decision criteria? What additional information must you uncover to understand them better? What additional criteria should you bring to the customer's attention? Which criteria must you influence to create a better fit with your product? Which criteria do you want to make *more* important? And which crucial criteria do you want to reduce in importance? Which of the methods for reducing the importance of crucial criteria should you use? How? Questions like these are an essential part of call planning for an effective selling strategy. And, in judging the success of your call, review it in terms of the strategic objectives. Did you uncover the information on criteria which you set out to find? Did you influence specific criteria? How much? Which criteria will require further selling in order to change them? Clear and conscious planning and executing of sales calls in terms of decision criteria and how to influence them is the secret of successful strategy during the Evaluation of Options phase of the sale.

Summary

We've covered a lot of ground in this chapter, and the conclusions we've come to here will be important when we move to the next chapter on competitive strategy. So let's review the main points we've made about decision criteria and how to influence them.

- Decision criteria are the criteria, standards, or dimensions which a person uses to make judgments or decisions. They are an essential part of decision making. Without decision criteria a buyer has no mechanism for making choices between alternative solutions.

- Decision criteria are particularly important to customers during the Evaluation of Options phase of the selling cycle, at the point when buyers are trying to assess the strengths and weaknesses of different vendors.

- As a seller you can, and should, influence decision criteria throughout the selling cycle. However, it's during the Evaluation of Options phase that the skills of uncovering and influencing decision criteria are most strongly related to sales success.

- There are four major strategies for influencing decision criteria. Some of these strategies are easier to use than others. In order of difficulty, starting with the easiest, they are:

  Develop decision criteria from needs uncovered during the Recognition of Needs phase of the sale.
  Reinforce crucial decision criteria you can meet.
  Build up incidental—or less important—criteria in areas where you are strong.
  Reduce the importance of crucial criteria which you can't meet.

- To reduce the importance of crucial decision criteria use:

  Overtaking, to build up the strength of other important criteria
  Redefining, to alter the way in which the buyer defines the criterion so that it becomes easier for you to meet
  Trading-off, to balance the criterion against limitations, penalties, or disadvantages which would come from meeting the decision criterion
  Creating Alternative Solutions, to produce new and creative alternative ways by which the criterion could be met.

By using these strategies and skills to influence decision criteria you can improve the fit between your products and the mechanisms by which customers judge you and your competition. The closer you can make the fit, the greater your chances of finally getting the business. If you can successfully influence decision criteria, particularly during the Evaluation of Options phase, then you put yourself in a commanding position for the rest of the selling cycle. And, as we'll see in the next chapter, you'll also be able to gain significant competitive advantage.

5
Differentiation and Vulnerability: More about Competitive Strategy

I was flying back from California to my home in Virginia. Next to me on the plane was a professor of physics. We were both writing technical papers—his was something to do with symmetry in fundamental particles, and I was writing on competitive strategy. "What I'm writing about," he told me, "really comes down to just two words—*truth* and *beauty*. In my area of physics we hunt for the delicate balance between what's beautiful and what's true." I'd not expected quite such a succinct piece of poetry from a physicist. When he asked me what I was writing about, I knew I'd have difficulty putting it so elegantly. I thought for a moment. "If I had to reduce competitive strategy to just two words," I told him, "then they would be *differentiation* and *vulnerability*. It's not quite *beauty* and *truth*, but those *are* the two keys to effective competitive strategy."

In this chapter I want to talk about those two words. *Differentiation* is how you convince the customer that you are different from your competition. Not just randomly different, but different—and superior—in terms of key dimensions which influence the customer's judgments. The other word which will appear prominently is *vulnerability*. That's a little harder to define. Successful sales strategists seem to have a sixth sense which tells them where they are strong or weak compared with their competition. They know when they are at risk—when they are vulnerable. And because they recognize their vulnerabilities in advance, they handle areas of competitive weakness in ways which prevent competitors from capitalizing on their vulnerability.

The Concept of Differentiation

Most of the published thinking on competitive strategy is in the area of marketing. Much of what's been written isn't directly relevant to selling. For example, there's advice about when to enter a competitive market and when to leave it, how to link competitive information with product design, and how to relate competitive pricing to product life cycle. None of these things is under the control of individual salespeople. But there's one important concept in marketing strategy which can be directly controlled by salespeople and which is vital to successful competitive selling. That concept is differentiation. The objective of competitive differentiation is to make your product distinct in the customer's mind from other available alternatives.

In global marketing terms, differentiation starts with product design. It continues through activities like pricing, promotion, and advertising strategy. Unfortunately, most writers on marketing lose interest in differentiation at this point. When the product is designed, priced, and promoted, then marketing has done its work. But, it's exactly at this juncture—when the product is ready to be sold to customers—that differentiation becomes even more important. Successful selling in competitive markets is all about how to differentiate your product from competing alternatives. However well your product is differentiated in the overall market in terms of design, price, positioning, or promotion, at the level of the individual, customer differentiation rests on how you sell. If I'm working with marketing people I find it helpful to use the term *micro-differentiation* when referring to how you differentiate the product to an individual customer during the sale itself. In this way I can avoid confusion with the more familiar marketing issues of macro-differentiation, such as pricing and advertising.

What's Unique about Micro-differentiation?

Overall marketing differentiation—what I'm here calling macro-differentiation—is, by definition, aimed at the whole market or at a particular market sector. Because of that it doesn't come down to the level of the individual customer. So, taking advertising as an example of macro-differentiation, good advertising will differentiate the product by emphasizing those areas where the product is strong and which *are likely to have the most impact on the majority of the buying population of the target market.* If you have the good fortune to be in a market where all customers behave in precisely the same way, and where what's important to one customer is likely to be equally important to another, then your advertising would have an equally powerful differentiating effect on each customer. But, inevitably, customers differ. It's quite possible that the differentiator which has the most effect on one customer may be unimportant to another. The classic marketing tools for macro-differentiation, such as advertising and promotion, can give overall positioning to a product, but they can't come down to the level of the individual customer. This can be a severe limitation, especially if your market has a widely varied buying population. To put it in the language of the last chapter, macro-differentiation is most effective when the majority of customers have similar decision criteria. But you can't rely on the effectiveness of macro-differentiation where there's wide variation in decision criteria.

The Dangers of Macro-differentiation in a Diverse Market

A new head of marketing joined a company which manufactured and sold industrial air-conditioning equipment. He wasn't impressed with sales results, and, after interviewing some of his company's salespeople, he wasn't impressed with the sales force either. "Most of them couldn't make a decent sales presentation to save their lives," he complained. He decided to remedy the deficiencies he'd found by adopting what he called "a marketing approach to sales." He hired marketing consultants to analyze his products and to identify where they were stronger than those of the competition. Then he designed a sales presentation which emphasized these differentiating dimensions which had emerged from his market research. His approach was the classic one which he'd used with great success to design advertising for his former company. When the sales presentation was ready, he insisted that everyone in the sales force should learn it by heart and use it in all their major customer presentations.

Unfortunately, despite the enormous energy which went into this project, sales didn't show any measurable increase. The head of marketing suspected one of the problems was that the sales force

(continued)

wasn't using the presentation he'd designed, so he asked us whether we could confirm his suspicions. We looked into what was happening. He was right that his presentation was not being used by some of the sales force. But he was *wrong* when he assumed that failure to use the presentation was losing him sales. On the contrary. His less successful people *did* use the presentation. But his top salespeople didn't like the presentation and used it only when senior sales management was present. As one of them put it to us, "This presentation would be fine if all my customers were the same. It shows how we're superior in terms of operating cost and of noise. But none of my last three customers gave a hoot for noise, and only one of them was interested in operating cost. If I'd have given that presentation it wouldn't have made any impact at all. Instead I emphasized speed of installation to the customer who was in a hurry. To another customer I made the sale because he wanted a system he could operate using his existing compressors, and I showed him how we could do that. And the final customer wanted a system which he could dismantle easily when he moved to a new site next year. If I'd talked about operating cost or noise he'd have thought I was off my rocker."

The head of marketing made the mistake of using a macro-differentiating approach which wasn't able to take into account individual differences in customers and which therefore couldn't cope with the diverse market in which he now operated. He didn't realize that it was the ability to differentiate *at the level of the individual customer* which brought sales success. His overall presentation was not able to provide this micro-differentiation; consequently, it was an ineffective sales tool.

Micro-differentiation is particularly important when there's wide variation in customers' decision criteria. It lets you position your product to an individual customer in a way which maximizes those dimensions which are important to the customer and where your product or service is strong. Even where, superficially, customers across a marketplace seem to have very similar decision criteria, closer examination reveals that many individual differences exist which can be used by effective salespeople. Over and over again I've been told by less successful salespeople that their customers are all the same. These salespeople generally go on to say that price is the principal criterion their customers use in making all decisions. Our evidence suggests that this isn't true. Even in the notoriously impersonal area of commodity sales to purchasing agents, individual variation among purchasers is the norm rather than the exception. As a result, it's possible for skillful sellers to use individual variations in decision criteria to differentiate their products effectively during the Evaluation of Options phase of the sale.

"Hard" and "Soft" Differentiators

When we introduced the idea of differentiators in the last chapter, we explained that, from the customer's point of view, a good differentiator must have two characteristics: it must relate to the customer's needs, and it must differentiate between competing alternatives. From the seller's point of view, a good differentiator should also be one where the seller's product or service should be measurably superior to the competition's. So, for example, machine speed might be an ideal differentiator for a seller offering the fastest machine on the market to a customer who needs speed. It relates to the customer's need, it clearly differentiates between competitors, and the seller's machine is objectively superior. Competitive success, particularly in the Evaluation of Options phase of the sale, rests on finding such differentiators and persuading the customer to use them as decision criteria. If all differentiators were as clear as "machine speed," then competitive selling would be relatively easy. You'd simply have to identify the dimensions where your products outperform the competition and find customers who needed products strong on those dimensions, and you'd have the basis for a sale.

But real life isn't quite that straightforward. Let's assume that your product is outstandingly reliable and that your customer badly needs reliability. So far so good, but how's the customer to know that your product will have fewer reliability problems than your competitors'? You *say* that it's reliable, but that's exactly what your competitors say about their products, too. Even the most honest of your competitors won't go out of the way to point out that their products are *un*reliable. Reliability isn't quite so easy to measure as machine speed. Until the machine breaks down after the sale, it's hard for the customer to decide whether or not the chosen machine has a reliability problem. Reliability may be just as important a criterion to a customer as machine speed, but because it's more difficult to measure, it will be harder for a customer to use reliability as a differentiator.

When I'm helping salespeople with competitive strategy, I invite them to write down the key differentiators which customers use as criteria to judge between them and their competition. Then I suggest that they divide these differentiators into two lists. One list should be the "hard" differentiators—those which can be objectively measured by the customer. Typical examples might be price, size, weight, speed, compatibility, or delivery. As we'll see later, some of these differentiators can turn out to be less "hard" than they might seem at first glance. The other list consists of the "soft" differentiators—those which are matters of judgment or which can't easily be objectively measured. Typical examples of "soft" differentiators might be quality, responsiveness, or standards of service. If a salesperson's "hard" list is much longer than the "soft" one, or if the person tells me that customers put more weight on the "hard" differentiators than the "soft" in making judgments, then competitive selling will be relatively straightforward for that seller. But if, as often happens, the "soft" are equally or more important criteria than the "hard," then it's likely that the seller will need considerable skill and careful strategic planning to succeed during the Evaluation of Options phase.

Competitive Strategy with "Hard" Differentiators

The ideal selling position is when your product has clear superiority in terms of its "hard" differentiators. If these differentiators are used as decision criteria by the customer, then your objective and demonstrable superiority will help you emerge from this phase of the sale as the top competitor. Under these circumstances, you don't need very elaborate selling strategies. You develop needs which can best be met in terms of your "hard" differentiators. So, as we saw earlier, if you happen to have the fastest machine on the market, you develop a need for speed.

How "Hard" Differentiators Make Selling Easy

A business-machines company had a dominant market position in the United States. However, a Japanese competitor had recently entered the market and was quickly taking market share. The U.S. company's initial response, seeing the impressive sales figures of its competitor, was to find out how the competitor's sales force was being trained and what selling strategies were helping the salespeople to achieve such remarkable sales levels. The U.S. company hired a number of the competitor's top performers to help it learn the "secret of success."

We traveled with some of these top performers and observed their selling skills now that they were working for a different company.
(continued)

We'd been told that we would be watching some of the superstars of the business-machines industry in action. What we saw was mediocre selling skill. These top performers had succeeded in their other company not because of sales strategy or selling ability, but because they had a product which was clearly superior in terms of three "hard" differentiators—price, speed, and ease of use. Because these three differentiators were generally important to customers and were therefore used as decision criteria, the so-called superstars were able to sell just by being there.

We found that the chief characteristic of these high performers was *energy*. They called on a lot of accounts. Because, in their original company, they were so well-differentiated from their competition in terms of three "hard" differentiators, they generally found it easy to come out ahead during the Evaluation of Options phase of a sale. But energy alone wasn't enough to bring them success now that they had changed companies. Their new organization had many competitive strengths, but most were in the "soft" differentiators. Quality was excellent, reliability was good, and company reputation was outstanding. But it took much more skill to sell using these "soft" differentiators, and few of the superstars could make the transition. Within a year, most of them had left the company.

Speeding Up the Decision Cycle

It's no coincidence that high-energy salespeople tend to be particularly successful when the "hard" differentiators are on their side. There's some evidence that the shorter the evaluation period, the more the customer will rely on "hard" differentiators and ignore "soft" ones. So, typically, a competitor with a price advantage will be more likely to succeed if the customer makes a quick decision than if the decision is drawn out over a longer evaluation period. High-energy people who pressure the customer to move quickly through the decision cycle, may—usually without realizing it—cause the customer to put more weight on the "hard" differentiators.

In some ways it's a counterintuitive idea that quicker decisions tend to favor "hard" differentiators. Conventional sales wisdom would predict the opposite. After all, everyone's familiar with impulse buying, which is a purchase made quickly—usually on the spur of the moment. It's generally made on irrational or "soft" grounds, rather than on the rational "hard" logic of measurable performance differentiators and identified needs. I was always taught, based on the phenomenon of impulse buying, that quick decisions tend to be emotional and that slower decisions are more rational. Doesn't that suggest that "soft" differentiators are used with quick decisions? So how is it I'm suggesting that quicker decisions put more weight on the "hard" differentiators? Shouldn't it be the other way around? In the small impulse sale, perhaps. But not in the strategic major sale. There are many counterintuitive differences between large and small sales. Some of these differences mean that the things which positively influence decisions when the sale is small will have a negative effect as the sale grows larger. If you'd like some research evidence on this point, let me refer you to my book *SPIN® Selling* which shows how the decision processes in larger sales are psychologically distinct from the ones which go on in small, one-call sales. And I must emphasize that I *am* talking here about major purchases, not about small impulse transactions.

"Soft" Differentiators Get a Second Chance

Because the big eight accounting firms are all very similar in terms of fee levels, skills, and range of services, one firm had set out to differentiate itself in the market in terms of its concern for its clients. However concern was a "soft" differentiator. Customers couldn't see concern as easily as they could see harder differentiators such as fees. Consequently, although customers wanted their consultants to show personal concern, it was a difficult decision criterion for customers to use to evaluate competing firms.

In one major sale, Tom L., one of the firm's consulting partners, was competing against two other big eight firms and a large local accounting company. The project involved helping the customer develop a new system for preparing operating budgets. Because the budgetary process was due to begin in less than a month, the customer felt under pressure to make a quick decision. After interviewing the four competitors, the customer's evaluation committee decided on the local firm which had proposed a fee level about 10 percent below that of the big eight competitors. "We liked what you said about personal concern for our problems," the customer told Tom, "but your competitor has a much lower fee level and that's got to be more important to us. Tomorrow I'm going to call them in to tell them that they've won the business." However, that afternoon, before the decision was announced, the customer's company was told

(continued)

to expect a hostile takeover bid. As it happened, the expected bid never materialized. But preparing to fight it took up so much of the financial staff's time that it was clear that there wouldn't be any chance of revising the system in time for that year's operating budget. So the consulting decision was put on hold.

Six months later, Tom was surprised to get a call from the customer, inviting him to a meeting. He was even more surprised to find out that his firm was now the front-runner. "We've had more thinking time," the customer explained, "and we now feel that even though you're more expensive, the personal concern your firm offers is worth a premium." Tom won the contract.

Tom was lucky. When the decision was urgent, the "hard" differentiator of fee levels was easiest to use to evaluate the competing firms. But when the customer had more time to think, "soft" issues, such as personal concern for the customer, became more important in making the differentiation.

Ask yourself how *you'd* behave if you were a customer trying to make a rapid decision in an area which, in all probability, you didn't entirely understand. It's almost certain that you'd differentiate using the easy decision criteria first. Few things differentiate more easily than the "hard" criterion of price. "Soft" criteria, such as quality, will be much more difficult for you to assess.

To take a personal example, right now I'm hoping to buy some ornamental trees to plant around the edge of a 3-acre lake at my office. I'm deep in the Evaluation of Options phase of the decision. I know what trees I want, and I've obtained prices and brochures from a number of commercial nurseries. I don't know much about ornamental trees, so I can't tell which nursery is offering the best quality or the healthiest stock. To understand those things would involve research, reading, maybe some expert advice, and, above all, *time*. But, without spending any time or effort, I can tell you that there are two "hard" differentiators which I can use. One is price—and I notice that some of these nurseries are offering cheaper trees than others. The second "hard" differentiator is size. Some nurseries offer 4-foot trees, some 5, and some 6. It's not difficult for me to make a decision if my objectives are to get the tallest trees for the least money. If I had to make the decision today, that's how I'd do it. But give me a few weeks to think, and I might be impressed by "softer" differentiators. One nursery, for example, offers frost-resistant stock. That's not so easy for me to measure—I don't know quite how I'd set about assessing the frost resistance of all the competitors—but it could be an important differentiator here in Virginia where the nights can get cold. Give me even more time, and I might learn to judge the disease resistance of trees. Again, this could potentially be an important criterion, but, for someone in my present state of knowledge, it's too "soft" for me to use effectively at the moment. Typically, the longer I'm able to think about how I'll make the choice, the more I'll learn about how to use "soft" differentiators as part of my decision.

Turning "Soft" Differentiators into "Hard"

An important strategic ability in the competitive sale is helping the customer turn "soft" differentiators into "harder" ones. If you're strong, shall we say, in terms of quality, then you want the customer to use quality as a decision criterion when evaluating you and your competition. As we've seen, if there's adequate time to make the decision, then it's possible that during the evaluation process the customer will come to understand how to judge "quality" effectively without requiring any help from you. But that's like saying that it's possible during the Recognition of Needs phase for customers to develop needs of their own accord. Of course they can. But the job of the effective sales strategist is to influence and guide the customer's decision process—not to sit back and wait for the decision steps to happen of their own accord. Just as you'd actively try to influence the development of needs, so you must actively influence the process by which the customer learns to use "soft" differentiators as effective decision criteria. A central skill in competitive selling, when your competitive advantages are in "soft" areas, is the capacity to help the customer use "soft" differentiators.

The Expert Judge

In the last chapter we said that one of the characteristics of experts was that they tended to have well developed decision criteria. I'd now like to refine that a little. The expert not only has well developed criteria, but can also use those criteria to judge "soft" areas with a precision and an objectivity which most people lack. Expert judges in any field, whether we're talking about gymnastics, ice skating, or dog shows, have learned how to turn "soft" criteria into "hard."

I once went to buy an oriental carpet with an expert. I'd picked out three carpets which looked very similar, and I wanted some help in knowing which to choose. One glance at my alternatives and he was able to say, "The one on the left is better quality than the others." I'd examined all three carpets closely, and I couldn't see any difference. "How do you know?" I asked. He explained that he looked for seven different factors in assessing carpet quality. He was able to describe each factor— I remember, for example, the number of knots to the inch was one—in "hard" differentiating terms. To me, quality was a "soft" differentiator. I wanted a high-quality carpet, but I didn't know how to measure quality, so I couldn't evaluate my options objectively. For the expert, however, quality was a "hard" differentiator. Using his seven factors, the expert was able to choose objectively in an area where I was just guessing.

We've looked at the case of the oriental carpet from the buyer's point of view. But now let's consider it from the seller's perspective. What if you'd been selling an oriental carpet to a naive buyer like myself? Suppose you were trying to sell me the high-quality carpet. Almost certainly your carpet would be more expensive than its two lower-quality competitors. And, as I've admitted, all three carpets looked to me to be the same in terms of quality. So how would I judge? I'd probably use the "hard" differentiator of price, and you'd lose the sale. How would you get me to buy your carpet? You'd have to be like the expert. You'd have to show me some "hard" ways to help me see the quality difference. So you'd have to educate me in how to make the choice—in the jargon of this chapter, you'd show me how to develop "hard" differentiators to help me judge a "soft" area.

IBM and Competitive Differentiation

Some years ago, IBM realized that acquisition decisions for mainframe computers were no longer the sole province of the boardroom, or even of the data processing department. New departments were springing up that needed computers of their own. Many of these departments—in functional areas such as design engineering or administration—had never bought a computer before. As a result, these new buyers tended to use "hard" differentiators such as price and performance specifications when judging IBM against its competitors. IBM was weak in terms of price and features and began losing business.

As part of a very successful strategy to regain dominance in this emerging market sector, IBM devised an educational program which was offered to potential users. "We don't mention IBM," its promoters told prospective customers. "All we do is to share with you some of the criteria you should be considering in the acquisition of *any* data processing equipment, whether it's ours or a competitor's."

The program was very popular. True to its word, no mention was

(continued)

made of IBM or IBM products. It was, as its promoters had promised, an *educational* program. It dealt with "soft" differentiators such
as service support. It showed, for example, just how important service support was in judging a data processing system, and it specified
the questions a customer needed to ask a vendor to ascertain whether
a sufficient support level was being offered.

This approach had a powerful influence on customer decision
making, and it brought IBM a lot of business in a sector where its
performance had been poor. The program's success rested on a simple concept. It took "soft" differentiators where IBM was strong and
defined them in "harder," measurable terms, which the customer
could use in making evaluation decisions.

Blurring "Hard" Differentiators

So far, I've made it sound as if your principal competitive strategy during the Evaluation of Options phase of the sale is to take the "soft"
differentiators where your product is stronger than the competition
and to make them "hard." It's certainly an important ability, but it's by
no means the only way to be competitively successful. Sometimes people
are very successful using the opposite strategy—they take a "hard"
differentiator and soften its outlines, making it more difficult for customers to use as an objective standard of judgment.

As an example, let's look at the case we discussed earlier of a "hard"
differentiator, machine speed. We said that if you had the fastest machine, and if speed was important to the customer, then you had an
ideal crucial decision criterion which would help you emerge from this
phase as the leading competitor. But what would you do if your machine *wasn't* the fastest? Clearly you wouldn't want machine speed to be
the crucial decision criterion. It's in cases like this that successful competitive salespeople may try to soften the differentiator. You might ask,
"How do you measure machine speed? Do you mean speed for continuous run, or speed for a one-off job? Some machines are very fast under
continuous run conditions, but they perform much more slowly if you
have one-off production needs." In this way, assuming that the customer
has a mix of continuous and one-off requirements, a potential "hard" decision criterion which seemed cut-and-dried has now become softened.

A similar method is often used by sellers to deal with price issues. I
once worked with a very successful seller from a computer company.
Her machine was about 15 percent more expensive than her key com-

petitor's but had more memory and a better display unit. When asked the price of her machine she would reply that the basic machine cost a little *less* than her competitor's. She'd then go on to say that, of course, its expanded memory version would cost a little more and so would its upgraded screen. However, she felt so strongly that these two enhancements were important that she didn't propose to offer this customer her "basic" version. Very few customers realized that, in reality, there was no such thing as the basic version. Every model had expanded memory and a high resolution screen. However, put this way, the "hard" differentiator of price became much more difficult for the customer to use when comparing her with her strategic competitor.

Using Differentiators in the Competitive Sale

Although you may sometimes want to soften a "hard" differentiator, generally your objective will be to make a "soft" differentiator harder. How do you do that? If you've established strong rapport and trust with a customer, you may be able to act like our examples of the oriental rug expert or the IBM educational program and *tell* the customer how to differentiate in the difficult but important "soft" areas. I'm frequently asked by companies to help them decide which type of sales training will have most impact on the productivity of their sales force—a "soft" area if ever there was one. Because they assume me to be an expert in these things, my clients listen carefully to the criteria I suggest that they should use in making sales training decisions. I'm usually able to give some "hard" and measurable ways which help them to evaluate competing programs. But I wouldn't get such a receptive response if I were a sales training vendor trying to convince a potential customer to look at sales training decisions my way. The customer would suspect me of being biased and wouldn't trust the impartiality of my advice. And the customer might be reluctant to accept me as an expert. Few salespeople have the luxury of acknowledged expertise.

So how do you help customers understand a "soft" differentiator, such as quality, in terms which will allow it to be used as an effective decision criterion? One of the most effective ways to harden "soft" differentiators like quality is to work through a 3-step process with customers—*define, refine,* and *reposition.*

- *Defining the differentiator.* First get customers to *define* the differentiator in their own words. Don't try to impose *your* standards of judgment. Instead, encourage customers to express their own thoughts about how to differentiate in "soft" areas. By talking about how they would make judgments, customers become clearer about how to assess "soft" criteria.

- *Refining the differentiator.* Don't be afraid to add information which helps the customer decide on what to look for in assessing a "soft" differentiator. However, it's equally important to be sure that your thoughts come as an extension of the customer's own definition. This process of adding to the customer's definition is what we mean by *refining.* To be effective, refining must build on the customer's own attempt to define the "soft" differentiator.

- *Repositioning.* If a customer is the sole person making the decision, then it may be less necessary to spend time defining and refining "soft" differentiators. For example, suppose that a sole decision maker thinks that the most important decision criterion is the product's quality. If, in the decision maker's eyes, your product has the best quality, then you have a significant competitive advantage, whether or not you try to define and refine the meaning of "quality." But now suppose the customer you're talking to *isn't* the sole decision maker but, for example, is just one member of a purchasing committee. Your customer may be personally convinced that your product has the best quality, but how can your customer communicate that to other members of the committee? In all probability, during the committee discussions, nobody will be able to agree on what "quality" means, or on how to measure it objectively. As a result, quality is no longer a useful decision criterion; it will—almost certainly—be downgraded and cease to be a crucial factor in making the decision.

  It's in the nature of shared decision making that criteria which are difficult to share will be discounted and will play a less crucial part in the decision. Conversely, measurable criteria will tend to become more important. So, assuming that you've succeeded in defining and refining "quality" so that the customer has some objective standards to measure it by, you may now be forced into a further step of convincing the customer to reinstate quality as a crucial decision criterion. This is what we mean by *repositioning.* It often happens that, during internal customer discussions in the Evaluation of Options phase, "soft" criteria fall by the wayside because people can't agree on their definitions. And, as we saw earlier, price notoriously comes to the fore as the one objective and measurable "hard" differentiator. After you've successfully defined a "soft" differentiator in "hard" terms, you will often need to reinstate it as a crucial decision criterion using the methods we described in the last chapter.

Consider your own products. Are they strong in areas which are "soft"? If so, how do *you* set about helping your customers to differentiate between you and your competitors? If you're like most salespeople, you'll be satisfied if your customer agrees that a differentiator is important. Many many times, for example, I've watched sellers of high-quality products get customers' agreement that quality will be an important factor in making the decision. Having established quality as a decision criterion the sellers feel they've achieved their objective and they move on to other topics. In contrast, I've noticed how top salespeople go to great lengths to *define, refine,* and *reposition* so that the customer is able to communicate the criterion to others involved in the decision.

Vulnerability

We've seen how differentiation (or *micro-differentiation,* as we used the term earlier in this chapter) is a crucial part of effective competitive strategy, particularly during the Evaluation of Options phase of the sale. Let's now turn to the other crucial concept—vulnerability. Vulnerability occurs when you are put at risk because a competitor is strong in an area which is important to the customer, and you are weak in that area.

Take a simple example. Suppose that you offer an 8-week delivery on one of your products, and you've a customer who's insisting on a 2-week delivery. Are you strong or weak? In the terms we've discussed so far, it seems as if you're decidedly weak. Early delivery is a crucial criterion and you can't meet it. But now suppose that your main competitors are all offering a 12-week delivery. Suddenly, instead of being weak you've become strong, compared with your competition. However, if you offer an 8-week delivery while your strategic competitors can deliver from stock, then your weakness is serious—you're *vulnerable.*

Vulnerability Analysis

There's a simple way to assess your vulnerability. It's called *vulnerability analysis* and it's illustrated in Figure 5.1. Draw three scales on a piece of paper. The left-hand scale should represent the customer's decision criteria ranging from crucial to incidental. On the center scale rank your product or service in terms of each criterion *as you believe the customer sees it,* ranging from strong to weak. Finally, use the right-hand scale to rank a key competitor in terms of the criteria, again being careful to rank each criterion as the customer sees it, not as *you* would judge it. Draw a line to link each criterion across all three scales. Whenever a *V* shape is visible, as with the "delivery" criterion in Figure 5.1, then you're vulnerable. This little tool is one of the simplest and most effective ways we've seen for assessing competitive vulnerability. What's

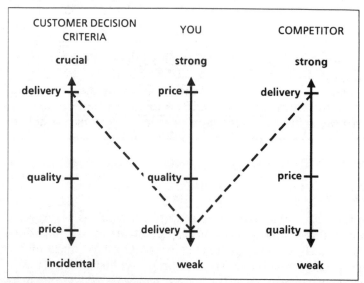

Figure 5-1. The V for vulnerability.

more, this method not only pinpoints your vulnerabilities, but it can also help you consider the strategic options which you can use to compensate for a vulnerability or to overcome it. But before we look at strategies for handling competitive vulnerability, let's pause for a moment to be sure we're clear what we mean by "competitor."

What's a Competitor?

We normally think of competitors as other vendors who offer similar goods or services which could substitute for our own. So, in analyzing vulnerability, we tend to think first of how we compare with other vendors. But that can be a dangerously limited view of competitors because it may lead us to ignore some hidden but strategically important sources of competition. Other demands on the same budget may be just as powerful a competitor as another vendor. I remember one sale in which I was locked in mortal combat with a rival consulting company trying to land a major research project with an airline in the area of sales training. Neither my organization, nor the other consultancy we were competing with, realized that the true competitor for the budget was an internal project in the area of flight crew selection. While we two consultants were competing energetically against each other, the sponsors of the selection project persuaded the key client executive to put his budget to flight crew selection and not to sales training research. I was stunned when I heard that neither of the consultancies would get the

When the Competitor Isn't a Competitor

I first met Donna Tanner when she was selling dedicated accounting systems for small- to middle-sized businesses. Her company installed both the hardware and the software that a business needed to enable it to budget, keep financial records, and prepare tax submissions. Several of her competitors offered similar integrated packages, and she was competing with one of them to install a system with Sound Inc., a publisher of audiotape learning programs. She had made two presentations to the head of administration and in each presentation she stressed the ways in which her package was differentiated from— and superior to—the competing package that Sound Inc. had been looking at.

Donna had done such a convincing job of differentiating her product from her competitor's that she was sure she'd get the business. Consequently, she was taken aback by the rejection letter she received from Sound Inc. But what surprised her most about the letter was that it explained that her competitor wouldn't be chosen either. "We have decided," the letter read, "not to buy a system of our own but to subcontract our accounting and tax preparation to a local accounting firm." Donna had never considered this a realistic option. It was riddled with disadvantages which she was sure that Sound Inc. hadn't fully considered. But now it was too late. She realized that she'd put her selling energy into defeating the wrong competitor. If only she'd realized that her competition wasn't limited to vendors of similar products, she might have convinced Sound Inc. that subcontracting had many drawbacks and it was better to have a system of their own. Her mistake was in taking too narrow a view of competition. Any alternative solution to a customer problem constitutes a potential form of competition which it's dangerous to ignore.

business. I'd never even thought about how an alternative use of the budget might be the competitor which lost the sale for both of us.

In assessing your vulnerability, an essential first step is to know who *all* your competitors are. There are two helpful questions for establishing the extent of competition, which you should always ask yourself to check that you're not thinking too narrowly:

- *Are there any alternative solutions to the problem?* There may be a different way for the customer to solve the problem, without using you or your obvious competition. If there *is* such an alternative, you should ask yourself whether it could be equally attractive to the customer. If so, then you're competitively vulnerable. In some market-places alternative solutions are more common than in others. There's rarely an obvious alternative solution open to a customer who's considering buying a new computer system, for example. Although the customer may be considering widely different architectures and configurations, the competition will, in most cases, be other vendors of computing equipment. But that's less likely to be the case in a services market such as consulting. An alternative to hiring a consultant, for instance, might be to do the project using internal resources or to hire a full time expert from outside. Neither of these alternatives involves a competing consultancy. It's much the same in the financial services area. Recently, several investment salespeople have been calling on me trying to sell their investment services. Each of them has probed carefully to find which other investment firms I've talked with, and each has done a fairly good job of differentiating themselves from competing investment houses. But what none of them knows is that at the moment I'm far more attracted to alternative solutions. I'm considering buying some land, and I'm also thinking about investing in a new business venture in Europe. Those are the real competitors. To

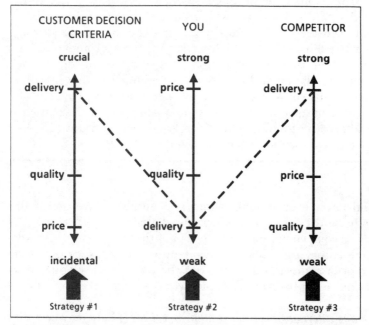

Figure 5-2. Three strategies for countering vulnerability. Strategy 1: change the decision criteria; Strategy 2: increase your strength; Strategy 3: diminish your competition.

sell successfully to me, investment advisors would have to successfully differentiate themselves in terms of superiority to my alternative financial options.

- *Are there any alternative uses for this budget?* Sometimes money is clearly set aside for a specified purpose. For example, a company may have earmarked half a million in its capital budget to replace its telephone system. But many other purchases, even major capital expenditures, can come from general budgets which could equally be used to support completely different purposes. Try to establish whether a specific budget has been set aside for the purchase. If so, then you're unlikely to have competition from alternative uses. But if you find that the purchase will be funded from a general budget where there are many competing demands, it's wise to ask the customer whether the purchase has high budgetary priority and whether any alternative demands on the budget are considered more important.

When you know the extent of your competition—whether it's just other vendors, or whether alternative solutions and budget demands must also be considered as competitors—then you're ready to assess and counter your areas of vulnerability.

Strategies for Countering Vulnerability

Fundamentally, you've three alternative strategies for handling vulnerability, as Figure 5.2 shows. They are:

- *Change the decision criteria,* so that the crucial criterion where you are weaker than the competitor becomes less important to the customer.

- *Increase your strength,* by changing the product you offer or the terms associated with it so that you are no longer perceived as weak. This approach, as we'll see in Chapter 7, is a key function of negotiation in successful sales.

- *Diminish your competition,* by reducing the customer's perception of your competitor's ability to meet the crucial decision criterion. This is the most risky of the three strategies and must be used with great caution.

Strategy 1: Change the Decision Criteria

In the last chapter, we discussed four methods for reducing the importance of crucial decision criteria which you can't meet. These methods were:

- *Overtaking*—building up a lesser criterion so that it becomes more important than the crucial criterion you're trying to reduce

- *Trading-off*—balancing the criterion against limitations, penalties, or disadvantages which would come from meeting the crucial criterion

- *Redefining*—altering the way in which the customer defines the criterion so that it becomes easier for you to meet it

- *Creating alternative solutions*—producing new and creative alternative ways to meet the crucial criterion

The first three of these methods, Overtaking, Trading-off, and Redefining, all influence the left-hand scale in Figure 5.2. We discussed each of these methods thoroughly in Chapter 4. There's nothing new to add here, except to say that it's probably wise to try to influence the customer's decision criteria *before* you attempt the other two strategies we're suggesting.

Strategy 2: Increase Your Strength

In the last chapter we showed how, by Creating Alternative Solutions, you could increase your strength in areas where the customer perceives you to be weak. The basic method involves probing a decision criterion to discover what lies beneath it and then finding a creative alternative way to meet the underlying need. There are two other ways to increase the customer's perception of your strength:

1. *Correct any misunderstandings.*   Sometimes the customer rates you as weak because of a misunderstanding or because the customer's information about your product is inaccurate. By correcting the misunderstanding, you'll no longer be seen as weak. Naturally, it's not quite so simple in real life. Remember that the customer perceives that you've a vested interest in appearing strong. Consequently, you won't be able to correct a misunderstanding by assertions alone. If the customer says, "I hear your machine is unreliable," then your saying "you've been misinformed; it's actually the most reliable on the market" is unlikely to change the customer's perception. You must offer *proof.* So in this case you'd ideally want to provide independent test statistics which demonstrate your machine's reliability. That's fine if such statistics exist, but what should you do if you haven't a source of objective proof to back your claim? It's here that an independent *person* can be so useful. A satisfied customer that the buyer can call, or a letter from a contented user, can give you the proof you need.

2. *Negotiate.* Another way to increase your perceived strength is through negotiation. The crucial decision criterion in Figure 5.2 is delivery. You're weak. Let's assume that you're offering a 10-week delivery and your competitors can deliver in 6 weeks. You might negotiate with the customer, offering to deliver half the order in 6 weeks and the other half in 10. Your offer reduces your perceived weakness and may do so sufficiently to influence the sale in your favor. As we'll see in Chapter 7, negotiation isn't to be entered into lightly. There are many negotiating traps for the unwary. But negotiation can have a useful and valid function in helping you vary the terms of your offer so that your perceived strength is increased.

Sometimes you're in the fortunate position of being able to compensate for perceived weaknesses by altering your product. Consultants, accountants, lawyers, and other professionals providing services often can change their proposed approach to remove any competitive weakness which their client perceives. Once I was sitting in the office of a friend who was vice president of a major consulting firm. Our conversation was interrupted by a phone call from one of his clients, who was about to turn down a proposal from my friend's firm. A competitive weakness had been created because the client wanted somebody with banking experience to head the consulting team. A rival firm of consultants was offering a project team with a banker in charge. My friend's firm had offered a team headed by a consultant who hadn't worked in banking before. Turning to a large planning calendar on his wall, my friend studied it for a moment and turned back to the phone. "If you think that banking experience is really important," he reassured the client, "then Paul Handry, who's a member of our banking practice, will be free next month and could head our team." In a matter of seconds my friend had "redesigned" his offering so that a vulnerability had been eliminated.

Strategy 3: Diminish Your Competition

The most difficult—and certainly the most dangerous—strategy for reducing vulnerability is to attack the perceived strength of your competitor so that the customer no longer feels that the competitor is strong. Why is it so dangerous to attack the competition? The traditional explanation is that if you attack a competitor or comment negatively on a competitor's product, then you reduce your own credibility. There's some evidence to support the truth of this widely held belief. One of our research studies showed that the more often salespeople mentioned their competitors during sales calls, the less likely they were to get the business.

Don't Knock the Competition

Diane Vail was a sales rep for a textbook publisher. She passionately believed in the superiority of the textbooks she represented, and, unlike most salespeople in her industry, she had actually read all of the books she was selling. What's more, she'd read all her key competitors' books as well. As a result, she was extraordinarily knowledgeable and other salespeople in her company would call her when they wanted answers to questions about the contents of a book or how it compared with the competition.

"You'd think that Diane would be one of our most successful salespeople," her manager complained to us, "but in fact she's a marginal performer. I can't understand it. She's bright, she's dedicated, and nobody in the whole company knows as much about the products as she does. What's going wrong?" It took just one visit to a customer with Diane to make the cause of her problem very clear. "Why is your intermediate level chemistry book better than the text we're using right now?" asked the customer. "There are three major things wrong with your present text," Diane replied, and went on for 10 minutes to demolish her competitor. After the meeting she was quite pleased with how the call had progressed. "I was able to show the customer that I know these books from cover to cover," she told us proudly.

Talking to the customer revealed a different story. "She certainly knows her stuff," he admitted, "but she's very negative about her competition, which makes me feel she's biased. So, although she's smart, I wouldn't want to trust her advice." Diane hadn't learned one of the elementary rules of discussing competition. Negative statements about competitors generally hurt *your* credibility more than they hurt the competitor.

Loss of credibility isn't the only danger from talking to customers about competitors. Another reason why it's risky is that discussion of another vendor takes time away from the more important area of understanding customer needs and decision criteria. You can't give 100 percent of your attention to the customer if you're concentrating on the competition. When the conversation gets diverted into a discussion of a competitor's product, you risk:

- *Lowering your own image.* Especially if you're ahead, you'll hurt your image by talking too much about the competition. You can see how true this is by looking at another highly competitive market-place—politics. Notice that the leading candidate is usually unwilling to debate with the others and that it's the candidates who are trailing behind who attack their competitors. The leader stays aloof. As politicians have discovered, talking about the competition only helps those who are behind. It hurts leaders.

- *Opening up areas you can't control.* It's true that you can sometimes score some quick points by discussing the competition's weaknesses. But you take the risk that once the discussion is focused around the competition, then it's not just weakness that will be discussed. The customer is also likely to introduce the competitor's strengths, which can put you on the defensive and open up areas you'd rather not talk about.

- *Building the competitor's importance.* The more something is talked about, the more important it becomes. By discussing your competitors, you build them up. Market leaders benefit enormously from the way their competitors unintentionally keep them in the customer's mind by talking about them. A senior IBM sales executive once told me that the best sales tool IBM has is competitors who never let the customer forget about IBM.

These reasons suggest that you should be very careful about adopting a strategy of attacking the competitor's strengths in order to reduce your own vulnerability. But does that mean you should *never* mention the competition? Unfortunately, in the real world, you can't altogether avoid discussion of competitors. But is it always damaging to talk about your competition? The answer is "No." Our evidence suggests that some highly successful salespeople *do* frequently raise competitive limitations during their discussions with customers.

Two Successful Strategies for Talking about Competition

We've observed two ways in which successful salespeople weaken their competition without damage to their own image. The first way is to mention competitive weakness *indirectly*. The second way is to focus on *generic* weakness, rather than the weakness of a specific competitor. These two methods are vitally important for reducing a customer's perception of a competitor's strength without damaging yourself in the process. Let's examine each more closely.

Raising Weaknesses Indirectly

Sometimes you're under pressure to discuss a competitor's weakness because customers ask you direct questions. You may, for example, be asked, "How does the speed of your product compare with theirs?" What's your best strategy for handling this kind of direct question from the customer about competitors?

Most such questions can be answered in one of two ways. Suppose the customer asks, "What's the difference between your product and EXCO's?" One way to answer would be to say, "EXCO is more expensive, it's slower, and it's not got a good reliability record." The answer analyzes the weaknesses of EXCO. The other way to answer the same question is to concentrate on your product, not theirs. "We are cheaper, our product is faster, and we've got a superior record of reliability." Both answers give exactly the same information, but their psychological effect on the customer is different. An answer which concentrates on the competitor's weaknesses will probably be seen as knocking. More dangerously, if you focus the discussion on the competitor, the customer is thinking about the competitor's product, not yours. As a result, it's common for the discussion to shift from a competitor's weaknesses to its strengths. Saying that EXCO is expensive, slow, and unreliable will often provoke a response from the customer such as, "Yes, but they have the only product which can handle oversize work—which is a key part of our business." You're then forced to discuss areas which you might prefer to leave alone.

So, one successful strategy for reducing a competitor's perceived strengths is to raise weaknesses *indirectly* by emphasizing your own contrasting strong points. But that strategy has its limitations. For one thing, it works best in areas where you have superiority. It's not a very effective method when you're no better than the competitor in the area you want to attack.

Exposing Generic Weaknesses, Not Specific Ones

A more versatile strategy for weakening the customer's perception of a competitor's strength is to expose *generic* weaknesses. Let's take an example. Suppose your competitor, whom we'll call SHAMCO, is offering a machine which the customer believes to be fast. It's clear that you won't get very far by offering statements like "SHAMCO's machine isn't as fast as you've been led to believe." From all we've seen, this approach would create an overall negative impression and leave you just as vulnerable as before. A more effective way to handle the direct discussion of SHAMCO's potential weakness in the area of speed would be to concentrate on the generic reason for the weakness, not on the specific weakness itself.

Let's illustrate how this works by comparing two extracts from a sales call. The first uses a specific approach.

CUSTOMER: I've heard that SHAMCO's processor is quite fast, so that a single cycle takes less than two minutes.

SELLER: Then I'm afraid you've been misinformed. It's well known in the industry that SHAMCO's got one of the slowest processors. It's lost them a lot of business.

CUSTOMER: But their reliability's pretty good, isn't it?

SELLER: Yes, but if it does break down, it's a real bear to fix, unlike our unit, which you can easily fix yourself.

CUSTOMER: On the other hand, if it doesn't break down often, then it might be worth the risk. I could always get a service contract from them.

SELLER: From SHAMCO? You must be joking. I've known people to wait days for a service call from them.

What's the general impression the seller is giving the customer? It's negative, it's knocking, and it certainly doesn't sound impartial. That's typical of what happens when you address the specific weaknesses of a competitor. In contrast, let's see how the same issues could have been dealt with using the approach of discussing generic weaknesses. A generic weakness is a flaw in the method or technology which the competitor uses, rather than a specific criticism of the competitor.

CUSTOMER: I've heard that SHAMCO's processor is quite fast, so that a single cycle takes less than two minutes.

SELLER: The speed of the cycle of all products in this market depends on the processing technology. SHAMCO uses a wet-image intensification process. Any machine based on that process can only use low-temperature fixers, which means it's forced to be slower than the advanced dry-image methods used in processors like the ones we offer.

CUSTOMER: But their reliability's pretty good, isn't it?

SELLER: True, the wet-image process *is* reliable. But a difficulty of machine designs where the whole processor's in one unit is that when it does go wrong, the fault's so inaccessible that you have to dismantle the whole thing—and that's a big job. On the other hand, modular processors like ours are much easier to fix because each part is separate; you can handle most problems yourself without needing an engineer.

CUSTOMER: But if their processor doesn't break down often, then it might be worth the risk. I could always get a service contract from them.

SELLER: When you're considering a service contract, a vendor's size can be very important. For example, a large company like ours has full national coverage. Smaller organizations like SHAMCO find it difficult to offer equivalent coverage.

Notice that this time the seller sounds much more objective. The same criticisms are being made, but they aren't directed specifically at SHAMCO. Instead the seller talks about the generic weaknesses of the processes and methods which SHAMCO uses. This has a greater impact on the customer and allows the seller to appear more professional and less prejudiced. In real life, the cumulative effect of so many criticisms in so short a span of time would probably have a somewhat negative effect. But if these generic weakness examples were scattered throughout a much longer conversation, it's likely that the seller could reduce SHAMCO's perceived strengths without too many penalties in terms of professional image.

As a general rule, I advise salespeople to use these two methods cautiously. I'd much rather see strategies for reducing vulnerability which either influence crucial criteria or build the customer's perception of your own strength. But I include them here because they *are* used by some very successful salespeople.

Leaving the Evaluation of Options Phase

The last two chapters have concentrated on one phase of the purchasing decision—Evaluation of Options. We've seen how to uncover and influence decision criteria, and, in this chapter, we've explored some elements of differentiation and vulnerability. If you follow the strategies we've described, then you've a good chance of emerging from this phase in a strong competitive position. But, even if your position is so strong that you've no serious opposition, it doesn't mean that you've made the sale. There's a potential minefield ahead when we come to the subject of the next chapter—the Resolution of Concerns phase.

6

Overcoming Final Fears: Strategies for the Resolution of Concerns Phase

I'd not even met David Davidson, yet his manager was apologizing about him in advance. "David's not the image of a super salesman," his manager warned me. "Don't expect too much from him. He's very quiet." "Yet he does have an outstanding record for closing major sales?" I asked. "Oh, yes," his manager assured me. "David's not the person I'd choose to go out and get a new prospect all excited, but once his sales have reached a certain point, then he's likely to get the business. Most other people in the branch win one sale in every five. David wins one in two."

When his manager introduced me to David, I soon realized the reason for his warning. David was quiet—almost shy. Many top salespeople radiate confidence, but not David. He was modest to the point of being reticent. If you'd lined up all 26 of the salespeople in his branch and asked people to guess who had the best closing record among them, I doubt if one person in a hundred would have picked out David. Yet, after an hour of talking with him, certain qualities shone through his apparent shyness. For one thing, he seemed disarmingly honest. He didn't act as if he had an ego to protect. So, when I asked him about his failures, he didn't make any excuses. He was candid, even when it didn't show him in a particularly good light. I recall that partway through the discussion I was thinking to myself, "I trust this man." What's more, the longer the discussion continued, the more I found myself telling him things that I normally wouldn't be sharing with the salespeople I was interviewing—things like uncertainties I felt about where the research was leading and my doubts about the data I'd been collecting. David was what's generally called a good listener—a rare type of creature that's easier to recognize than to describe to others. As we'll see later in the chapter, some of his qualities were major assets in helping him be successful in closing difficult and complex sales.

Resolving Concerns in the Larger Sale

But before we look at why David, and others like him, are successful in the closing phase of a major sale, let's first remind ourselves of the point we've reached in the purchasing decision.

As Figure 6.1 shows, once the customer has recognized a need and decided which options for meeting the need best fit the evaluation criteria, the sale may enter a final phase called the Resolution of Concerns. I say "may" because one of the curious things about this phase of the

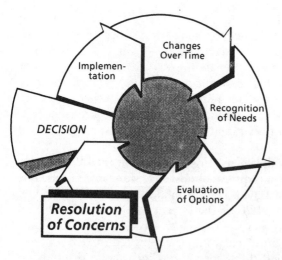

Figure 6-1. The Resolution of Concerns phase. Fears, worries, or concerns which are barriers to the final purchasing decision.

sale is that sometimes it happens and sometimes it doesn't. In small sales, or when the customer is making repetitive purchases from existing suppliers, the Resolution of Concerns phase is generally a nonevent. In contrast, when it's a large competitive sale, and when the customer is new to buying in a market, the Resolution of Concerns phase can be the hardest part of the whole sale. What is it about large, complex sales which makes the Resolution of Concerns phase so much more prominent? Let's briefly review some of the differences between simple and complex sales and look at how each of these differences can influence customers' concerns.

Bigger Decisions

In a complex sale, the customer's decision is normally large, not only in financial terms, but also in terms of its impact on the business. It's common for complex sale decisions to affect the customer's whole operation.

Result: As the size of the decision grows, so does the buyer's concern about risks—risks of making an expensive mistake and risks of disrupting the business.

More People

Any significant decision is likely to involve several people, departments, or levels of management.

Result: Organizational decisions involving more than one person are liable to generate political concerns—such as risks of upsetting influential individuals or functions—which don't generally arise in simpler sales.

More Competition

The bigger stakes involved in complex sales will attract competitors, and their activity is likely to be more intense than in simpler sales.

Result: With stiff competition, issues of vendor credibility and competence become important customer concerns.

Longer Selling Cycle

A complex sale may take many months, giving buyers plenty of time to become aware of risks and develop doubts.

Result: It's common, in longer selling cycles, for customer concerns about a vendor or a product to increase slowly over time. Worries about technical issues or post-sale support are examples of concerns which often develop as the sale progresses.

More Implementation Issues

As we'll see in Chapter 8, complex sales generally involve a continuing relationship between customer and vendor, particularly during the Implementation phase when the product or service is being introduced. In contrast, it's not uncommon in simpler sales for customers to buy from a vendor they may never see again.

Result: The customer is likely to have more concerns about relationships—concerns about the vendor company, its people, and the support it offers.

What's the common factor here? The one word which best sums up the customer's concerns in a major sale is *risk*. The size, complexity, and business importance of the decision all make it more risky for the customer. Some of these risks may be real—a vendor may genuinely lack the right technology, support capability, or business stability. Other risks may exist only in the customer's mind, and a vendor able to provide everything the customer needs may nevertheless arouse doubts and concerns. Whether the concerns have a basis in fact or are only imagined, they are real to the customer and can affect the outcome of the sale.

Risk in the Resolution of Concerns Phase

By far the most difficult customer concerns arise in the Resolution of Concerns phase. As the decision approaches, the customer's feeling of risk increases. In a simple sale, where the product costs very little, the worst penalty from a wrong decision is that the buyer has wasted a small amount of money. But in a complex sale, where the purchase is not only expensive, but also affects the customer's business, it's not uncommon for a wrong decision to damage a buyer's career. Consequently, because the buyer's risks are so much greater, some special concerns may arise during this phase of the sale which don't usually occur in simpler sales. The rest of this chapter examines these special concerns in more detail, showing what they are, why they arise, and the best strategies for dealing with them.

The Making of a Cautious Buyer

Keith G. was a management trainee, fresh out of college, who had just joined a major food-and-soft-drink conglomerate. His first job was in the purchasing department. He was responsible for buying supplies and non-capital goods items for the administrative functions. Most of his purchases were small—a few hundred dollars on average. Keith, like many ambitious young graduates, wasn't delighted to be placed in purchasing. "This is a dead-end function," he confided to us. "It's for people who have failed in real jobs. Everyone here seems to be a deadbeat. All they want is safety. Nobody's prepared to take any risks."

Keith was determined to change all that. He sought out new suppliers, he bought unusual items just to test them out, and he persuaded the management of the administration department to change and to experiment with new materials. Many of his introductions were welcomed by management. He was so successful that he was promoted, within the purchasing department, to a position which gave him responsibility for acquisition of big-ticket capital goods. "This is my chance," he told us. "I'll bring some innovation and some life into our purchasing."

Eighteen months later we interviewed Keith as part of a study on lost sales. Keith had turned down a vendor we were working with, and we were trying to find out why. "Well," Keith explained, "I liked his equipment, but it's new and that could be risky, so I went with another vendor I thought was safer." "That doesn't sound like you, Keith," we told him. "You were the one who used to make speeches about the importance of taking risks." "I've changed," he admitted. "Last year I bought a very expensive and untried piece of bottling equipment from an unknown supplier. If it had worked I'd have been a hero. It didn't—and we were left with a million-dollar mistake. When the purchasing manager's job became vacant, it went to one of my colleagues who's never taken a risk in his life. I wanted that job and I lost it because of one error. Nobody remembered my dozens of successes. From now on, I'm being careful."

Keith had learned two unpleasant lessons which explain why capital goods purchasing agents are so cautious. First, the risks of failure in large sales are very visible. Second, few organizations encourage risk. His colleague, who won the management job by playing safe, had a more accurate finger on the pulse of the typical purchasing department.

Consequences: The Risks of Going Ahead

What are the risks which buyers fear during the Resolution of Concerns phase? They can take many forms. The simpler risks are little more than the natural business anxieties which accompany any major decision: "Will the equipment arrive on time?" "Will there be any difficulties with installation?" "Is the training support going to be enough?" Other fears may be more deep-seated, such as, "Do I really want to do business with this vendor?" "Will our people accept the change?" or "What will happen to my career if this goes wrong?" It's these deep-seated concerns which are the dangerous ones. We call them *Consequences*. Some customers will voice them openly, but more often they remain lurking beneath the surface, influencing the decision without your even knowing it. Many sales which have moved promisingly through the Recognition of Needs and Evaluation of Options phases are lost because the seller didn't recognize and deal successfully with Consequence issues.

Objectives for the Resolution of Concerns Phase

We've seen how success in each phase of the sale so far depends on meeting specific strategic objectives. The Resolution of Concerns phase is no exception. Its strategic objectives are as follows:

- *To find whether Consequence issues exist.* We've found that some sales have serious Consequence issues, while in others there are no Consequences at all. The first strategic objective for this phase is to determine whether Consequences exist. As we'll see, this can be harder than it sounds.

- *To uncover and clarify any Consequence issues.* If you've reason to suspect that a Consequence issue exists, then your next sales objective must be to uncover it and ensure that you understand it. Again, this can be tougher than it sounds. Many major sales are lost because the seller dealt with minor symptoms and didn't ever get to the customer's real concern.

- *To help the customer resolve Consequence issues.* Finally, when you've a clear understanding of the real issue, you must aim to help resolve it. Notice that I say "help." As we'll see, Consequences are psychological issues which exist in the customer's mind. Only the customer can resolve them. Your role is to help the customer, not to try to resolve the concern on the customer's behalf.

What Causes Consequence Issues?

Consequences are the penalties or risks the customer believes could result from making a decision in your favor. But what causes Consequences? We were able to gain some insights into the nature of Consequences and their causes from a study we carried out about customer concern with price and how it changes during the selling cycle. Sellers with extensive experience in major sales usually report that the level of customer price concern isn't constant across all phases of the selling cycle. It's common for price concerns to be high during the early stages of a sale. Often the customer's very first question is "What does it cost?" One of the reasons for this early concern with price is that the customer hasn't yet fully recognized needs. As a result, the seller's product or service can't be judged in terms of the problems it solves and must therefore be judged on cost, not on value.

As the graph in Figure 6.2 shows, price concern tends to drop as the sale progresses, usually reaching its lowest point in the middle of the cycle. In its place comes an increased interest in applications—in the capabilities which the product or service offers the customer. Finally, just before the decision, there's often a sharp increase in price concern, with cost issues frequently becoming the central issue on which the whole decision seems to rest. What accounts for this sudden increase in price concern? One explanation is that the seller's efforts earlier in the cycle have tried to build up the customer's perception of value by emphasizing all that the customer would get from making a decision in the seller's favor. The seller tries to influence the value equation by developing solutions, savings, and benefits. However, as the decision approaches,

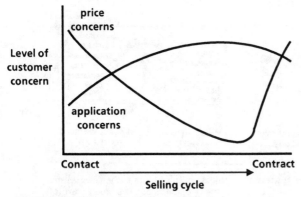

Figure 6-2. How price concern changes.

the customer naturally looks at the other side of the equation and begins to assess what all these things will cost. Figure 6.3 illustrates this change in the customer's value equation.

Cost isn't just a question of purchase price. Part of what the customer must pay is measured in less tangible terms—the decision has costs in terms of risks, implementation hassles, political dangers, and other things which could go wrong. These form the basis for the Consequence issues which often lie under the surface. So when a customer expresses a concern about price, that may not be the only factor present. Working with a major business-machines vendor, we carried out follow-up interviews in 50 lost sales where the customer had turned the seller down on the grounds of price. In 64 percent of the cases, interviews revealed that price was not the most important factor. The real issues were Consequences—risks and penalties which the customer feared would come from making a decision in the seller's favor. Typical customer responses included:

> "My V.P. came from one of their competitors and still has a lot of contacts there. I wasn't going to stick my neck out and risk upsetting him."

> "Their system is good—maybe the best on the market—but I'd heard they didn't put much effort into customer care, and that made me nervous."

> "Oh, I'm quite sure that their product would have been a big improvement on what we finally bought. But I just wasn't prepared to go through all the work and trouble of changing vendors again."

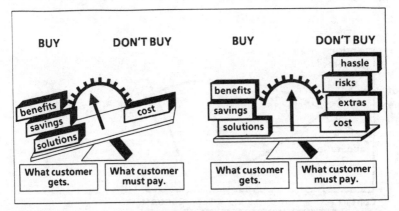

Figure 6-3. How the value equation changes.   LEFT: Early in the sale, sellers build up what the customer gets. RIGHT: As the decision nears, customers start to worry about what they must pay.

Price is the "respectable" way to express Consequences. Customers find it much easier to tell you they've decided not to buy because of cost than to explain issues such as mistrust, politics, hassle, or risk. And, because price-based decisions have business respectability, they can also be a convenient explanation within the buyer's own company. As a result, price is often used as a smoke screen for other concerns.

Price Is a Smoke Screen for Consequence Issues

Sam F. had worked hard for almost 8 months as head of a sales team which had been selling automated kitchen units to a fast food chain. Individually the units weren't expensive, but, because the sale would mean supplying more than 800 outlets, it was the biggest sale ever, not only for Sam but for his whole company. Everybody, from the company president down, was anxious as the decision approached. In one of his meetings with the fast food purchasing committee, Sam decided to take his president along to assess how the sale was progressing.

It wasn't as easy a meeting as Sam had hoped. Several members of the committee quibbled over minor points which Sam thought he'd already dealt with satisfactorily in earlier meetings. Worse, the head of the committee said, "Now we've got your president here, Sam, we'd like to take this opportunity to point out that your price is a lot higher than we'd expected. It may lose you the sale." Sam was astonished. His sponsor had told him just 2 weeks earlier that one of the strongest points in his proposal was his price—which was about 5 percent lower than the bid from a better known competitor.

Back at the office, the president was worried. "I think we're in danger of losing this one unless we do something about our price," he told Sam. After much internal discussion, Sam was told to revise his bid and cut another 9 percent off his overall contract price. "We might even lose some money on this contract," the president explained, "but it's worth it, because it gives us a presence in fast foods which we haven't had before."

Within a week Sam heard that he'd lost the sale. Several months later, when the dust had settled, Sam went back to his sponsor to find out what had happened. "Frankly," his sponsor explained, "we'd been told that you were moving out of the commercial kitchen business. We figured that was plausible because we knew that you didn't have much commercial business with other fast food chains, so this couldn't be as important for you as your domestic kitchen business.

(continued)

We didn't want to take the risk of a vendor who wasn't committed to our business." "But," Sam protested, "we were serious about commercial business. That's why we cut our price so much on our resubmission." "Your price cut had the opposite effect on us," explained his sponsor. "We thought it was a sign that you wanted to unload your commercial kitchen stock at cut prices so that you could get out of the commercial kitchen business."

Sam's president made a big mistake. He didn't understand that, as the decision nears, price issues are often raised as a respectable way to let a vendor know that a deeper discomfort exists. In this case, neither Sam nor his president realized that the Consequence issue was commitment to the commercial market. Had they known, they could have resolved the customer's fears. But, by treating the price issue at its face value, they only intensified the customer's true concerns—and it cost them a sale which would have been the biggest in their company's history.

The tendency of customers to raise a price smoke screen can have serious implications for how you handle price issues. If the issue is truly a concern about cost—and frequently it is—then it may be appropriate to negotiate and to offer some price reduction. However, if price is merely a smoke screen for a Consequence issue, then price reduction isn't the answer.

Recognition—The Essential First Step

Before you can handle Consequences you must be able to recognize them. That's why the first strategic objective for this phase of the sale is recognition—finding out whether Consequence issues really exist. And, as we've seen, Consequences can be difficult to recognize because (1) they are often under the surface, influencing the customer's decision without ever being discussed with you—so you may not even realize that they exist—and (2) when they do surface, they are often in the disguised form of a price concern, which leaves you with the problem of deciding whether the cost issues the customer is raising are real or are—at least in part—a smoke screen for Consequences the customer may be reluctant to express.

Some Early Warning Signals

Even before a face-to-face meeting with the customer in this phase of the sale, there are some indicators which can help you predict whether Consequences are likely to intrude. Remember that we've said that Consequence issues arise because the customer perceives a risk from doing business with you. Factors which increase that risk—and which therefore make Consequences more likely—would include:

- *Large decisions.* The larger the decision, the greater the risk to the buyer if something goes wrong. Decision size isn't measured only in dollars. Psychologically there may be fewer perceived risks—and therefore fewer Consequences—for the president of a large corporation making a million-dollar purchase than for a departmental manager who's spending $50,000. To assess whether Consequences may exist, you've got to ask yourself the question, "Is this a big decision for this individual?"

- *High-visibility decisions.* Sometimes the decision isn't particularly large, but it does have high visibility within the purchasing company. In such cases, with senior management showing interest, buyers may feel themselves under increased pressure and are likely to have more Consequence issues as a result.

- *Better known competitors.* If you're competing with other vendors who have a stronger reputation in the marketplace than you, a decision in your favor may be seen as risky. In contrast, a decision to go with the market leader is easier to justify. The competitor with the strongest market reputation will often use its position to raise Consequences about other vendors.

- *Competitor's account.* If you're selling into an account where a competitor is already well entrenched—particularly if the competitor has given good service—the buyer may be worried about the risks of changing.

- *Different technology.* If your product or service is based on technology or ideas which are new to the customer, then its unfamiliarity may raise Consequences. This is particularly likely if your competitors are proposing more conventional solutions which the customer understands better. The competition's more familiar approach may make your less conventional solution seem risky by comparison.

By asking yourself how many of these factors are present, you can estimate whether or not Consequences are likely to arise later in the selling cycle. The more factors you find, the more likely there will be Consequences.

How Safe to Be a Market Leader

Jan T. was very successful selling mid-size IBM computers. We'd been talking to Jan as part of a study we were promoting to find out how technical salespeople explained their products to nontechnical customers. Jan's success with first-time buyers led us to think that he was probably doing a good job of educating potential customers. But talking to Jan revealed a different story. "I don't sell computers," he told us. "I sell safety." If the customer wants to understand technicalities, I call in a support specialist. My job is to make the customer feel that IBM is the safest place for a first-time buyer to be. So I carefully—and in a responsible, professional way—raise concerns about the risk of dealing with a computer vendor. I raise risks about service, risks about reliability, and risks about software support. Then I show the customer that risks are much lower with IBM. IBM is safe."

Jan's success came because he did such a good job of raising Consequence issues which IBM could solve better than other vendors. And, of course, IBM marketing must take credit for building safety deeply into their overall marketing strategy. By recognizing that the ability to resolve Consequence issues is more important to the customer than a price premium, IBM has, until very recently, been able to keep outstandingly high margins on a product range which lacked superiority in terms of its features.

Detecting Consequences
Face-to-Face

As we've seen, it's relatively easy to predict in advance whether there are likely to be Consequences which will influence the sale during the Resolution of Concerns phase. But how do you recognize whether a Consequence is troubling a buyer when you're sitting face-to-face?

Sometimes, of course, the buyer will raise the Consequence directly. Most sellers can recall meetings in which a buyer has said something like, "Let me be frank: I'd like to do business with you, but I'm afraid of all the disruption which this new system would cause." When a buyer raises perceived risks like these, it's a sure sign that you've built a sufficiently good personal relationship so that your customer feels comfortable sharing such information with you. The issue is now on the table and it can be addressed. But even when you do have a good relationship with the buyer, there may still be Consequences which haven't been shared with you and which—if you don't resolve them—will influence the decision against you. These are by far the most dangerous of Consequences. The customer may have a misperception about you, your product, or your company which will damage you if it goes uncorrected. But how do you know whether such issues actually exist? What are the signs you should look for to tell whether a Consequence may be lurking under the surface?

Signs Which Suggest Consequences

There's no single sure sign that a Consequence exists in the customer's mind. But there's a high chance that some undisclosed issues do exist if one or more of the following signs are present.

- *Resurfacing of previously resolved issues.*   Suppose, for example, that last month one of your customers raised a quality issue about your product. You produced samples and a whole lot of other evidence to show that your quality exceeded their specifications. They seemed quite satisfied. Now, when you thought the whole quality issue had been finally put to bed, they begin raising it all over again.

  Cases like this, where a previously resolved issue resurfaces, are a clear sign that a Consequence may exist. Not always, of course—it's possible that the buyer is merely verifying a crucial issue before moving on—but experienced people generally take the resurfacing of old issues as a signal that the real concern is a Consequence which the buyer isn't yet sharing.

- *Unrealistic price concern.*   Many price concerns are just that—genuine budgetary issues about the cost of buying your product. But, as we've seen, price can also be a respectable way to express Consequences. How can you tell whether you should take price issues at face value, or whether they are being magnified out of proportion because of an unresolved Consequence?

  The safest course is to accept price issues at face value unless they seem to be unrealistic. For example, if a competitor is offering a similar product at a cheaper price, then accept price concern as genuine. But if your price is close enough to your competitor's for the concern to seem unrealistic, it probably signals that a Consequence issue exists.

- *Unjustified postponements.*   Postponements and delays are normal facts of business life as priorities and people in the account change. But if there's no apparent reason for postponements—if, for example, a presentation you've scheduled keeps getting put off without explanation—there's a strong possibility that Consequences exist which are making the customer reluctant to proceed.

- *Unwillingness to meet.* Another sign that Consequence issues are troubling the customer is persistent unwillingness or refusal to meet with you. Obviously your customers, particularly at a senior decision-making level, will not be available to you whenever you want to see them. But if you had easy access to a customer earlier in the cycle, and access is now being withheld, then suspect Consequences. Be particularly suspicious if one or more of your competitors is getting the access which you're finding hard to achieve.

- *Withholding of information.* Customers may be reluctant to give information to vendors, particularly if a decision is being made through formal processes like bid specifications or committees. So the customer's unwillingness to give you information may not, in itself, indicate that Consequences are present. However, if the customer freely gives information to your competitors while withholding it from you, it's a clear warning that Consequences may exist.

Discrepancies: The Common Factor

The common factor which underlies these signs is that each one shows a discrepancy between what should be happening and what's actually happening. When a resolved concern resurfaces, there's a discrepancy: the issue has already been resolved, yet here it is coming up again. If price concern is unrealistic, there's a discrepancy between a legitimate level of price concern—which is what *should* be happening—and an inflated and unrealistic price concern—which is what's actually happening.

So the basic principle of recognizing Consequences is to look for discrepancies—things which don't quite add up. If the customer says one thing but does another, or if an issue seems quite out of proportion, there's a strong possibility that the discrepancy is caused by an underlying concern which the customer isn't sharing with you.

How Do You Handle Consequences?

We've seen what Consequences are, why they arise late in the selling cycle, and how to detect whether they are present. Now comes the key strategic question: What's the best way to handle Consequences? Many sellers don't handle Consequences at all. They believe that any issue under the surface is best left alone. By trying to uncover Consequences, they argue, you'll make matters worse. So unless the customer raises an issue, it's better to ignore it.

Other people, particularly those with long experience in major sales, recognize that Consequences will affect the customer's decision. They believe that it's better to get the issues out on the table where they can be handled and resolved, rather than to have them lurking under the surface. But even these experienced people, who recognize the importance of dealing with Consequence issues, may have difficulty in uncovering and resolving Consequences successfully. By their very nature, Consequences aren't easy to uncover and, once uncovered, will often require delicate handling. What are the basic principles which can help you deal successfully with Consequences?

Some Basic Principles

There's no magic formula for handling Consequences. As in other areas of selling, no single approach will be successful 100 percent of the time. However, there are some basic principles, and some specific skills, which can help resolve Consequence issues and increase your chances of getting the business.

- *Don't ignore Consequences.* A Consequence issue doesn't go away if you leave it alone. That's an important and fundamental principle. Those salespeople who would rather ignore Consequences than face the risks of dealing with them are taking even bigger risks. They are letting damaging customer concerns continue unresolved—those concerns may ultimately cost them the sale. Whether you like it or not, unresolved Consequences hurt your chances of success, so you can't afford to ignore them. Because the customer doesn't tell you a concern, you shouldn't assume that it's unimportant. Often, the most damaging concerns are the ones which the customer is most reluctant to share. So, if you've reason to believe that a Consequence issue exists, get it out on the table and resolve it; don't ignore it.

- *Build relationships early.* The easiest Consequences to deal with are ones the customer shares with you and seeks your help with. If, for example, a customer asks your advice on how to handle a V.P. who prefers one of your competitors, then the Consequence is out on the table and it can be addressed. It's far harder for you if the buyer says nothing but thinks, "It's too risky to go with them because I don't know how to convince the V.P."

  The first step in handling Consequences is to get customers to share them with you. And that depends on how well you've built confidence and trust. Trust can't be switched on instantly like a light. The whole history of your relationship through the earlier parts of the selling cycle will determine whether the customer feels confident enough to share things with you. No strategies or techniques at the end of the sale can substitute for careful, professional relationship-building earlier in the cycle.

- *Only the customer can resolve a Consequence—you can't.* Consequences are risks or penalties which the customer perceives will result from making a decision in your favor. The risks exist in the customer's mind. That doesn't make them any less real—but it does mean that their solution must come from the customer, not from you. You can't resolve other people's fears for them. All you can do is create the right conditions to allow them to resolve their fears for themselves. Even experienced salespeople fall into the trap of trying to resolve Consequences for customers, rather than helping customers to provide their own solutions. Remember that Consequences belong to your customers, not to you. You can help your customers resolve Consequences, but you can't do it for them.

It's the Customer Who Resolves the Consequence

While working with an industrial insulating materials manufacturer, we had an excellent example of how important it is to get the customer to suggest solutions to Consequence issues. Larry Polermo, one of their salespeople, had for 3 years tried unsuccessfully to make sales to a particular customer who was the largest commercial builder in his territory. "The problem," Larry told us, "is that the buyer is afraid that his boss won't like it if he changes from a local supplier. I've tried everything. I've brought written costings he can show his boss to prove that we'll save him money. I've urged him to go to his boss and tell him that our material has a higher coefficient of insulation. I've even pushed him to just take the risk and make the decision himself—after all, he is responsible for purchasing. But nothing seems to work."

"Perhaps you're trying too hard," we suggested. "You're the one who's coming up with all the ideas. Why don't you ask the buyer what his ideas are for handling his boss?" Larry was skeptical. "It won't do any good," he warned us. "That's the problem—this buyer hasn't got any ideas." However, Larry agreed to try and, at his next meeting, asked the buyer for suggestions about how to convince the boss. After the call Larry telephoned us. "It's just as I said," he told us. "I

(continued)

asked him and he didn't come up with anything." We admitted that our suggestion had failed. Selling's an uncertain business—you win some and you lose some. This one we had lost. Or so we believed until 2 weeks later when Larry called us again. "I got my first order," he told us cheerfully. "The buyer says he thought about our discussion over the weekend, and the more he thought, the easier he felt it would be to convince his boss to give us a small trial order. So he talked to his boss on Monday, and now I'm in the account."

Larry's success came because, instead of pressuring the buyer with his own suggestions, he tried to get the buyer to come up with possible solutions. The psychological barrier was in the buyer's mind. Larry couldn't remove it by pressuring the buyer—his pressure may even have strengthened the barrier. But, by encouraging the buyer to think about solutions, the barrier weakened and, finally, crumbled.

The Three Deadly Sins of Handling Consequences

The qualities which make a person good at handling Consequences are difficult to develop. As we've seen, they include empathy, sympathetic listening, and an ability to take an honest look at yourself through your customer's eyes. I've tried hard to train people to be more skillful in these areas, but, to be frank, I don't know how well I've succeeded. These aren't easy qualities to develop. The necessary interpersonal sensitivities are subtle, and the skills can take years to learn. But, if I'm not sure how to train salespeople to create the trust necessary for good Consequence handling, I am sure about how to help people avoid some common strategic mistakes which most sellers make. In particular, there are three deadly sins of Consequence handling which are committed by salespeople with the intention of helping to resolve Consequence issues.

If the customer raises a Consequence issue, many salespeople make the fundamental mistake of trying to overcome it as if it were an objection. They ignore the principle that a Consequence is the customer's problem and only the customer can resolve it. This leads them to try solving the problem for the customer, using counterproductive methods which reduce the chances of dealing with the Consequence successfully.

1. Minimizing

Minimizing, the first of the deadly sins, is making light of a customer's concern by denying its importance or by offering baseless reassurance.

Typical examples of Minimizing would be statements such as "Don't worry about it," "Someone of your experience shouldn't be concerned about that," and "Trust me."

Telling someone not to worry doesn't resolve fears, as anyone should know who's tried to tell a frightened child there's nothing to be afraid of in the dark. Similarly, your customers aren't going to be reassured simply because you tell them there's nothing to worry about. Yet, in a variety of ways, most salespeople try to reassure customers by minimizing their concerns. Minimizing will not help you deal with the customer's Consequence issues for the following reasons:

- *Minimizing doesn't resolve the Consequences.* Minimizing may temporarily relieve a concern, but, because it doesn't actually resolve it, the concern will soon come back.

- *Minimizing drives the Consequence underground.* Minimizing a concern makes the buyer feel that the seller thinks it trivial, so the buyer no longer wants to share it. As we've seen, the most dangerous Consequences are the ones under the surface. Minimizing a customer's concern will drive it underground, where it will continue to create doubts.

- *Larger Consequences remain hidden.* When buyers decide to share Consequences, the first one they choose to reveal is often a lesser concern. This relatively minor issue is put forward by the buyer as a kind of test, to see how sympathetically the seller will deal with it. If it's minimized, then the buyer may decide not to share the more important Consequence issues. It's possible, for instance, that the more important Consequence in this example is that members of the board have doubts about whether the seller's company can handle a complex installation. By Minimizing a smaller Consequence, the seller may never hear about these larger concerns until the contract is awarded to a competitor.

2. Prescribing

The second deadly sin is Prescribing—pushing the seller's own ideas, solutions, and recommendations for how the Consequence should be resolved. Typical examples of statements which are used when salespeople prescribe include: "The way to handle that concern is...," "If I were you, what I would do is...," and "My recommendation would be..." If a Consequence is creating a problem for the customer, then common sense suggests that it would be helpful if you could offer a way to solve it. And that's just what Prescribing is—offering solutions to customers' problems. So why is it counterproductive to use Prescribing behavior? To understand why Prescribing doesn't help resolve Consequences, it's important to be clear about the difference between an ordinary problem and the special type of problem which we call a Consequence.

Most ordinary problems are difficulties which exist for us out there in the real world—my car won't start, the roof is leaking, the cat's hurt its tail. We're generally grateful to anyone who can solve these problems for us. If you can start my car, fix my roof, or put the cat's tail in a splint, then I'm glad to have your help—I may even pay you for it. A Consequence issue is different. Here, the most important part of the problem isn't out in the real world—it's in a person's head. A Consequence is a fear, concern, or doubt. If I'm afraid to do something, then you can't resolve that fear for me. All you can do is help me solve it for myself. Some people, like therapists, counselors, and psychiatrists, make a career out of helping others resolve inner concerns. Although these people in the helping professions disagree about most things, there's one area where they are in full accord: never try to solve a client's problems—always help clients solve problems for themselves. The problem with "If I were you" advice is that I'm not you. The way I'd tackle a problem would be different, and, even if my advice were good and you accepted it, you might have real difficulty putting it into practice.

Prescribing—telling customers what you think they ought to do—is rather like offering product solutions too early in the sale. Sellers who give solutions before they've developed needs tend to receive more objections from their customers. Prescribing has the same effect—it raises resistance in the customer. So don't try to resolve Consequence issues by recommending solutions to the customer.

3. Pressuring

The third deadly sin, Pressuring, pushes the customer for information or decisions. Typical statements indicative of pressuring might be, "I must have a decision right away" or "Unless you give me that information, I can't produce the proposal in time." A customer with a Consequence issue will often seem indecisive. The nature of most Consequences is that there are factors in favor of a decision almost exactly balanced by factors against. If all the factors point the same way, then the customer doesn't usually have worries about making a decision. Customers rarely lose sleep over how to tell an overpriced, underfeatured vendor that their after-sales service has a poor reputation. Consequences arise when positives and negatives appear to be evenly balanced—when the customer wants to do business but has doubts or fears large enough to make a commitment seem risky.

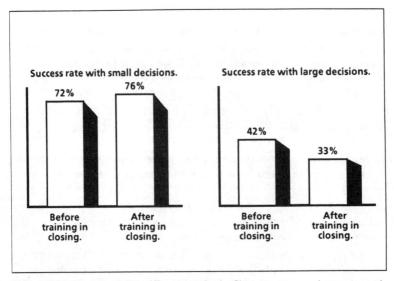

Figure 6-4. Closing and its effect on sales.   Closing increases sales success with *small decisions*, but decreases success with *larger decisions*.

Many salespeople have been taught that the best way to handle an indecisive customer is to use closing techniques, such as assumptive or alternative closes, to get a decision. This may be an acceptable strategy in simpler sales, but it becomes dangerous and counterproductive as the sale grows more complex and Consequences begin to influence the decision.

In *SPIN® Selling* I describe a whole series of studies which show that pressure generally has a negative impact on the customer as the size of the sale grows. In one of those studies we investigated the relationship between the effectiveness of closing techniques and the size of the purchasing decision. As Figure 6.4 shows, when the decision is small, using closing techniques increases the chances of making a sale. However, with larger decisions, the use of closing techniques reduces sales significantly.

Why should closing work with small decisions but fail with larger ones? The explanation lies in the psychology of pressure and its effect on decision making. Closing is one of the ways in which a seller can put pressure on a buyer to make a decision. If the decision is small, pressure can have a positive effect on an uncertain buyer. That's not only true in selling. If, for example, you want a friend to go with you to a concert, and she's undecided about whether she wants to go, use a little pressure and she'll probably be at the concert with you. But if the decision's a large one—for example, if you're trying to persuade her to change her job—then pressuring her is likely to generate resistance and counter pressures which may make her less likely to change.

Why doesn't pressure succeed when the decision is large? It's because large decisions have Consequences, which, as we've seen, are fears, worries, and concerns. Putting pressure on a person who is worried about making a decision will increase the worries and make the person less likely to decide in your favor. So pressuring the customer is a dangerous way to handle Consequences.

The Dangers of Pressure

The Newhall Corporation, a major supplier of industrial robots, is a subsidiary of a giant multinational. As often happens with subsidiaries of large corporations, performance had been judged by the corporate board as mediocre and a complete change of management was ordered. The new vice president of sales began by analyzing the record of his sales force. Only 26 percent of bids resulted in orders. "Too low," he thought. "I'd better do something about it." He decided that many members of his sales force weren't taking an aggressive enough approach to closing sales. So he called together all sales managers and firmly instructed them to send their people out to every customer to whom a bid had been submitted and try to aggressively push the customer into signing the contract. He confidently expected that this strategy would greatly increase the present 26 percent hit rate.

Three months later, when final figures were available, he was alarmed to find that the result of his blitz, as he called it, was a sales rate of 19 percent. By pressuring his customer base he'd lost orders, not gained them. The vice president of sales didn't understand that many of his customers had Consequence issues. They were worried because it had been reported in the press that the multinational giant might leave the robotics business. If that happened, customers faced the serious risk that their equipment would be unsupported. The sudden pressure from the sales force only increased the feeling of risk. Many customers responded to pressure by moving to safer competitors.

The three deadly sins of Minimizing, Prescribing, and Pressuring are three common but counterproductive ways to deal with Consequences. Each one may be used with the genuine intention of helping the customer resolve concerns, but, as we've seen, they usually have the opposite effect.

Handling Consequence Issues Successfully

In this chapter we've talked about how important it is to understand whether Consequence issues exist during the Resolution of Concerns phase of the sale. We've looked at some of the telltale signs which show whether Consequences are present—resurfacing of old resolved issues, unrealistic price concerns, unjustified postponements, unwillingness to meet, and withholding of information. All these things indicate that a discrepancy exists—that something doesn't quite add up.

We've said that the reason why Consequences are so difficult to handle is that they often lurk under the surface and that buyers may be reluctant to share them. So, before you can deal with a Consequence, your initial strategic objective must be to uncover whether or not one exists. We've also said that the first Consequence which the buyer raises often isn't the most important one. So your next objective must be for you to clarify the Consequence you've uncovered—to find out whether it's just a symptom for other more significant concerns and to gain a clear understanding of the issues which are troubling the buyer. Finally, we've said that a Consequence is a concern which exists in the buyer's mind. Only the buyer can resolve it. Your role isn't to provide the solution, it's to help the buyer resolve the Consequence.

To achieve the strategic objective of uncovering, clarifying, and helping to resolve a Consequence issue, we've suggested that you should keep in mind three basic principles:

- *Don't ignore Consequences.*   Consequences will be more likely to hurt you if you leave them unresolved. Don't kid yourself that they'll go away of their own accord.

- *Build relationships early.*   Consequences are easier to talk about if you've built up trust earlier in the sale.

- *Only the customer can resolve a Consequence.*   Consequences are in the customer's mind. Your job is to help the customer discuss and think about Consequences. You can help your customers resolve Consequences, but you can't do it for them.

Finally, we've talked about the three deadly sins of Minimizing, Prescribing, and Pressuring. When you're handling Consequence issues, watch out for these three perils and try to avoid them.

I started this chapter by describing David Davidson, who had such an outstanding record for closing major sales. Many of David's colleagues, including his manager, had trouble understanding how someone like David could be so successful. He was shy and quiet, a listener rather than a talker, and a sensitive, sympathetic person. His manager, like many of us, had been brought up to believe that "super closers" should be dynamic, energetic, dominant, and extroverted. How could David be successful if he so clearly lacked these classic traits?

I hope, if David's manager ever reads this chapter, that he'll now find it easier to understand why David was so successful. Sympathetic listening and a genuine regard for the concerns of others are clearly helpful characteristics for handling the Consequence issues which arise in major sales. In smaller sales, there is some evidence that you can use a pushy and assertive style to close successfully. In my book *SPIN Selling*, I present several studies which show that a high-energy, forceful, and dominating style can succeed in small sales. But not in major sales. As the size of the sale grows—and as Consequence issues become more frequent and more severe—it's the empathetic questioning style of a David Davidson which is needed for success.

And Finally...

If you've followed all the advice we've offered so far, you'll now be mercifully near to the decision itself. In the first phase of the sale, the Recognition of Needs, you'll have developed needs in those areas where you're best able to provide a solution. In the next phase of the sale, the Evaluation of Options, you'll have influenced the customer's decision criteria, differentiated yourself from competitors, and reduced any competitive vulnerability. Now, during the Resolution of Concerns phase, you've uncovered, clarified, and helped to resolve any Consequences. What other barriers could possibly exist between you and that elusive decision? Just one: negotiation. In these final stages of a major sale—just as the decision approaches—the customer will often attempt to negotiate better terms. Unfortunately, few of the salespeople we've met are good at negotiation. They find it stressful and difficult when, at the end of all this selling effort, the customer asks to negotiate changes in specification, price, or delivery. Yet there are some simple rules which can help make negotiation easier—and they are the subject of our next chapter.

7

Sales Negotiation: How to Offer Concessions and Agree to Terms

On the surface, selling and negotiating may seem very similar. They have the same aim—reaching an acceptable business agreement. They both involve persuasion skills, and they both require relationship building. But there's one big difference, and if you don't understand it your whole selling strategy is in trouble. The difference is this: when you're negotiating you have the ability to vary the terms in order to get an agreement. To negotiate, you must first have the authority to change something—such as price, delivery, or contract terms. People don't normally expect to negotiate for a can of beans in a supermarket because the checkout person has no authority to change the price. But they *do* negotiate when they are buying a house, or a used car, because they are dealing with a vendor who has the authority to change the terms and to make concessions. In other words, when you're negotiating you're prepared, if necessary, to give something away in order to do business. That's not true of selling. When you're selling you don't give anything away. Your success rests on persuasion skills alone.

Why the Difference between Selling and Negotiating is Important

The most common mistake people make when they're not clear about the difference between selling and negotiating is to begin negotiating too soon. In one major organization I worked with, the sales force was given negotiating authority to offer a discount of up to 10 percent in order to get the business. Management, when introducing this negotiating authority, stressed to the sales force that negotiation was to be used *only if it was absolutely essential* to achieving the sale. When this new policy was evaluated 6 months later, it was discovered that the full discount had been offered in almost every case. The final result was equivalent to an across-the-board price cut of 9.8 percent. This was, of course, disastrously different from the effect which the company had intended. The company had given away its margins and, worse, hadn't even taken a higher sales volume in exchange. A closer analysis showed that the sales force had been offering customers the 10 percent discount very early in the selling cycle as a means of gaining initial interest. Their salespeople were negotiating—by giving away the maximum discount— when they should have been selling. Late in the selling process, when the discount could have been a powerful tool, it was no longer available. It had already been given away and its impact lost.

Negotiating Too Soon

Ian Gilmore sold document binding machines in the office products market. He was one of his company's most successful salespeople, and, because of that, he was given responsibility for several national accounts, including a major engineering organization which had the potential for a very large contract. At a company sales meeting it was announced that the national accounts representatives, including Ian, would be given the power to negotiate substantial discounts for bulk purchases. And, as often happens at such meetings, management issued dire warnings about how this negotiating authority was only to be used when absolutely necessary. Ian wasn't too concerned about the warnings—he was too delighted at the thought of being able to offer a discount.

"This will make life a whole lot easier," he thought to himself. One reason for Ian's delight was that he'd just heard that his big engineering customer had decided to produce most of their documents inter-

(continued)

---

nally, and, inevitably, they would need to buy a substantial number of document binding machines. "What a break," Ian thought. "In the same week I find that my biggest customer has finally decided to introduce binders I'm given the power to negotiate discounts. This sale is being handed to me on a plate." The next day Ian rushed out to visit the engineering company buyer. "Good news," he told her. "Because you're a potential national account, I'm able to offer you a special quantity discount, which is up to 15 percent below our published prices." The buyer was delighted. "That's really good news," she told Ian, "and I'm sure that it will make us *much* more interested in your machines."

A month later the engineering company published specifications and invited bids from Ian and three of his competitors. "I'm glad I was able to offer that extra discount," Ian told his boss. "It's helped us get in the door." The selling cycle progressed until, ultimately, only Ian and one competitor remained. In his final proposal Ian emphasized that, with his special discount, he was almost 10 percent cheaper than his competition. He was confident that his price advantage would give him the business.

The day before the decision was due, the buyer called Ian and told him, "Your competitor has just offered us a price reduction. We'd like you to think about whether you can do the same." "But I offered you a price reduction right at the start," Ian protested. "You've already had a greatly reduced price from us. I can't offer any more." "As you wish," the buyer told him, "but I warn you that your competitor's price cut has made a very positive impact on us." Ian called his boss. "We've got to reduce our price," he insisted. "Impossible," his boss told him. "You've already gone to the maximum special discount. We can't do more." There was nothing Ian could do. The following day he learned that he'd lost the sale. Ian's mistake was to begin negotiating too soon. He offered his maximum discount as a means of creating interest. He would have been more successful if he'd followed his competitor's example and waited until nearer the decision when his price concession would have maximum impact. Negotiating too soon is the most common mistake of inexperienced negotiators.

There are many other case studies I could quote of sales organizations which have made the mistake of allowing their people to negotiate price if that became necessary to take the business. Results of this strategy have almost invariably been disappointing. In most cases, salespeople have offered the reduced price too soon in the sale, and consequently their concessions have had minimal impact or have resulted in giving away more than was necessary.

The Key Rule: Negotiate Late

The cases I have given are not isolated examples. Most people begin negotiating much too soon. Successful sales negotiation depends on a clear understanding of one key rule: *never negotiate before you must*. The earlier you give concessions, the less impact they will have. Don't begin to modify your terms until it's clear that you have no alternative. Negotiation never has been, and never will be, a substitute for effective selling. There are obviously good business reasons for waiting as long as you can before negotiating and, once negotiation becomes inevitable, for making as few concessions as possible. Why make costly concessions in a negotiation if you can get the same business by using your selling skills without giving so much away?

There are also good psychological reasons for holding back as long as possible before negotiating. By giving things away early, you may create an expectation that even larger concessions will follow later. And as we've said, a concession given early has less impact than the same concession offered later in the sale.

Why don't early concessions work? After all, you would expect that giving concessions to the customer early in the sales process would get you in the door, establish goodwill, and put you one step ahead of the competition. However, it's not a good strategy to begin with concessions because you are influencing the wrong half of the customer's value equation. As Figure 7.1 shows, in making any decision to purchase, customers must balance two opposing elements. One of these is the seriousness of the problems which your product would solve. The other is the cost of your solution, measured in terms of money, inconvenience, or risk. If the problem is so serious that the cost of solving it seems small in comparison, then the customer will probably buy. But sometimes it's the other way around. The problem may not seem significant enough to justify the price of your solution. In this case, the customer will probably continue to live with the problem or will look for a cheaper source of help.

In selling, you generally try to build customers' perception of problems, but in negotiating you tend to concentrate on the other side of the value equation. By making concessions during negotiation, you attempt to reduce the side concerned with cost. If, for example, you offer a 5 percent discount, what you are doing is making your product solution seem less expensive to the customer. However, if you've failed to build a sufficient need before offering your price concession, then you've adopted a risky and potentially expensive strategy.

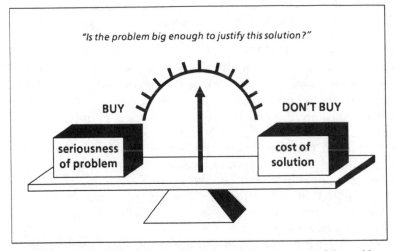

"Is the problem big enough to justify this solution?"

BUY   DON'T BUY

seriousness
of problem

cost of
solution

Figure 7-1. The customer's value equation.   If the seriousness of the problem outweighs the cost of solving it, there's a basis for a successful sale.

Which Side of the Value Equation?

An overhead-projector dealer authorized its sales force to offer a 15 percent discount to corporate clients buying two or more projectors. In other words, it gave its sales force the authority to negotiate price. One of the dealer's salespeople was John Connally. To gain interest from his prospects, he usually mentioned, in setting up the appointment, that he could give a discount. By doing this he was operating on the "cost of solution" side of the customer's value equation, making his solution seem cheaper than expected. Predictably, his offer of a discount was a remarkably effective attention-getter, allowing him to set up an increased number of meetings. However, because the projectors he was selling were expensive, even with a 15 percent discount he had no real price advantage over most of his competitors. As a result, although his order rate rose a little, it wasn't enough to compensate for the lost profit from a 15 percent price reduction.

His lack of success convinced John that he should change strategy. So he shifted his attention to influencing the other side of the customer's value equation. Instead of initially promising a specific discount, he used terms like "very competitive" to gain an interest without giving anything away. When customers asked about price or discount, he would reply, "That would depend on things like quantity or which machine best meets your needs. Let me get an under-

(continued)

standing of those needs, and then I'll be able to give you a price."
Turning to the "seriousness of problem" side of the equation, he uncovered dissatisfactions and built up their implications. In one case,
for example, he found that the customer's present projectors would
sometimes overheat. As a result, more than $2000 of damage had
been done to one set of transparencies. Because he was able to show
that his products were cooler in operation, he took an order on the
spot for three new projectors without giving any discount. In the customer's mind, a problem which could cause thousands of dollars
worth of damage was severe enough to make John's price differential
seem insignificant. Increased attention to developing problems
meant that John sold more effectively and therefore took more business. And, by selling better, there were fewer occasions when he was
forced to negotiate discounts.

The case of John is a simple one in a straightforward selling situation. But even in complex sales, the same principle applies. Give
your primary attention to developing the "seriousness of problem"
side of the customer's value equation. It's better to get the business by
building stronger needs than by trying to make your solution
cheaper.

Negotiation: A Costly Way to Resolve Consequences

Using negotiation too early, so that it becomes a substitute for selling, is
the most obvious mistake that sellers make. Giving away concessions
early in the sales process is not the smartest way to gain customer interest. But there's another, less obvious area where people make the mistake of negotiating when it would be far more effective to be selling instead. This danger point comes at the end of the cycle, just when
negotiation would seem to be the most sensible strategy for getting the
business.

Sometimes, as the final purchasing decision approaches, we've seen
that customers experience concerns or fears about the consequences of
buying from a particular vendor. These Consequence issues are rarely
expressed openly but may nevertheless lurk under the surface. Typical
Consequence issues might be a customer's doubts about the stability of a
vendor, concerns over the integrity of the seller, or worries about how
the customer will convince key internal people that the decision is the
right one. As we saw in the last chapter, customers may be reluctant to
express some of these reservations directly and may therefore choose to

raise them in the "respectable" form of price issues. We once carried out a follow-up study of 50 lost sales where the customer had turned down a vendor on the stated grounds of price. Interviews with these customers revealed that in 32 cases out of 50, price was only a secondary concern. The real grounds for rejecting the vendor were unresolved Consequence issues. In cases like these, where price isn't the real concern, how effective will it be to attempt to negotiate by making price concessions? Almost certainly negotiation isn't the best answer. It will be more effective to uncover and resolve the Consequence issue, as this next case study shows.

When Price Isn't the Issue

Two small vendors were competing with a computer giant in selling a central electronic filing system. The customer was concerned that in the highly volatile state of the computer industry, the small vendors might not survive. Naturally, given that the decision involved several hundred thousand dollars, the customer was afraid of buying an installation from someone who might go out of business and leave the system unsupported.

This type of concern isn't easy to express. So the customer, as often happens, chose the easy way out and raised price as a reason for not wanting to go ahead. One vendor took these price concerns at face value and revised its proposal, shaving another 4 percent off the cost of the system. The effect on the customer was the opposite of the one intended. "They must be desperate for business; it's a bad sign, and we should steer clear of them" was the consensus among members of the customer's purchasing committee.

The second small vendor adopted a different approach. "We're already cheaper than the big competitor," the vendor's management reasoned, "so price is a smokescreen for some other concern. We'd better find out what the *real* problem is." By probing for the Consequence issues, they revealed the customer's concern about vendor stability. They then arranged a series of actions designed to reassure the customer, including a meeting with the vendor's bankers, discussions with existing key accounts, and a confidential inspection of the vendor's order books. Reassured, the customer went ahead and signed the contract at the originally proposed price. The first small vendor who, in reality, was every bit as financially viable as the second, lost the business by negotiating when there was still an important selling job to do.

Larger vendors must also contend with Consequence issues, although these may take a different form. For example, it's common for customers to have concerns such as, "How do I explain this to my V.P., who prefers their competitor?" Negotiation about price, delivery, or support won't make the fundamental fear go away. It's better to resolve the real issues, rather than bargain your way through a smoke screen.

Showstoppers

So far we've talked about when *not* to negotiate. We've said:

- Don't negotiate early in the selling cycle; negotiation should never be a substitute for selling.

- Don't try to negotiate your way out of Consequence issues or nonspecific concerns.

In summary, the best strategic advice is to negotiate late and negotiate little. But, however well you sell, and however hard you try to avoid negotiation, there will be times when the customer will not do business unless you can change your product offering or your proposed terms. These are the *showstoppers*—barriers to moving forward which can't be overcome by selling skill alone. For example, a couple of weeks ago one of my customers called to ask whether we could bid on a consulting contract which involved designing and delivering a program in French. The sale was clearly in the Evaluation of Options phase. The customer had identified a need to provide a program for French-speaking salespeople. By inviting bids from consulting firms like mine, the customer was beginning the process of choosing between vendors. Normally we'd feel this would be much too soon in the selling cycle for us to begin negotiating. However, the reality was that we didn't have the capability to design a complex program in the French language. We faced a showstopper. Either we would lose the sale or we'd have to negotiate an alternative, such as designing the program in English and getting the client to translate it into French. Selling skill alone couldn't solve the problem because it couldn't alter the fact that the customer had a need that we were unable to meet. Unless we could find an acceptable alternative way to satisfy the customer's specification, we couldn't bid on the contract.

Most showstoppers arise because the customer has needs or requirements which you can't meet. But it's not only the customer who introduces showstoppers. Sometimes the seller's company can create them too. My organization, for example, has a policy that we won't provide sales training for companies selling tobacco products. More than once that's been a showstopper which has prevented us from doing business.

There are two pieces of strategic advice for dealing with showstoppers. First, be sure that the barrier *is* genuinely a showstopper. I've heard negotiators talk of showstoppers when a competitor has access to a decision maker and they don't, or when their price is marginally higher than the competition's. These are difficult selling situations, but they are *not* showstoppers. The definition of a showstopper is that it's a barrier which is insurmountable using your present products or terms. You can't move forward unless you change your approach in some way—for example, by offering a different product, different terms, or a creatively different approach. If you treat every competitive disadvantage as a showstopper, it leads you into making too many concessions too early in the sale.

The second piece of advice is to deal with showstoppers relatively speedily. If you identify a potential showstopper, address it quickly; don't postpone it. One of the common strategic mistakes I see in less experienced people is that they generally wait as long as possible before confronting any showstoppers. Their reasoning, I imagine, is that they want to build up a positive relationship with the customer first. They believe that the customer will be more likely to make concessions—or even give way entirely on the showstopper—if the tough issues are avoided until the last possible moment. But, plausible though this may sound, it's not what most experienced negotiators believe. If it's a *real* showstopper, then by definition it's likely to prevent the sale, so the sooner it's raised with the customer, the better. If it's so serious that there's no way around it—if, in other words, it stops the show—then by raising it you've made sure that neither you nor the customer has wasted unnecessary time in a fruitless selling cycle. But if, as sometimes happens, there are creative ways to remove the showstopper, then the sooner you and the customer start problem solving, the better.

Remember that we're talking here about *real* showstoppers—where the customer won't move ahead unless you radically change something. In order to advance the sale you may have to consider major modifications to your selling strategy, such as offering a completely different product, substantially varying your price or payment terms, or drastically modifying your proposed approach. None of these options will be desirable and sometimes none will even be possible—hence the name "showstoppers." Although our general advice is to negotiate little and late, showstoppers are an exception. Because of their nature you *must* negotiate or you're out of the sale. Showstoppers are the only things you should negotiate during the Recognition of Needs or the Evaluation of Options phases of the sale.

The Right Time for Negotiation

If you've been fortunate enough to progress through a sales cycle without any showstoppers, you may find that you've successfully resolved Consequences and there are now some last points remaining which need to be hammered out before the final decision can be made. This is the point in the selling cycle where negotiation is an effective strategic tool.

The first question to ask yourself before any negotiation is, "Do I have the power to vary the terms?" Unless you have authority to change something, such as delivery, support, or contract terms, then you're not able to negotiate, and it's dangerous to give the customer the impression that you can.

Everybody Negotiates

People tend to think of negotiation as a process which only takes place across a formal bargaining table. As a result, they see negotiating as a very unusual, and very threatening, activity. This narrow view of negotiation is dangerous. It leads people who have little experience in formal negotiation to feel insecure and ill equipped. "I'm not a negotiator," they typically say, "so I don't know anything about how to negotiate." If that's how you see negotiation, you're missing a vital point. Everyone negotiates, and most people have developed their negotiating skills to a higher level than they may realize. In an average day you're likely to be involved in dozens of negotiations. You negotiate about priorities at work and at home, about budgets, targets, and use of time. Whenever a resource is scarce and there are competing views about how to use it, you are likely to be negotiating. So don't think of yourself as knowing nothing about negotiation or as being totally inexperienced. You've probably developed negotiating skills which you haven't recognized.

Defining Negotiation

Negotiation, as we've seen, is more than just a formal bargaining process. That's too narrow a way to look at it. It's an integral part of our everyday life. Some writers, taking account of this, have defined *negotiation* in very broad terms as "any conversation with a purpose." But that's too broad. A more balanced definition of *negotiation* is that it's an attempt by two or more parties to reach an agreement when the following three conditions are present:

1. *Both parties can vary the terms.* That's the difference between negotiation and selling. If you can't vary the terms, you must sell, because you can't negotiate.

2. *The resource is scarce.* When there's enough of something we generally don't bother to negotiate about it. In a meeting where there's enough coffee to go around, we don't negotiate about who should get a cup. But if there are eight people in the meeting and only enough cups for five, then coffee may become a negotiable issue. We negotiate about money and time because they are such scarce resources.

3. *Agreement and conflict exist simultaneously.* Every negotiation can be seen as two overlapping circles, as illustrated in Figure 7.2. In one circle are the things *you* want, in the other the things that the customer wants. In the overlapping area there are needs in common to both of you. For example, the customer wants to solve certain problems. You also want to solve those problems—by selling your product or service. Some of the customer's wants may not be in your circle. It's probable, for example, that getting the lowest price is desirable for the customer but doesn't suit you. Or *you* might want something, such as the business the account is giving to your competitors, which the customer will be unwilling to provide.

It's *not* a negotiation if your circle and the customer's don't overlap at all. When that happens, you've a customer who doesn't want what you have to offer and isn't prepared to pay for it. Without common ground, neither party has anything to offer the other, so there's no

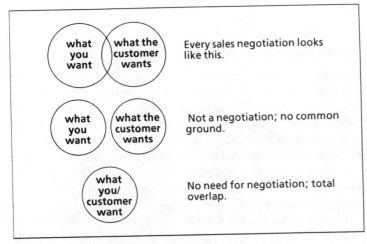

Figure 7-2. The overlapping circles of sales negotiation.

basis for negotiation. If your circles overlap completely, then that's not a negotiation either. It means that you and the customer are in complete agreement. If that's so, why negotiate? There's nothing to negotiate about. Just go ahead and do business.

The two-circles diagram clearly shows one of the most important characteristics of negotiation. In every negotiation, potential agreement (the middle ground) exists side by side with potential conflict (the areas which don't overlap). One of the things which makes negotiation difficult is that you must deal with agreement and conflict in the same meeting. Negotiation simultaneously contains hopes and frustrations.

Studies of Expert Negotiators

Some years ago, with the help of Bill Allen, I studied 51 expert negotiators during 107 negotiating sessions. By comparing the behavior of these experts with results from a parallel study of average negotiators, we found that the experts showed marked differences in how they handled negotiations.

We defined an expert negotiator as one who:

- was rated as effective not only by the negotiator's own company, but by the other party in the negotiation as well
- had a proven track record of negotiating complex deals successfully
- had a low incidence of implementation problems, so that once an agreement was negotiated, it was carried through with a high level of customer satisfaction

Short-term versus Long-term

Many of the books you see on airport bookstands about how to negotiate are based on techniques for gaining a short-term advantage over a person you'll never see again. These books usually contain clever tricks and deceptions for pressuring the other party. Beware. In a complex selling environment there's no place for tricks and gimmicks. The lessons in these books only work in on-off negotiations where you don't expect to have further relationships with the customer. They are dangerously counterproductive if your objective is to build an effective long-term business relationship.

The skills and strategies which we investigated were those needed for developing a solid basis for future business. It's worth noting that the expert negotiators were chosen not just for their negotiating skill, but also because the deals they negotiated were implemented successfully and therefore contributed to an effective long-term customer relationship.

The main purpose of our studies was to build behavioral profiles of skilled negotiators. We weren't specifically studying strategy. However, our contact with the expert negotiators gave us opportunities to talk with them about strategic issues. From our conversations, and from watching them during actual negotiations, we were able to draw some conclusions about common factors in their approaches to negotiating strategy. We observed five ways in which the skilled negotiators seemed to execute strategy differently from their less skilled counterparts. These were:

- focusing on areas of maximum leverage
- establishing and narrowing ranges
- planning and using questions
- separating understanding from agreement
- rigorously testing for misunderstanding

Let's look at these in turn and see how the points we observed in each area can help you implement an effective negotiating strategy.

Focusing on Areas of Maximum Leverage

When less experienced negotiators meet to plan their negotiating strategy, price reduction tends to be the most frequently discussed element. Inexperienced negotiators generally think of concessions largely or solely in terms of price. I've sat through dozens of meetings watching sales teams plan their negotiating strategies for key accounts. With depressing frequency the issue of price emerges, predominates, and finally swamps all other items. I recall one such meeting that was opened by the team leader with the words, "Ladies and gentlemen, there are three items on the agenda. The first is price, the second is price, and the third is price. Then, if we've any time left over, there are some price issues we should discuss." Sometimes these strategy meetings don't even mention the customer. All their energy is taken up figuring out how to persuade their own senior sales management to offer a bigger discount. Less experienced negotiators act as if price is the only concession that will have an impact on the customer.

It's different watching very experienced sales negotiators discussing concession strategy during a planning session. Although price *is* sometimes the central topic of the strategy discussion, it's more likely that experienced negotiators will focus instead on other potential concession areas. The first question skilled negotiators ask themselves when they think about making a concession is "How important will the concession be to *this customer?*" It sounds like such an obvious question that you might assume that *every* negotiator asks it when thinking about concession strategy. Alas, that's not so. Most people don't ask themselves which concessions—of all the ones they might offer—will have the most impact on a specific buyer. I strongly suspect that the reason most people don't ask the question is that they couldn't come up with an answer. And the reason they haven't an answer is that they've not done a good job of uncovering decision criteria during the Evaluation of Options phase.

The better you understand a buyer's decision criteria, the easier it will be for you to decide which concessions will have maximum leverage during a negotiation. If, for example, you've discovered that early delivery is a crucial criterion to a customer and price is only moderately important, then a concession which offers delivery a week early might have more impact than a sizable price cut. Unfortunately for many salespeople, they haven't been trained to uncover decision criteria. As a result, they never discover what's crucial and what's incidental to the buyer making the decision. But their lack of knowledge doesn't entirely explain why they should assume that price is the only important decision criterion. Why do they act as if a price reduction will outweigh all other concessions in its impact? There are several reasons. For example:

- *They don't see how decision criteria influence concession impact.* When you stop to think about it, it's obvious that if you can give the customer a concession in an area which is crucial, then you'll have much more impact than giving a similar-sized concession in an area which is incidental. For example, assume you've a potential customer who is not particularly sensitive to price but whose most crucial decision criterion is that the equipment has good after-sales service. This customer might be greatly impressed if you offered an extended warranty as a concession, because your offer is in an area which is perceived as crucial. Offering the warranty would cost you much less than, say, a 5 percent price reduction and would have—in this case— much more impact. In contrast, you might have another customer who hasn't even thought about after-sales service and who would be totally unimpressed by the offer of an extended warranty. But obvious though this is, most people don't automatically think about how the impact of a concession depends on the importance of a decision criterion. Consequently, for most salespeople, a direct $5000 price concession feels like it *must* be worth more to the customer than $4000 worth of concessions in terms of other commonly negotiable items like warranties, delivery, or training support. But if, for example, it's training support which is crucial to the customer, then $1000 of increased support may easily psychologically outweigh $5000 of price reduction.

- *They are misled by customer references to price.* We saw in Chapter 6 that customers tend to make more frequent references to price late in the selling cycle during the Resolution of Concerns phase. And, as we also saw, many of these references are a smokescreen for deeper Consequence concerns. Less experienced salespeople generally take price concerns at their face value. They will usually go back to their company and seek price concession authority from their sales management rather than try to uncover and resolve Consequence issues.

Focusing on Areas of Maximum Leverage

An example of how to maximize negotiating leverage was given to us by a seller in the computer assisted design (CAD) business. He told us about a competitor, named Paul K., who was competing against him for a CAD contract. The customer was a high-prestige engineering consultancy whose offices were located in a beautiful old mansion just outside Boston. Paul K.'s system was about 8 percent more expensive than his rival's, but, because the engineering firm was so well known, Paul's manager thought that this was an important enough account to justify negotiating additional price discounts. So he told Paul, "Get this business at all costs. I'll let you cut our price by 10 percent if you need to, so that we come in a little below the competition."

Paul was a very skilled seller, and he had uncovered a crucial decision criterion which he hoped would make a price cut unnecessary. He had noticed during the Evaluation of Options phase that the customer had questioned him closely about whether the equipment could be installed without damage to the building. "We're asking all vendors about this," the customer told him, "because this is a fine historic building, and we don't want you knocking holes in it when you install your communication cables."

In the final selection process, the customer was negotiating with Paul and his competitor. The competitor, equally anxious to get this high-prestige business, had made a significant price cut which made Paul's machines approximately 20 percent more expensive. Paul knew that, even with the authority to make a 10 percent price cut, he

(continued)

couldn't match the other vendor on price. So he played his trump card. "You said that it was crucial to install this equipment without any damage to the building," he reminded the customer. "We believe we've found a way to do that. We propose to employ a skilled craftsman to install ductwork so that it will be invisible. The whole installation will be under the supervision of an expert in historic buildings. But, unfortunately, because this will be costly work, I can't offer you any additional price concessions." "That's fine," replied the customer. "If you're prepared to install the way you're describing, then that's far more important to me than a few thousand dollars price reduction."

Paul got the business. When all the costs of the expert installation were added up afterward, they amounted to an equivalent of only a 1½ percent price reduction. Paul succeeded because he realized that the value of concessions is measured by the customer more in terms of the importance of decision criteria than in terms of dollars. His competitor (who told us this story) failed because he didn't understand that simple principle. He told us the story to illustrate the incomprehensible nature of customer behavior. "I offered a discount ten times the value of their installation gimmick," he complained, "and I still lost the business. I can't understand why."

Experienced negotiators have often told us how important it is to understand decision criteria in order to find which concession areas will offer maximum leverage. I recall that we trained some major-account salespeople in the Health Sciences Market Division of Kodak in how to uncover decision criteria. Bill Irvine, who was at that time a Kodak negotiator deeply involved in major-account negotiation, called me to say how much easier it was to negotiate after the salespeople had been trained. "Since the training," he told us, "I'm getting a much more useful briefing from salespeople. Instead of just price, price, price, I'm hearing about a far wider range of negotiable issues which are important to the customer, like technical support or customer training."

Establishing and Narrowing Ranges

Some of our earlier work in negotiation showed that less skilled negotiators tend to set fixed-point objectives, while skilled negotiators tend to set objectives in the form of ranges. Let me give you an example to show what this means. Assume that there's a negotiation pending for which it's necessary to make a price reduction in order to get the business. A less skilled negotiator, planning a strategy for this negotiation, will tend to think of a *fixed point* when considering price reduction. So, typically, the negotiator might decide, "I'll reduce the price by 5600 dollars" or "I'll offer a 3 percent reduction." The figures in these examples—$5600 and 3 percent—are examples of fixed points. In contrast, when skilled negotiators plan strategy, they usually think in terms of *ranges*. In an equivalent situation, a skilled negotiator would be more likely to decide, "I'll reduce the price by somewhere between 4000 and 5800 dollars" or "I'll offer a reduction of between 2 and 3½ percent." Put this way, it sounds as if the less skilled negotiators are precise and the more skilled negotiators are vague. The unskilled negotiators seem to know what they want, while the skilled negotiators sound as though they haven't really thought carefully about their objectives. But nothing could be further from the truth. The reason why skilled negotiators think in terms of ranges is to keep maximum flexibility during the negotiation. As the negotiation progresses, skilled negotiators will gradually narrow the range until, finally, they can agree on a fixed point with the customer. So, in essence, less skilled negotiators tend to jump straight to a fixed point, while more skilled negotiators—although they end up at a fixed point—only arrive there after setting a range and progressively narrowing it.

This is one of those findings where, at first, it's hard to see how to use it to help your own negotiating strategy. When I've been teaching sales-negotiation programs, I've found that most people react with a polite yawn to the discovery that skilled negotiators set ranges and then progressively narrow them. I remember, during a coffee break in one such program, overhearing one member of my class saying to another, "The only reason why he made such a big deal about setting ranges is that he had fifteen minutes to spare before coffee and he didn't want to start on a *serious* topic." "Yes," agreed the other, "after all, *everybody* knows how to set a range." I wish that were true. The reality is that very few salespeople know how to set effective ranges and even fewer know how to progressively narrow them toward a point of agreement. Let's look in more detail at how to set and narrow ranges by considering a typical price negotiation.

Step 1: Set Your Upper and Lower Limits

At the start of most price negotiations, all you usually know is that the customer is expecting some kind of price reduction and that, without it, you're likely to lose the business to your competition. It's at this stage, as we've seen, that the inexperienced or unskilled negotiator will often set an arbitrary fixed point—say a 10 percent discount—and offer it to the customer. What's wrong with offering a fixed discount? Mostly that, at this early stage in the negotiation, you don't have enough information to know whether a 10 percent discount is too high or too low. If, for example, it turns out that the customer will accept 5 percent, then by offering 10 percent you've unnecessarily given away your margins. So, until you've had an opportunity to assess the customer's expectations more accurately, you should start by setting a broad ballpark range. The purpose of this first range is to help you establish your upper and lower limits. As we'll see later, you will have to *narrow* it before it can help you during the negotiation itself. The top of your initial range, as Figure 7.3 shows, is what you'd like best. In this case, you'd ideally like no discount at all—so you might set 0 percent as the initial top of your range.

At the bottom of your range comes the highest discount you would be prepared to offer. Let's assume that—at an absolute maximum, and if you successfully convinced your management to treat this customer as a strategically important account—you could get the authority to offer a 20 percent discount. Then the initial lower limit of your range would be 20 percent, and the top would be 0 percent. You've now established your ballpark. You're negotiating a discount which will be somewhere between 0 and 20 percent. This is a very simple example where your upper limit offers no concession at all and your lower limit is the most that your management will allow you to give. In real life it's sometimes

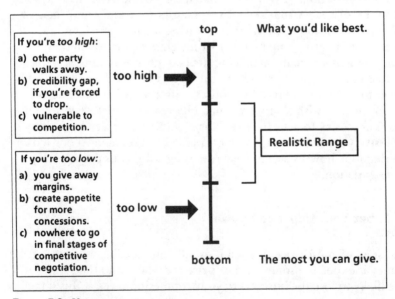

Figure 7-3. Using ranges.

much less simple to establish limits—particularly at the lower end of the range, where you're trying to decide on the maximum concession which you would ever offer this customer. This is a fascinating and important area of negotiating strategy, but it's too detailed to discuss in a general work like this. If you'd like to read more, then try Ury and Fisher's book, *Getting to Yes*. You'll find that their concept of a BATNA (Best Alternative To Negotiated Agreement) gives useful advice on how to set the lower end of a negotiation range.

Step 2: Refine Your Upper Limits

Your initial ballpark range will normally be too broad to serve as an effective negotiating tool. The upper point on your range, because it's what you'd like best, will almost certainly be an unrealistic expectation—like the 0 percent discount in this example. So you must temper your upper limits by deciding what's the *realistic* best case. It's important to be realistic when you refine your upper limit, because if you're too high in negotiating with the customer you face risks such as the following:

- The customer may walk away from the negotiation and decide not to negotiate further because—in the customer's eyes—your position is unrealistic. If you miscalculate your initial position in this way, there's a high chance that you'll make the customer more entrenched and more demanding. There's some evidence that people who initially negotiate for an unrealistically high point on their range will end up making greater final concessions than those whose initial offers are less extreme.

- You may create a credibility gap. Suppose, for example, you offer an initial 1 percent concession, knowing that if the customer doesn't accept then you'll be quite ready to offer, shall we say, 8 percent. Because your initial 1 percent offer clearly wasn't a serious negotiating position, the customer will question whether your 8 percent offer is just another negotiating ploy, too. Remember that giving concessions often creates an appetite for further concessions. The higher on your range you start, the more concessions you'll be forced to give—and the more concessions the customer may come to expect from you.

- If your initial point is too high, then you may become vulnerable to competition. I recall sitting in a negotiation where the negotiator I was watching started right at the top of his range and offered only very small initial concessions. His strategy was to return the following day with larger concessions which, he hoped, would impress the customer and lead to an agreement. "Talk tough to start with," he told me, "and you can always soften up later." Unfortunately, his unrealistic starting position was unsatisfactory and irritating to the customer. As soon as we left the meeting the buyer called a competitor. The competitor was prepared to make a more realistic offer, and, as a result, the meeting intended for the following day never took place. The sale was lost.

So your first step in narrowing the range is to set a *realistic* upper limit. It must be high enough to give you some negotiating latitude but low enough not to violate the customer's expectations. It must also take into account your competitive strength. In our example we had an initial range from 0 to 20 percent. Refining the upper limit would mean that you must start from a point more realistic than 0 percent. Suppose you're not quite sure what the customer will demand, but you think it probable that the buyer will be expecting *at least* an 8 percent discount and probably more. If you were the competitive front-runner, you might set, shall we say, a starting point of 6 percent as your upper limit. In doing so you've established a realistic starting point, but you've kept a couple of percentage points of negotiating latitude in hand. But if you were competitively in a weak position, you might decide that even an 8 percent cut would not be enough, and you might set a realistic upper limit of, shall we say, 12 percent. Of course, as we've said a number of times earlier in the chapter, you have to be very careful not to use price reduction as a substitute for effective selling and—as we saw in the last section—you shouldn't be making price concessions if you can achieve negotiating leverage more effectively in other areas.

Step 3: Refine Your Lower Limits

Next, turn your attention to the other end of your scale—the maximum you're prepared to concede. This end must also be refined. If your lower limit is *too* low you run risks such as the following:

- You may be giving away margins. If the customer isn't expecting a 20 percent discount, you shouldn't let 20 percent enter into your thinking. The more you allow yourself to see 20 percent as acceptable, the more likely you'll be to offer larger discounts than you need. So, irrespective of whether you have the *authority* to offer a 20 percent discount, your range should never be greater than the customer's probable expectation. In our example, suppose that the customer's probable expectation was 15 percent; then 15 percent should become the bottom of your range, rather than 20 percent.

- If your lower limit is too low, you may create appetite for further concessions. In our example, suppose that you believe the customer is expecting a discount of 10 percent. The bottom of your range is 20 percent, so you've a lot of latitude. When the customer asks you for a 10 percent price cut, because it's so comfortably within the initial range you've set for yourself, you're likely to agree. Unfortunately, if you agree too readily, smart customers will conclude that because you gave in so easily, they should have asked you for more. They may press you for additional price concessions, or they may try to gain concessions in other areas—such as delivery, add-on extras, or after-sales support.

- If the bottom's too low, then you've nowhere to go. By negotiating near the bottom of your range, you've left yourself with very little latitude in the event of a competitive negotiation. If a competitor unexpectedly makes a further price cut, you won't be able to match it if you're already at or near the bottom of your range.

Start Too Low and You've Nowhere to Go

Julian G. was negotiating a consulting project with a bank. The bank had chosen three final potential consultants from an initial list of 20. Julian's firm was one of the three. All three finalists were well equipped to do the job, so in preparing a negotiation strategy Julian and his manager decided that price would be the key issue rather than other factors such as professional qualifications or experience. One of the three competing firms was very expensive, and Julian wasn't worried about it. But the other competitor was almost exactly the same price.

"We should take the initiative here," Julian suggested to his manager. "We know we could afford a 10 percent discount on fees. Let's get in first and offer the discount, so that we become the front-runner." Julian's manager agreed. The following day Julian met with the bank and offered the 10 percent discount. As he'd expected, the bank was delighted. However, what he *didn't* expect was that the bank's negotiators immediately pressed him for further concessions in other areas—in particular they wanted the work to be carried out on site, which would add about 4 percent to Julian's costs. "I'm sorry," Julian told them, "I've already given you everything I've got—there's no way I can add another 4 percent to my costs." Still, he wasn't unduly worried because he'd taken the initiative and his overall price was less than his competitors'. He was especially pleased to hear

(continued)

during the meeting that his closest competitor had just offered a 5 percent reduction, which meant that his own 10 percent offer really looked good.

In the week which followed, the bank eliminated the most expensive competitor, leaving just Julian and his rival—who was now priced about 5 percent higher than Julian. Then, early one morning, the bank called Julian. "We're going to make the decision today," they told him. "We'd like you to think about whether you could include the extra on-site expenses in your price." Julian and his manager spent all morning recalculating their figures. "There's no way we can absorb that extra cost," his manager decided. "We're on a very slim margin as it is." "But we've got to do *something*," said Julian, "because I sense that our competitor may be offering another reduction." In the end, Julian's manager authorized him to absorb half the incremental on-site expenses—the equivalent of a further 2 percent cut. Julian was delighted. He telephoned the bank with his offer and sat back to wait for their decision, confidently expecting that he'd won the business.

At the end of the day he received the awaited call from the bank. "Sorry," they told him, "the business went to your competitor who was prepared to absorb *all* the incremental on-site expenses." Julian was stunned. "They only cut their price by an equivalent of 9 percent," he told his manager, "while we cut ours by 12 percent. I can't understand how they got the business."

Julian's mistake was that he started negotiating too near the bottom of his range. His strategy had the advantage that it made him an early front-runner, but—just before the decision, when concessions really count—he ran out of negotiating latitude.

Step 4: Negotiate within Your Narrowed Range

Once you've refined the top and bottom of your initial range, you've arrived at a realistic narrowed range which you can use for the actual negotiation. So, in our example, if we assume that you're in a strong competitive position and the customer isn't expecting a reduction greater than 15 percent, your range might have narrowed from its initial ballpark of 0 to 20 percent to a more realistic negotiating range of 6 to 15 percent. There are three useful rules for negotiating within your realistic range.

1. *Start at, or near, the top of your range.*   If you've narrowed your range realistically during your planning, then the customer shouldn't be surprised—or have his or her expectations violated—if you begin at the top of your range. Take our example of a 0 to 20 percent initial range which has now been narrowed to a 6 to 15 percent realistic negotiating range. If you started at the original top of your initial range and offered no concession at all, you'd almost certainly upset the customer's expectation and create a negative impact. But if you've set a realistic top of 6 percent, then that would probably be your best opening position.

2. *Make concessions in small increments.*   Don't jump straight from a 6 percent discount to, say, a 12 or 13 percent discount if you intend 15 percent to be your bottom limit. Remember that the customer's negotiators are trying to judge how big a discount you're really prepared to offer. If you make a large initial concession, they are likely to judge that you've still got a long way to go. Moving from a 6 percent concession straight to an offer of 12 percent might unintentionally signal that you intend to give a lot more than 15 percent and may cause them to pressure you for much more than you're able to give. On the other hand, if your initial concessions are relatively small, say an offer to increase from 6 percent to 8 or 9 percent, then you signal that large extra concessions are less likely. Of course, you must also bear in mind that your concessions mustn't be *too* small. I once saw a multimillion-dollar negotiation collapse because the negotiator—having been asked for a concession of about $85,000, infuriated the customer by coming back with an offer of less than $3000.

3. *Signal the bottom by making increasingly smaller concessions.*   Less experienced people generally give concessions until they reach the lower limit of their range and then they stop. But experienced negotiators don't just stop making concessions. They signal to the other side that they are approaching their limit by giving concessions more and more unwillingly and in smaller and smaller increments. They may also start making concessions reciprocal by saying, for example, "If we give you extended maintenance, then you must give us an assurance that only trained and licensed operators will use the equipment." So, if you feel that you've not much more you can give, make sure that your final concessions are small and are only offered under protest.

The ability to set and use negotiating ranges, which I've briefly described here, is an essential part of effective negotiation strategy.

There've been whole books written on how to establish ranges. Many of these books, particularly the ones based on the mathematics of decision theory, are incomprehensibly complex. Even after three years of postgraduate study in statistics I can't understand some of them. Unfortunately, this mathematical overkill has tended to give range-setting a bad name. That's a pity. Many practical negotiators have been frightened away from thinking about ranges because they are afraid they won't be able to understand how to use them. Like anything else, it's usually easy enough if you start simply. Follow the four steps I've discussed here:

- Set your ballpark upper and lower limits.
- Refine your upper limit in terms of customer expectations and competitive strength.
- Refine your lower limit in the same way in order to arrive at a realistic range.
- Negotiate, starting at the top of your realistic range and making concessions in increasingly smaller increments until you reach agreement.

You'll find, if you follow these simple steps, that you can use the basic concept of ranges to improve the effectiveness of your negotiating strategy without getting into the complexities of decision theory models.

Planning and Using Questions

The next general area of competence we observed in effective negotiators was the way in which they used questions. In any form of persuasion, questions are central to success. People are persuaded much more effectively by questions than by statements. In selling, however well you describe your product, it's the questions you ask which will have the greatest influence on whether you make the sale. Because negotiation is a form of persuasion, it's reasonable to expect that questions would be just as important to success in negotiation as they are to successful selling. Our research confirms this. Skilled negotiators ask lots of questions. People who don't use questions aren't likely to be effective negotiators.

Anyone who can sell successfully goes into negotiation with some useful questioning skills already established. And, although there are some differences in emphasis, there are also some clear parallels between the way questions work in selling and the way they can help you in negotiation. For example:

- *Questions reveal needs.* In selling, a primary function of questions is to uncover and develop customer needs. Questions have a similar function in negotiation. Frequently customers put forward positions which you can't accept. For example, a customer might push you for immediate delivery, when you can't supply for several weeks or months. The only way you can avoid deadlock is to ask questions to reveal the needs which underlie the position the customer is taking. So your questions might reveal that the underlying reason the customer wants immediate delivery is to allow payment in this year's budget rather than next. By finding ways to phase the payment, you may be able to alter the urgency of delivery dates.

  The taking of fixed positions in negotiation often leads to a frustrating deadlock or stalemate wherein neither party is satisfied and each becomes increasingly reluctant to shift. Vendors rarely win out if the negotiation enters a stalemate. Using questions to break this kind of deadlock is one of the oldest and most useful negotiating strategies. To understand how it works, it's important to be clear about the difference between a *position* and a *need*. When someone takes a *position* in a negotiation, the person is adopting a narrow point of view based on just one possible solution to an underlying need. A *need* generally has several potential solutions, while a *position* is the single solution which the negotiator prefers. By getting behind the position and finding out what the need is which motivates it, you can often come up with acceptable alternative solutions.

- *Questions expose problems.* In both selling and negotiating, asking questions is a powerful way to uncover and develop problems. In selling, your objective is to uncover a problem your product can solve and to make that problem more significant and more worth solving. Your objective in negotiating is usually a little different. Often, in a negotiation, you want to show that the position a customer is taking has problems or disadvantages. Rather than disagree directly with the customer's position, it can be more effective to reveal the difficulties by asking questions.

  Asking about problems and their implications is particularly important as an acceptable means of exposing flaws and disadvantages in customers' proposals. This weakens customers' enthusiasm for their positions and makes them more receptive to any alternative solutions which you might introduce.

- *Questions reveal strategic information.* In both selling and negotiating it's valuable to have as much information as possible about what the customer is thinking. In negotiation, this information is especially important. The more you know about the cards in the customer's hand, the easier it is to form an intelligent strategy for playing your own. Negotiation, as we've said earlier, involves an ability to make concessions—to vary the terms of the agreement. Unless you have an accurate picture of the customer's positions and the needs underlying them, it's hard to know which concessions you must make to get the business. The better the information you've uncovered, the better your strategy will be.

- *Questions control the discussion.* In selling, the person asking the questions is controlling the discussion. The same is true in negotiation. But while it's generally accepted by both parties that the seller should ask most of the questions in a sales call, that acceptance is often challenged in negotiation. In negotiation, customers usually want to maintain control and may try to do so by asking most of the questions.

  Many salespeople are surprised by this change in customer behavior and respond to a sudden increase in customer questions by meekly answering each one. As a result, they leave negotiations having given customers a lot of ammunition and having found out very little in return. In short, they've lost control over the discussion. Skilled negotiators don't let the other party use questions to control the negotiation. When two expert negotiators face each other, they even negotiate about who should be asking the questions. It's common to hear an effective negotiator say, "I've answered one of your questions, now it's your turn to answer one of mine."

- *Questions are an alternative to disagreement.* Because negotiation always contains a possibility of conflict, the potential for disagreement is usually present. How do skilled negotiators handle situations in which there's a potential conflict of views or positions? One of the most effective methods they use is to ask questions as an alternative to direct disagreement. For example, an unskilled negotiator might say, "I disagree with your proposal because it would be unworkable." A statement like this not only sets up a confrontational position, but it also invites the other negotiator to ask the question "Why?" The unskilled negotiator is now forced to defend the statement, giving the other negotiator opportunity to expose weaknesses in the reasons given.

  In contrast, a skilled negotiator would be more likely to express any disagreement in the form of a question, such as, "How would your proposal work in practice?" If a proposal really *is* unworkable, it will be hard to defend. So the negotiator who has asked the question is now in a strong position. And, by using questions instead of disagreeing, it will be easier for the other party to admit to difficulties without loss of face.

  There's another bonus to putting disagreement in the form of a question. Suppose that the other side's proposal *is* workable. If you say, "I disagree—it won't work," you commit yourself to an untenable position. You'll later be shown wrong and be forced to back down. But asking "How would it work in practice?" gives you a simple insurance policy. If their proposal does prove workable, you can gracefully accept it without losing face.

- *Questions give thinking time.* We can only handle one complex thing at a time. While talking we can't simultaneously do a good job of thinking. If you are asked a question during negotiation, answering it will take most of your thought and attention. And while you are answering the question, with most of your attention focused on giving your answer, you can't adequately be thinking about your position or planning your next move. Many experienced negotiators use this to their advantage. When they are under pressure and need time to think, they will deliberately ask a question in an area where the answer will be time-consuming but unimportant. While the other party is answering the question, the one who asked it doesn't even listen to the answer, instead using the time to plan the next move.

  By asking questions you can take away some pressure and give yourself thinking time. Questions can also be used for the reverse purpose: to *reduce* thinking time for the other party, thus exerting additional pressure. One of the reasons why questions give control over a discussion is that the person answering questions is under pressure and unable to think, while the questioner gets a breathing space and can plan ahead.

Of all the tools and techniques which a negotiator has available, questions are probably the most important. A negotiator who doesn't ask questions is at a severe disadvantage. As Figure 7.4 illustrates, our research shows that skilled negotiators ask more than twice as many questions as average negotiators.

The surprising thing about this research isn't the high level of questions used by skilled negotiators. After all, questions are clearly very powerful negotiating tools, and it's predictable that any successful negotiator would be asking lots of them. What *is* unusual is the low level of questions which average negotiators ask. Why is this so low? Even a totally inexperienced negotiator should realize that questions are important. But, strangely enough, many salespeople who are successful because of their ability to ask questions, suddenly stop asking them when they get into a negotiation. Unfortunately, people don't always apply their sales skills to negotiation. As a result, some experienced salespeople who would never dream of trying to sell by giving features do al-

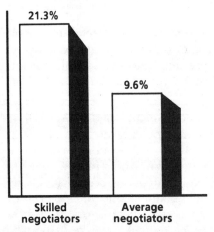

Figure 7-4. Asking Questions. Questions as a
percentage of negotiators' behavior.

most the equivalent in negotiation. They try to persuade by giving reasons. The most important message we can offer to you as a negotiator is
this: reasons don't persuade. Questions are just as crucial a part of successful persuasion in negotiation as they are in selling. The questioning
skills which help you sell effectively will also help you negotiate.

Selling Helps You Negotiate

When we were looking for successful negotiators to include in our
research study, Bill Allen introduced me to Tom T., one of the labor
negotiators in Esso. "I'd judge Tom to be one of the half-dozen best
negotiators I've seen," Bill told me. That was praise indeed—Bill had
worked in high-level negotiation all over the world, and he knew
what he was talking about.

We were able to watch Tom in several negotiations, and, as Bill had
promised, he was clearly very skillful. After one of these negotiations,
in which Tom had successfully resolved a very difficult issue, I was
talking to him over a cup of tea. "Where did you get your training in
negotiation?" I asked him. "I've never been trained," he told me.
"But I was in selling for eight years before I moved into labor relations.
I've tried to treat negotiation as if I'm still selling. So I ask questions and
I look for benefits for the other side. That sales approach has paid off
for me—it's helped me handle some difficult negotiations."

Plan Your Questions in Advance

Average negotiators spend most of their planning time thinking about how they will explain their position to the other side. As a result they plan reasons, not questions. Good questions don't come any more automatically in negotiating than they do in selling. Planning the right questions is the foundation of a good sales call. It's equally important to plan them in negotiation. Before you go into any negotiation, produce a list of the key questions which you will ask to:

- *uncover information* which will help you plan a better strategy. These are mostly factual questions and typical examples would be "How many units are we talking about?" "Does it come into this year's budget?" or "How has our competitor proposed to handle this issue?"

- *reveal underlying needs* which may be causing the customer to take a particular position. These questions typically ask "Why?" Examples might be "Why do you want delivery so urgently?" "What's the reason for insisting on a six-hour maintenance time?" or "Is continuity of supply your *real* concern?"

- *expose problems* with the customer's position which may make it impractical or untenable. The purpose of these questions is to show disadvantages. They are similar to the Problem Questions you would use during a sales call. Examples might include, "Could that cause a problem in this area?" "Wouldn't that clause create difficulties with other suppliers?" or "It sounds good in theory, but how would it work in your Denver laboratories?"

- *get agreement* from the customer to key points in your case. These questions get the customer to tell *you* the value of the points you wish to make. Typical questions might be "If we assigned a technical advisor to work with you throughout the implementation, what advantages would that have for you?" "Why would it be useful to you to have the Q-unit installed first?" or "It's clear that these payment terms would suit us, but wouldn't they have some value for you too?"

By planning questions like these, and by asking them during the negotiation, you'll be more persuasive and, therefore, more effective. But remember that questions *do* need to be planned—they don't just happen. Effective negotiators, like effective salespeople, put time and effort into the planning and preparation of their strategy.

Separating Understanding from Agreement

A great deal of time is wasted in negotiation, and enormous frustration is generated, because each side commonly believes that the other isn't really listening and isn't interested in understanding his or her position. How does this happen?

In most negotiations, people are reluctant to agree with points made by the other side because they are afraid that acceptance will weaken their case. As a result, when one side puts forward a point, the other side rarely shows any positive reaction to it. This is often interpreted as failure to listen or failure to understand. Consequently, the side putting forward the point will frequently repeat it several times at length, hoping that it will finally be understood. This constant repetition slows the negotiation and creates unnecessary barriers between the parties.

Skilled negotiators prevent this barrier from arising by continually expressing *understanding* of what the other side is saying, but doing so in a way which doesn't suggest agreement or acceptance. So they tend to frequently summarize their interpretation of what the other party has said. They use phrases like "If I'm understanding you correctly..." or "What I hear you saying is...." By doing this they show that they are listening, and, as a result, they reduce some of the time-wasting repetition which is such a common feature when inexperienced people negotiate.

Rigorously Testing for Misunderstanding

The final difference we observed in how skilled negotiators implemented their negotiation strategies was that, throughout the negotiation, they continually probed and tested to ensure that both parties clearly understood the areas of agreement and—equally important— the potential areas of disagreement. What's the objective of a negotiation? The simple answer is that the purpose of negotiation is to achieve an agreement. But that's *too* simple. What's the use of an agreement if it can't be implemented successfully? Or if the customer later challenges important parts of it? The objective of a negotiation is not just to achieve an agreement, it's to achieve an agreement which *works*. A signature on a piece of paper is worth nothing if the whole contract collapses and results in recrimination and legal action.

Why Negotiations Go Sour

Too many sales negotiations end up with a contract which later becomes a source of dispute between the parties. Why does this happen? Why do some implementations go sour? The most common reason can be traced back to the process by which the original agreement was negotiated. The average negotiator often thinks no further ahead than getting the signature on the contract. So, if there are potentially delicate areas where the customer might interpret the agreement differently—implementation schedules, warranty rights, penalty clauses, and guarantees would be typical subjects—the average negotiator may try to skate over them quickly, so they don't interfere with the all-important objective of getting the signature. So, unless the customer makes an issue of an area, the less skilled negotiator may try to rush ahead and get the agreement signed. But failure to establish a common understanding of a key point during negotiation can lead to expensive trouble afterward. Worse, the longer a misunderstanding is allowed to go on, the harder it becomes to correct.

We've said that the aim of a negotiation is to achieve not just an agreement, but an agreement which works. And to survive all the tough and testing pressures of implementation, a successful agreement must be based on a common understanding between the parties. How do skilled negotiators ensure this common understanding? First, they recognize that it's important. They don't believe that leaving ambiguities alone will somehow make them go away.

Bill Allen, whom I regard as the best negotiator I've ever seen, has some simple maxims about negotiation which reflect the importance most skilled negotiators attach to making sure that each key point in an agreement is clearly understood by both sides. The advice he gives to other negotiators is as follows:

- Any point too delicate to stand up to rigorous discussion *during* the negotiation will never survive the strain of implementation after it.

- Ambiguities worsen like a cancer: an ambiguity during the negotiation grows into a misinterpretation afterward. This, in turn, grows into the most fatal of all negotiating illnesses—mistrust.

- You can't undo history; once mistrust exists, there's lasting damage. Misunderstandings which could have been cleared up earlier are magnified by mistrust into insurmountable barriers.

- When you're negotiating, *never* let misunderstandings or ambiguities go unchallenged.

It's good advice. Yet one of the most common strategic errors of inexperienced sales negotiators is to focus all their attention on getting the signature and, as a result, to skate quickly over potential areas of misunderstanding.

Misunderstandings Come Back to Haunt You

Pam G. had just succeeded in making the biggest sale of her career—and one of the biggest in her company's history. She was meeting with the customer to tie down some final details before the contract was signed. Only one point worried her. As a matter of policy, her company insisted on charging a standard $200-per-unit fee for on-site installation. This flat fee was not subject to any quantity discount, and, because the revenue went to the service organization, the sales function had no authority to reduce or change it. In a smaller sale $200 wouldn't be an issue—the installation was complex, and, for the work involved, $200 was a fair charge. However, Pam had sold 200 of the machines in this deal, and she was afraid that the customer might protest at the thought of a total installation charge of $40,000.

During the meeting, Pam ran through the contract terms with her customer's lawyer and financial controller. When they reached the installation clause the contract read, "There shall be a machine installation cost of $200." "You'd think we'd get that free," grumbled the controller. "It's not worth worrying about," the lawyer reassured him. "After all, 200 dollars is only one dollar a machine." Pam realized that the customers had misunderstood the installation charge. What should she do? If she corrected their misunderstanding, then it was clear that they would be unhappy about a $40,000 charge, and it might keep them from signing the contract. "I'll pretend I didn't hear that comment," she decided, "then we'll sort it out after the sale."

Two weeks later, when the customer found out what "machine installation cost of $200" *really* meant, there was an uproar. The customer canceled the order and threatened legal action. The issue ultimately reached the president of Pam's company, who decided, in the interests of good customer relations, to give free installation. But, by this time, the customer had become so angry that this concession was no longer enough. In the end, the customer reduced the order to 120 machines but retained the discount level for 200. Pam's company gave free installation and lost money on the deal.

Pam's mistake was to believe that significant misunderstandings during negotiation can be overlooked and sorted out afterwards. She learned the hard way—and so did her company—that in negotiation it's dangerous to allow a misunderstanding to pass uncorrected.

A Final Word on Negotiation

Before we leave negotiation, I'd like to summarize some of the ways in which you can apply the key ideas of this chapter to your own negotiations.

- *Differentiate between selling and negotiating.* Most people begin negotiating too early in the selling cycle. Remember, in dealing with your own customers, that you should never allow negotiation to become a substitute for selling. In particular, never fall into the trap of offering discounts—or other negotiable items—as a means of generating customer interest early in the selling cycle. Think of negotiation as something which will only be effective *after* you've done the best possible job of selling.

- *Don't try to negotiate Consequence issues.* As we saw in the last chapter, Consequence issues are resolved by discussion and confidence-building, not by bargaining and negotiation. Negotiation is a very expensive way—and not a very successful one—to deal with Consequences. In your own accounts, try to handle Consequence issues before you enter into final negotiation.

- *Focus on areas of maximum leverage.* Price concessions are often less important than you think. In this chapter we've seen how skilled negotiators use their understanding of customer decision criteria to focus on other areas where they have negotiating leverage. In your own negotiations, particularly if you're trying to handle price concessions in an area where you've very little latitude, look hard at the decision criteria which are crucial to the customer. As we've seen during the chapter, a relatively small concession in an area which is crucial will often outweigh larger price concessions.

- *Establish and narrow your negotiating range.* We've seen that there are four steps involved in setting and using a negotiating range:

  Set your ballpark upper and lower limits.
  Refine your upper limit in terms of customer expectation and competitive strength.
  Refine your lower limit in the same way so that you arrive at a realistic negotiating range.
  Start at or near the top of your range, making concessions in increasingly smaller increments until you reach an agreement.

- *Plan and use questions.* Planning your questions is just as important to negotiation as it is to selling. Few of the inexperienced negotiators I've seen do an adequate job of planning questions. One cause of their neglect is that they become too concerned with putting across *reasons* and *arguments*. Remember that questions are generally more persuasive than reasons. In planning your own negotiation strategy, be sure to make a list of questions you intend to ask.

- *Separate understanding from agreement.* You may not be able to agree with the customer, but you can—and should—show that you *understand* the customer's position. When you hear something which you can't agree with—and if you don't want to challenge with a disagreement—it's important that you don't just ignore what the customer has said. Acknowledge that you've heard and understood, using phrases like "If I'm hearing you right, what you're saying is…" This shows that you're listening and reduces the time-wasting repetitions of position that are so common in negotiation.

- *Never allow misunderstandings to persist.* In your own negotiations, never be afraid to probe and explore areas where the customer may have misunderstood what you are offering. Remember that it's much easier to deal with a misunderstanding *before* the agreement than afterward when an angry customer feels cheated.

We've found that, with a little effort, most salespeople can put these suggestions into practice. And the effort is worthwhile, because negotiation is a neglected area of sales performance. Many times we've seen sales lost because these rules were ignored. But, more important, we've also seen many occasions where one or more of the suggestions we've made here has been the turning point in winning a major sale.

8

How to Ensure Continued Success: Implementation and Account Maintenance Strategies

It was Friday afternoon on a warm spring day. The branch office was almost deserted. Many people had left early for what promised to be the first glorious weekend of the year. I was sitting at a vacant desk, gazing idly out of the window, as I waited for Gino Torri. Gino was the top major-account salesperson in the branch, and I was hoping to arrange a schedule for traveling with him the following week. One of the younger salespeople was busy at the next desk packing his things so he was ready to leave before the rush hour.

"It looks like a great weekend," I said. "Yes," he replied, "and I'm all set to enjoy it. I've made a big sale this week, and I think I'll take a couple of days' vacation. Now that the final contract's signed on this sale I can afford to relax for a while." My reflex action, as a sales trainer, was to ask him, "Do you think that's wise?" Misinterpreting my concern, he responded, "Oh, I won't neglect my other accounts, if that's what you mean. In fact now that this sale is finished, I won't be spending any

167

more time on the account, so I can give my other customers 100 percent of my attention as soon as I get back. Nice to have met you—I must rush." Picking up his coat he dashed from the office. I looked out of the window, watching him as he crossed the street. He was making one of the most common strategic errors in selling. It was serious enough to damage his sales career, yet he was totally oblivious to his mistake as he rushed off to enjoy his spring weekend.

When Gino arrived I told him about the incident. "Yes," Gino remarked, "I was that way myself once—which is why I recognize his mistake. Like most inexperienced people, he thinks he can put *less* effort into the account now that he's made the sale. But a good sales strategist would know that immediately after the sale you must put in *more* effort, not less." Gino clearly deserved his reputation as a top major-account seller. It's amazing, even among experienced salespeople, how few realize the dangers of reducing their involvement in an account immediately after a sale is made.

The Implementation Phase

A constant theme of this book is that, just when you think it's safe to ease off your effort, there's another vital phase of the selling cycle waiting to bite you. For example, early in the sale, in the Recognition of Needs phase, you work hard to do a thorough job of developing needs using the SPIN® questions. You'd imagine, after all the effort involved in good needs development, that you deserved a rest. But no—competition rears its ugly head, and, before you've had time to catch your breath, you're deep into all the problems of influencing decision criteria during the Evaluation of Options phase. What's more, you're also wrestling with issues of differentiation and vulnerability. Assuming that you succeed in influencing the decision criteria in your favor, differentiating yourself convincingly from your competition, and successfully eliminating any vulnerabilities, can you sit back and relax? Only if you're *very* lucky. Chances are that during the Resolution of Concerns phase you'll have to resolve Consequence issues, or even negotiate. This phase at least has the compensation that it leads to a sale, but by this time you clearly deserve a vacation. That's certainly how many major-account salespeople feel. And who can blame them, because successful major-account strategy is hard work. However, as we'll see in this chapter, it can be a fatal mistake to ease off on your effort once the contract is signed. In most major sales, once the formal decision has been made the account enters a whole new phase of the selling cycle—the Implementation phase, illustrated in Figure 8.1.

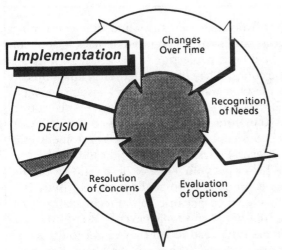

Figure 8-1. The Implementation Phase. The installation of your product; account development.

All That Effort for Nothing

Betty O. had just won a major contract to install automated inventory-tracking equipment in a warehousing company. Her customer had 80 warehouses spread across a large geographical area, and Betty's equipment was being installed to keep track of stock levels of more than 25,000 separate stock items spread across the 80 locations. Because the project was so large, an initial pilot implementation was set up involving just three warehouses in one metropolitan area. The agreement between Betty's company and the customer was that if the project performed to expectations during the pilot, then it was to be extended in a number of phases until all 80 locations were included in the system.

It had taken Betty 10 months of excruciatingly hard work to get the contract. First she'd had to convince the very traditional customer that there was a need to automate. Then she'd had to fight off an aggressive and capable competitor. Finally, because the customer hadn't done anything like this before, she'd had to do a lot of hand-holding during the Resolution of Concerns phase of the decision. The intense effort had inevitably led her to neglect some of her other customers. After the contract was signed, Betty breathed a huge sigh of relief and quickly turned her attention elsewhere. She was glad of the chance to take a rest from this account—especially from the cus-

(continued)

tomer's logistics manager, who had been fussy and time-consuming throughout the sales cycle—and to turn her attention back to some of the smaller customers she'd been neglecting.

About a week after the contract had been signed, she came into the office to find a phone message waiting from the logistics manager asking her to call. "Let him wait," she thought. "He's kept me waiting enough during the last 10 months. It won't hurt *him* to wait a day or two." Consequently, she busied herself with other customers and didn't return his call for several days. When she did call him, he was downright rude. "You'd better get yourself over here right away," he told her. "Your scanning equipment is worse than useless." Betty was alarmed, so she immediately called her installation technician. "It's a fuss about nothing," he told her. "The fools haven't entered the bar codes right, so the scanners can't read it. All they've got to do is follow the software prompts, and everything will be fine." Relieved, Betty called the logistics manager back. "My technician says it's not a problem," she assured him. "There's nothing wrong with the scanners. I'll try to visit the installation site next week, when I'm a little less busy."

Over the weekend Betty received an unexpected call from her regional sales director. "I need to see you in my office in an hour," he told her. She quickly realized trouble was brewing, especially when she found her boss waiting in the regional director's office. "We've had a lawsuit from your customer," he told her. "They're taking our equipment out and suing us for damages." That started a nightmare for Betty. In the weeks that followed she struggled unsuccessfully to change the customer's mind, and she found herself under increasing pressure and criticism from her own management.

Finally she left the company and took a job at a lower salary with an office products sales force, where she participated in a training program we were running. When we got to the section of the program on the importance of giving the customer extra attention during the early stages of Implementation, she stood up and told this story. "I made the worst mistake," she said, "and it cost me my job. I thought I could afford to give the customer *less* attention after the sale was made. It's an easy mistake—but I'll never make it again."

The Implementation phase begins with installation—the introduction, testing, and initial evaluation of your product or service. Psychologically, installation can be an anxious period for the customer. What if something goes wrong? Has it been a bad choice? This is the moment when the purchasing decision faces the acid test in terms of results. Until this point in the selling cycle all the customer has seen is promises of performance. Now those promises must be delivered. What strategies should you, the seller, use to make sure that installation is smooth and successful?

As a necessary first step toward forming an effective overall implementation strategy, you must understand something of the psychology of implementation *from the customer's point of view.* You must be able to anticipate how your customer will be feeling at different stages of the implementation process. Most implementations go through three distinct stages, illustrated in Figure 8.2. The better you understand each stage, the easier it will be to predict how your customers will react.

1. The "New Toy" Stage

Immediately after the sale, in the very early period of implementation, customers are usually excited and interested because something new is happening. As we all do with new things, people in the account will initially "play" with the product which is being installed. They enjoy finding out about the product, and if they find it can be made to perform little tricks they are delighted. In this "New Toy" stage, your product or service hasn't yet settled down to performing a serious job. So users try out those things which can be done simply, with little effort, and which produce some immediate visible result. If users are unsophisticated, they are most likely to be attracted to the entertaining or superficially impressive aspects of your product or service. When automatic sta-

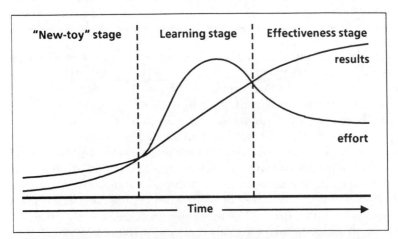

Figure 8-2. Stages of Implementation. "New Toy" stage—a few simple successes with little effort. Learning stage—hard work but not much to show for it. Effectiveness stage—full results achieved with much less effort.

pling was first introduced as a feature of copiers, one test machine stapled 600 documents in its first day of operation. More than 500 of them were totally unconnected with the machine's work purpose. They were demonstrations to a stream of curious visitors who came to see the "new toy."

Sophisticated users, of course, behave very differently in the "New Toy" stage. They pick out the more unusual and interesting capabilities to try. But they still explore and play a little before getting down to serious application.

A "New Toy" Paralyzes the Government

There's a story told in Xerox about what happened when they introduced their information processing system—at that time code-named "alto"—to the White House. It was intended to be the first of a new generation of professional workstations, and, with one of its capacities, users could print their documents in different type sizes and type styles. Few of the senior White House officials had ever seen anything like this before. For the first couple of weeks, top White House aides spent much of their time printing out profound messages like "I love Kansas City" in every imaginable type size—first in italics, then in bold.

When it was whispered among members of Congress that the officials of the executive branch were so busy playing with their new machines that they didn't have time to become involved in government, one senior member of the House was reported to have considered introducing an Appropriations Bill to buy the White House new toys more often.

Everybody plays with things when they are new, and the exploration process which includes playing serves a useful purpose. It gives people a brief overview and an initial understanding of the capabilities they've bought. It builds customer confidence in the correctness of the buying decision. By gaining a few simple successes for little effort, the customer feels positive about the purchase and motivated to go on to the next stage, where things will generally be much less easy. So the "New Toy" stage serves a useful purpose. In terms of your selling strategy, it's therefore smart, in the early part of an implementation, to encourage people to "play" with any aspect of your product or service which gives quick results for little effort. This increases a customer's confidence and motivation to learn the more serious capabilities you're offering.

It's easy to see how there's a "New Toy" implementation stage when the customer is adjusting to a high-technology product. But how about routine products? How about services? How about commodities? Does the same thing happen with them? The answer seems to be "Yes." Even in less glamorous sales there can be a little of the "New Toy" phenomenon.

I recall working with a chemical company which sold commodities and which had a free hot line that customers could call with technical queries. "We get a flurry of calls on the hot line whenever we have a new customer," their technical supervisor told me. "Most of these calls are just excuses to try out the hot line." It's another example of the "New Toy" stage in action.

In my own case of selling services, I developed a video-based sales-training program for Citibank. You wouldn't think that a training program offered very much opportunity for the "New Toy" phenomenon; however, some of the vignettes in the tape which showed how *not* to sell were quite funny. A couple of weeks into the implementation I was walking past an office in Citibank when I heard one of our videos being played, accompanied by loud sounds of laughter. I looked in the office to find a group of senior bankers—whom I'd normally regarded as very sober people—winding through the videos to find the funny bits. The "New Toy" stage had struck again.

So, although your products or services may not create the obvious "playing" which happens with high-technology gadgets, a toned-down version of the same basic principle may still be present. Encourage it; the more people feel happy about exploring your product's capabilities through "playing" with it, the easier a time you'll have during the next stage of implementation.

2. The Learning Stage

The Learning stage is usually the most difficult stage of the implementation process and the one where the customer's confidence may fall to crisis levels. Let's look at the psychology of what's happening. It's true of most systems that the benefits you get are in proportion to the efforts you put in. Most complex products or services require hard work from the customer in order to get the best results. After the superficial exploration of the "New Toy" stage, the customer has to begin the more difficult process of learning how to achieve full potential from the product. And learning is hard work. As Figure 8.2 illustrates, the effort required is greater than the results it brings. This is true of all learning. When you are first learning to ride a bicycle, it's quicker and more comfortable to walk; during the Learning stage of installing an automated system, it's usually easier to do things manually.

What effect does this need for greater effort have on the customer? It's generally true that unsophisticated customers will underestimate the effort and difficulty of the Learning stage. They may expect instant results and will feel cheated if they don't get them. This is a vulnerable time in the implementation process. Later in the chapter we'll look at strategies for reducing some of the problems you will commonly meet during this stage.

Beware the Learning Stage

I asked a group of salespeople from a communications company to each describe the worst mistake they had ever made in terms of sales strategy. One of them offered a perfect example of how dangerous it can be if you don't realize that customers go through difficulties during the Learning stage of installation. "My worst mistake," she told us, "was when I was selling telephone PBX equipment. I'd just made a sale to a small customer who seemed happy as a clam with our product during the first couple of days while we were installing and testing it. I naturally thought that if the customer was this happy right at the start of installation that he'd be even happier as the installation progressed. So I used his name as a reference. I was bidding on a huge contract for another customer, and I thought that an enthusiastic report from this small customer would help.

"My big customer, I now realize, was in the Resolution of Concerns phase of the decision. He was worried about implementation difficulties and he badly needed some reassurance. I naturally urged him to get in touch with the small customer who had seemed so happy at the start of the installation. I now understand that my small customer was initially in the 'New Toy' stage of implementation and hadn't seriously started the tough process of really learning how to use the full potential of the equipment. A week later, when my big customer called to check my reference, things had changed. The small customer was trying to program in stuff like call-forwarding and budget center billing. These operations were proving difficult, and the customer was feeling very negative and discouraged. A week before, in the 'New Toy' stage, he would have gone out on sales calls for me. Now, in the Learning stage, he really gave a bad reference, and he played up all the difficulties he was having. It frightened my big customer, and I think that was what lost me the biggest sale of my career."

Her mistake is an example of one of the most common strategic errors which salespeople make during the Implementation phase of the sale. Not realizing that the enthusiasms of the "New Toy" stage usually give way to difficulties in the Learning stage, she had mistimed her reference to come at the worst point of the installation cycle.

Sophisticated customers normally have less trouble in the Learning stage than unsophisticated customers have. In many cases they've already implemented installations of comparable complexity, so they know what to expect. They usually have a realistic implementation plan which takes into account the inevitable difficulties associated with learning to achieve full potential from a purchase. Also, their experience means they already know how to cope with the kinds of problems which could create major learning difficulties for less sophisticated users.

3. The Effectiveness Stage

As the customer gains a full understanding of your product or service, the effort which must be put into learning is dramatically reduced. At the same time, as Figure 8.2 shows, results increase, so the overall impact on the customer is a positive feeling that things are getting easier. This is the Effectiveness stage, when customers make comments like "I'd never go back to the old way of doing it" or "How did we manage before this came along?" The more smoothly you can help an account reach the Effectiveness stage, the more successful your implementation.

The Motivation Dip

Understanding the three stages of implementation will help explain an important concept called the *Motivation Dip*, shown in Figure 8.3,

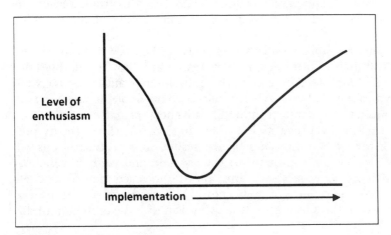

Level of
enthusiasm

Implementation

Figure 8-3. The Motivation Dip.

which illustrates how the level of customer enthusiasm changes during the implementation process.

During implementation, a customer's motivation—or enthusiasm for your product—is not usually at a constant level. Just after the purchasing decision, during the "New Toy" stage, it's common for customers to have high expectations and motivation. Generally, customers' enthusiasm will drop off rapidly as they enter the Learning stage. This isn't something unique to the implementation of purchasing decisions. It's a fundamental part of everyday psychology.

Think about what happens when people take up a new sport or hobby. At first they are so motivated that they can't talk about anything except their new enthusiasm. Then, when the magic wears off and is replaced by the need for hard work—by the Learning stage in other words—most people experience a real dip in their motivation level. It's at this point in everyday life that many people become discouraged. The dieter starts to overeat again, the hobbyist gets an urge to spend the evening watching television, and the potential athlete can't summon the energy to go out and exercise. This is the high risk point in *any* implementation, whether we're talking about one person on a diet or a major account in the midst of a multimillion-dollar product installation. During the Learning stage it's necessary to put in extra effort without necessarily seeing extra results. When your customers discover that getting the best from your product or service involves effort on their part without immediate visible reward, their enthusiasm may fall. There's another danger here. The higher the customer's initial level of enthusiasm and expectation, the farther the fall when the customer enters the Motivation Dip. Many salespeople, misled by a customer's tremendous enthusiasm during the "New Toy" stage, are quite unprepared for the sudden fall in motivation when the customer comes face-to-face with the awkward reality of the Learning stage.

However, the Motivation Dip doesn't last, as Figure 8.3 shows. If people persist, their efforts begin to show results and they regain their motivation to continue. The dieter who gets slimmer and fitter feels encouraged to stay that way. When results become visible, motivation rises again. This is what happens in the Effectiveness stage. Your product or service can finally prove itself by showing payoff which greatly outweighs effort. When this happens, the results your product brings will generate increased motivation for the account, and your implementation problems are usually over. But, in order to reach the Effectiveness stage and the high level of motivation that comes with it, you need to help an account to survive the Motivation Dip with the minimum of difficulty and pain.

Three Strategies for Handling the Motivation Dip

We've observed three ways in which successful salespeople ensure that customers get through the Motivation Dip without difficulty.

- *Strategy 1: Start before the Contract Is Signed.* In the installation phase, an anxious customer will look critically for any sign that things are going wrong and, because of anxiety, may overreact to minor difficulties. The better you've done your job earlier in the sales process, the less anxious the customer will feel and the less likely that small problems will cause disproportionate reactions. An important area for resolving implementation anxiety comes in the Evaluation of Options phase of the buying process. If you can ensure that the customer genuinely feels that your product matches decision criteria better than the competition's, you'll remove much of the post-decision anxiety.

  Even more important is your skill in handling Consequences during the Resolution of Concerns phase. A customer who has unresolved Consequences will be half expecting something to go wrong and, while acutely aware of any faults, may fail to see the positive successes of your implementation. So if you detect a potential Consequence issue during the sales process—for example, if the customer feels nervous about your company's reputation—it pays to resolve the issue *before* the signing of the contract, so it won't resurface in the form of damaging negative reactions during implementation.

- *Strategy 2: Involve the Customer.* Bringing any change to an organization has risks, and installation of a new product or service, however carefully you plan it, will sometimes go wrong. Making an installation plan—deciding step-by-step the most effective way to introduce your product—is essential to implementation success. But it's never a guarantee against the unexpected. How can you ensure that your customer will remain loyal and satisfied with your efforts if an unanticipated problem occurs?

  The best way is to involve the customer in the installation planning process. The more that installation is based on the customer's own plan, the more forgiving the customer will be if something unexpectedly goes wrong. Salespeople who are outstandingly effective implementers usually get the *customer* to play the central role in suggesting the implementation plan. The seller's role they see as a secondary one of helping and improving the customer's ideas—not taking the lead in suggesting the plan itself.

Involving the Customer in the Implementation Plan

Larry T. was a partner with a well known financial services consulting firm. He had succeeded in selling a major project to a new client which involved a total reorganization of the accounting functions of two divisions. Because this was a vitally important project, Larry put literally hundreds of hours into planning the implementation process for the first of the divisions. His plan was elegant, meticulous, and—in technical terms—near perfect. However, the one thing Larry *didn't* do was to involve his client in the detailed planning of the implementation. When, inevitably, the installation of the new system proved to be harder work than his client had expected, the Motivation Dip hit with a vengeance. Divisional executives became very critical of the new system, and Larry was forced to spend all his time attending meetings to explain the system and to justify his implementation plan. With enormous effort Larry was able to help the client through the Motivation Dip, but it took 2 months of full-time effort before the new system began to produce worthwhile results and the divisional executives slowly turned from criticism to praise.

Although Larry had succeeded in retrieving the first implementation, he realized with alarm that he was just about to run into difficulties with the second implementation, which was due to begin in the other division, the Light Manufacturing Group. Because of the extra effort which the first implementation had required, Larry hadn't had time to produce a detailed implementation plan for the Manufacturing Group. And because the structure of the Group was very different from the structure of the other division, he knew that he couldn't make use of the plan he'd so carefully made for the first implementation. He was caught. Without enough time to plan, he was sure that the Manufacturing Group implementation would be a disaster. Even with the hundreds of careful planning hours he'd put into the first division he'd had severe implementation difficulties. Now, with no time to plan and with the reputation of the Manufacturing Group for being difficult and uncooperative, Larry saw an inevitable failure staring him in the face. "I've no choice," he reasoned to himself. "I've no time to plan the implementation alone, so I'll have to get people from the Manufacturing Group to work on the plan with me." So he set up a number of planning committees. Each committee was headed by an executive who would be affected by the changes that Larry was introducing.

(continued)

The eventual implementation plan produced by these committees had Larry in despair. It was messy and only partly thought out. "This is the end," thought Larry. "They can't possibly put this mess into practice. The whole thing will collapse and I'll be fired."

Nothing could have been further from the truth. The plan *did* get into real difficulties. But whereas the first division had blamed all their difficulties on Larry, the people in the Manufacturing Group—because the implementation plan was *their* plan—took responsibility for their own problems and worked nights and weekends to put things right. The overall implementation was completed in record time, and the Manufacturing executives congratulated themselves, and Larry, on a fine implementation.

When we interviewed Larry he told us, "I used to think that a good plan was one which was technically good. Now I realize that what makes a plan good is whether people are committed to making it work. An average plan which gets real commitment from the people implementing it will always beat a great plan which forgot to involve people." Nobody needed to convince Larry that involving the customer in implementation planning is one of the best ways to overcome the Motivation Dip.

- *Strategy 3: Put in Effort Early.*   People who are effective in implementing any new idea, or installing any new process, tend to concentrate their efforts in the early stages of the implementation. Less experienced salespeople generally don't understand about implementation stages and the Motivation Dip. Consequently, they make a serious mistake during the "New Toy" stage. They see that the customer is positive and excited, so they expect that the whole implementation will continue in an equally positive way. Because of this, they give the account less attention, so they fail to pick up early warning signals of customer learning problems.

During the Learning stage, when customers begin to experience the Motivation Dip, average salespeople are taken by surprise. Because they are unprepared, they wait too long before taking corrective action and then are forced to put in extra effort in attempting to correct the difficulty. It invariably takes longer to retrieve something that's going badly than it does to maintain something that's going well. And retrieving problems not only means additional time, it also creates unnecessary dissatisfaction. Fire prevention is a better strategy than fire fighting. The Motivation Dip will be easier to handle if you put your effort into making sure that fires don't start.

From Installation to Account Development

After you've successfully guided the customer through the installation portion of the cycle, you enter the stage of the Implementation phase which is usually called *account maintenance* or *account development*. I must confess that I much prefer the term *account development*. Although *account maintenance* is widely used to describe all those activities which take place after the contract has been signed, including installation and customer care, in some ways it's a misleading term. "Maintenance" implies that your primary objective is to keep things running the way they are now. Effective account development is much more than that. It's a positive, active process for extending and developing your business.

Sometimes the account development job is relatively simple. Your existing sale gives you access within the account to areas where new problems exist which your products can solve. If you're in the fortunate position of having additional sales opportunities presented to you in this way, then account development begins a new sales cycle, starting with the Recognition of Needs phase. In theory—and, usually, in practice—things are likely to be much simpler the second time around. You already know the account and some of the people. Your product is already established in part of the account. It's easier to find strong internal sponsors. Assuming your product performs well from the first sale, additional sales to an account should require less selling effort.

Why Is Account Development So Important?

But it's not just reduced effort which makes account development attractive and strategically important. Good management of your existing accounts is important because, in the majority of markets, it's the most effective strategy for limiting the opportunities of your competition. Analysis of companies which have lost market share to their competition shows that inadequate attention to existing accounts is often a key reason for competitor success.

Your existing accounts are also an invaluable source of recommendations and third party references. The larger and more complex the sale, the more likely the customer will be to investigate your reputation in existing accounts as a key factor in making the buying decision. In many markets customers talk with each other. Good account development can be a powerful sales tool, making a satisfied customer do some of your selling for you. On the other hand, inadequate attention to existing accounts can give your competitors damaging case study material to use against you. My research team at Huthwaite once followed up 50 lost sales in a capital goods marketplace. In each of the 50, the customer had turned down the final proposal on the grounds of price. In 32 cases out of 50, interviews revealed that price—the "respectable" way to say "No"—was not the primary cause of lost sales. One of the key reasons for customer refusal was that competition had used examples of poor account maintenance to develop insecurity and concern.

But clearly the most important reason for good account maintenance and development is that your existing accounts represent a significant opportunity for increasing business. Particularly if your strategic objective is to maximize short-term sales, existing accounts are the quickest source of additional business.

Five Simple Strategies for Account Development

In many cases, an account that has recently purchased from you doesn't have immediate business potential. Your product or service satisfies the need, and, until something changes, there's no clear opportunity for further sales. Many salespeople play a waiting game, just calling on such an account occasionally, hoping that the inevitable changes over time, such as changes in people, products, or needs, will generate new opportunities. This waiting strategy, although common, is one of the least successful and most expensive ways to do business.

A more positive, and more effective, approach to account development is to use five simple strategies to ensure that visits to existing accounts yield the maximum business benefit.

Strategy 1: Develop, Don't Maintain

When they don't have a concrete sales goal, many salespeople shift their attention to maintaining good personal relationships with existing customers in the account. They feel that a visit, a lunch, and a social chat is worthwhile from time to time just to make sure that the relationship continues. Their objective is often to protect existing business from competitors and to ensure that the customer keeps them in mind should new business opportunities arise.

Unfortunately, this strategy is generally ineffective. Studies of salespeople who are most successful in protecting their existing business base show that the ones who succeed are *not* the ones whose main objective is protection and maintenance. The people who protect their business most successfully are those who are always actively looking for new opportunities in the account. Ironically, if your objective is to maintain or protect, then you'll be more likely to fail than if your objective is to sell. By making every customer care call into a sales call which tries to extend your business, you stand the greatest chance of protecting the business you've already got. So concentrate on account development, not on account maintenance.

Strategy 2: Document the Good News

When things go wrong, we're on the phone; we're visiting; we're writing letters. In other words, we're giving tremendous attention to trouble and how to correct it. What happens when things go right? Most salespeople are so busy that they let success pass unnoticed: nothing is recorded; nothing goes into the files. What's wrong with that? Imagine that a couple of years ago you made a major sale to a company. On the whole your product performed well, but, inevitably, there were a few small problems during the installation stage. As a result, half a dozen letters were written by you and your customer about the problem and how to solve it. Now, 2 years later, imagine there's a new decision maker about to make a repurchase who reads through the file to assess how well you've performed. All the letters are about the problems and trouble. The cumulative effect of the problem letters in the file gives a bad impression because there's no mention of the 95 percent of things which went right.

A quick, easy, and productive strategy in account development is to ensure that your customer's files contain letters about successes, not just problems. Best of all, get these letters and memos from satisfied people in the account. Failing that, write to the customer yourself, outlining the positive and successful impact your product has had, and offering any further help and assistance which the customer might need. In that way, when it's time for repurchase or renegotiation of a contract, you're in a stronger position.

Strategy 3: Generate Leads and References

The problem with satisfied customers is that the better you've satisfied their needs, the less of an immediate business opportunity they provide; but satisfied customers can be invaluable in other ways. Instead of making a visit just to chat with a satisfied customer who doesn't have any needs, use part of that visit to get the customer's agreement to act as a reference for other interested prospects. Or ask for some names of people the customer knows whom you could contact. A satisfied customer who doesn't have any immediate business for you is often delighted to give you contacts and introductions to potential customers in other companies.

However, remember that the customer's enthusiasm is likely to be at its lowest during the Learning stage, when implementation is at its most vulnerable point. So generate leads either very early in the installation process, during the "New Toy" stage, or else wait until your implementation is complete and producing maximum results before asking for introductions and references.

Farmers and Hunters

A few years ago, the popular idea was introduced that there are two types of successful sales personalities, "Farmers" and "Hunters." Farmers, so this idea suggests, are the relationship-oriented salespeople who will "grow" existing accounts and develop more business from them. Hunters are more aggressive salespeople who are best at opening up new frontiers and tracking down new business opportunities. The idea is appealingly simple, but, like many simple concepts, it turned out to be naive and dangerous.

One organization in the computer industry was so taken by this idea that they reorganized their sales force into a hunter group and a farmer group. They gave the hunters responsibility for new accounts and the farmers responsibility for maintaining existing accounts. The policy was a disaster. As one of their executives told us, "Our farmers lost the business to the competition's hunters. We found that the best way to protect an existing account was hunting, not farming."

Our research comes to the same conclusion. If a seller's objective is merely to maintain or modestly develop existing business, then there's a good chance that the business ultimately will be lost to a competitor. We found that the people who did the best job of protecting their existing accounts from competition were those whose objectives were to uncover new and additional business opportunities.

Strategy 4: Reassess Your Understanding of Customer Needs

People who are effective in developing more business from existing accounts will, once or twice a year, visit each of their existing accounts and treat them as if they were new business opportunities. By carefully probing to uncover and develop any needs which have changed, they thoroughly review what's happening in the account. Too many sellers feel this approach is unnecessary because they think they already know all the needs of their existing accounts and feel it would be artificial and time-wasting to go through such a process. In one major company, a group of experienced salespeople were each asked to check out the needs in five of their existing accounts. Although they were initially skeptical and felt the exercise unnecessary, in an average of two accounts out of five, important business opportunities were uncovered. Remember, if *you* don't reassess your understanding of your customers' needs, the competitors will. Competitors get into your accounts by uncovering and developing needs which you've neglected.

Strategy 5: Influence Future Decision Criteria

Even when you find that an existing customer has no needs and can't provide you with leads, a visit can still turn into a positive selling opportunity. By developing the customer's decision criteria you can ensure that, in the event of future needs, your products or services will be judged as stronger than your competitors'. Many salespeople, if they don't see any need, just talk about non-business matters. It's much more powerful to work on decision criteria.

A Strategic Error to Avoid

There's a simple mistake that people make in the strategy they use with existing accounts which results in an enormous loss of potential business. When a new product is announced, most people try to sell it to their key existing accounts first. This is generally a poor strategy. When a product is new, it takes time to learn how to sell it well. Studies show that, at first, salespeople sell new products by talking about the product, not about the customer's needs. Reference to features is, on average, three times as high in calls where a new product is being sold. Start the introduction of new products in your smaller accounts and don't approach your key existing customers until you're confident that you can make a strong needs-based sales call.

A Last Word on Account Development

Your business relationship with an account is never static. It's either getting better, or it's decaying. Never delude yourself into believing that you have a stable relationship which will continue indefinitely and remain invulnerable to competition. Complacency is the worst of all sins with existing accounts. Face the uncomfortable fact that what you did yesterday is history. What counts with most customers is what you're doing for them today and what you can do for them tomorrow. That's what good account development is all about.

9

Anatomy of
a Sales Strategy

In this final chapter I want to bring together the major lessons of the book into a single, complex case study. Inevitably, I'm forced to invent an artificial case—no single real case has all the necessary elements neatly sequenced. So I've constructed this case by combining elements from five different real cases I've worked with. The product I've chosen is a new pump which is being introduced by the Towtron Corporation. Our hero—if you could call him that—is Harry Katt, a bright young business school graduate just beginning a career in major-account selling. Before we start, we know that this will be a tale with a happy ending, unlike so many competitive sales in real life. But, despite its cheerful outcome, notice that even this ideal textbook sale is hard work. Harry Katt's success will come not by chance, but by the careful and painstaking planning and execution of a sales strategy.

February 15: The Product
Launch

Harry Katt sits among the audience of salespeople at the Towtron Corporation's launch of its new product line. The launch has been delayed 6 months because of technical difficulties, and the sales force is now impatient to see the new pumps which are rumored to be a significant technical breakthrough. In particular, Harry is anxious to hear about the Meterflo product, which is the first pumping system in the industry to be microprocessor-controlled. With all the usual fanfare, the new Meterflo pump is presented and members of the launch management

187

team describe all its features. In addition to microprocessor control, it has a newly designed impeller system, and it's much smaller than competitors' pumps of similar capacity.

Everyone in the sales force, including Harry, is excited at what they see. "This will give us the competitive edge we've been waiting for," remarks someone seated near Harry. "At last," says another, "we've something we can use to fight Niagara." (Niagara Pumps is Towtron's chief competitor and, in recent years, has started to eat away at Towtron's share of the specialist applications market.) However, excitement is tempered a little when the sales targets are announced. "I know it's a good pump," Harry tells the person sitting next to him, "but those targets are going to be tough to meet."

February 15: First Thoughts

Back at the office, Harry and several of his colleagues sit around and discuss initial strategy for selling the new Meterflo pump in their territories. The general consensus is that it would be best to start by approaching the biggest existing accounts. Harry is the only dissenting voice. "I think that's dangerous," he explains. "I'd rather practice on a small account first. I've a hunch that this pump isn't going to be an easy sell. I don't want to waste my best accounts by using them for practice." His colleagues laugh. "You're only saying that because you don't *have* any big accounts," teases one of them. Harry shuts up. He knows that what his colleague says is true. His territory has great potential, but he hasn't yet penetrated any of the three large prospects it contains. Nevertheless, he's full of enthusiasm and confident that the new Meterflo pump will be his passport into at least one of these large prospects. "But for now," he decides, "I'll try a couple of smaller accounts first."

February 22: Mistakes in a Small Account

Harry visits a small account. He finds his enthusiasm runs away with him, and he spends almost half an hour telling his customer about every imaginable feature of the new pump. The customer, who knows Harry well, tells him, "You're obviously very excited about this new pump, Harry. But for me it's just another way of getting liquid from point A to point B." Driving back to the office, Harry thinks about what his customer said. "Perhaps I'm *too* enthusiastic," he thinks. "Perhaps I'm letting my enthusiasm get the better of me—I'm giving more attention to the product than to the customer." The more he considers this possibility, the truer it sounds. He realizes that although he would normally ask a lot of questions on a sales call, on this occasion he didn't. Instead, he let the product take over. "Well, I learned something from calling on a small account first," he decides. "In the future I'll be careful not to let my enthusiasm for the product get the better of my concern for the customer."

February 23: Finding a Point of Entry

Harry's manager calls him in. "Where are you going to sell the Meterflo?" she asks him. Harry is cautious. "I'd *like* to sell it to Youngs," he tells her, naming one of the three big prospects in his territory which he is hoping to penetrate. "They have a lot of sophisticated pumping equipment, and, according to some people, they maintain a state-of-the-art system for liquid handling. If I could get in there, then I'm sure that other accounts would follow." "Do you know anyone at Youngs?" asks his manager. "No," concedes Harry, "Niagara has a stranglehold on Youngs, and it's hard to make any contact at all." "I may be able to give you a lead," his manager offers. "It's not a great lead, I'm afraid, but at least it's a start. I know one of their industrial engineers. He wrote an article on handling corrosive liquids a couple of years ago in *Materials Handling,* and some of the article was about pumps. His name's Jim Flood. Give him a call; perhaps he'll see you."

February 25: First Contact with the Account

On his third attempt, Harry gets through on the phone to Jim Flood. "I know you're interested in pumps," he explains, "because I read your article in *Materials Handling.* We're just launching an advanced-technology pump, and I'm trying to get some initial reactions from people like yourself who know about advanced applications." Jim Flood sounds suspicious. "You're not trying to sell me something, are you?" he asks. "Because I have nothing whatsoever to do with the purchase of pumps." "I won't deny that I'd like to make a sale to Youngs," Harry tells him, "but that's not what I want to talk with you about. Youngs is supposed to be very advanced in this area, and you're the person in Youngs who's written about it. I'd be genuinely interested in hearing your thoughts." "Okay," agrees Flood, "I'll give you half an hour on March second. But remember, I hate salesmen."

March 1:   Initial Entry Strategy

The day before his meeting with Flood, Harry sits down to think about strategy. He decides that it's important not to sound as though he's selling something. "I'm not going to try to uncover needs," he thinks. "Instead, I'll genuinely try to find out what Flood feels about things like microprocessor control. Half an hour isn't long. Perhaps I should start with a ten-minute overview and then get Flood talking about what *he* thinks is important in a specialist pumping system."

March 2:   Initial Meeting

The meeting with Flood doesn't turn out as expected. Halfway through the overview Flood is called away. He comes back apologetically 20 minutes later. "I'm sorry," he explains, "an emergency cropped up. I haven't any more time today. Perhaps we could meet again some other time." They agree to meet in a week. Harry leaves disappointed. Was Flood's disappearance a true emergency, or was it a sign of disinterest? Harry decides that Flood's ready agreement to meet again means that he's at least a little interested, so the emergency was probably genuine.

March 9:   Entry Strategy—At the Focus of Receptivity

Harry meets again with Flood. This time Flood does most of the talking. He has strong opinions on current developments in pump technology. Some points in the Meterflo pump he likes and others he doesn't. Harry is very careful not to treat Flood's dislikes as if they are objections to be overcome. "I'm not selling," he reminds himself. "I'm here to listen to a receptive person." Flood has so much to say that he dominates the conversation. At the end of the meeting, Harry still hasn't found out anything about pumping applications in Youngs and about who—if anyone—has problems which the Meterflo pump could solve. Once again, time runs out, and Flood rushes off to another appointment. Harry's only compensation is that Flood declares how much he enjoyed the meeting and suggests a further meeting over lunch in 2 weeks time. "I made progress," Harry thinks to himself afterward, "but I can't afford too many meetings like this one. This sale could take forever."

March 14:   Slow Progress for Harry

There's a team meeting back at the office. Most people are reporting tremendous customer interest in Meterflo which they predict will turn into sales in a couple of months. Harry is despondent. He doesn't see any short-term opportunities and can't believe that people are expecting major sales during the next 2 months. He doesn't take much part in the overall feeling of euphoria in the office.

March 23:   Entry Strategy— Stuck at the Focus of Receptivity

Lunch with Flood. Harry has decided that his objective for this meeting is to find the name of someone at Youngs who has a problem which the Meterflo pump could solve. An even better objective, if Flood will cooperate, is to get an introduction from Flood to this person. "Flood is at the focus of receptivity," thinks Harry. "I need to get to the focus of dissatisfaction."

Flood wants to talk technicalities throughout lunch. Eventually Harry steers the conversation around to whether anyone in Youngs has a problem which Harry's pump could solve. "I guess that the Pigments Department would be the most likely," Flood tells him. "They have to mix very precise amounts of pigment into paints, and your microprocessor technology might be a way around some of the accuracy problems they've been having." Harry tries the big question. "Would you be willing to give me an introduction to them?" he asks. "Sure," says Flood. "Come back to the office with me, and I'll call Keith Bright right now."

Flood is as good as his word. Back at the office he calls Bright. "I've a young fellow here," he tells Bright, "who has a pump which could be just what you're looking for in Pigments. I'd like to fix for the two of you to get together." So a meeting is arranged for March 25th, and Harry leaves feeling very good about the way the account is progressing. "I've moved from the focus of receptivity to the focus of dissatisfaction," he tells himself. "I'm getting deeper into the account, and, judging from what Flood says, they really like the Meterflo concept."

March 25:   Entry Strategy—
Moving to the Focus of
Dissatisfaction

Before the first meeting with Bright, Harry reviews his objectives. "The number one objective," he reminds himself, "is to get Bright's agreement that he's got problems which we could solve with the Meterflo system. That should be easy, given Flood's introduction." His confidence has been given a further boost because Flood called him the previous day to say that, the more he thought about it, the more convinced he was that the Meterflo system would solve the Pigment Department's problems.

But the meeting with Bright is much less smooth than Harry had expected. "Who told you we had a problem?" Bright demands. "Those interfering fools in Industrial Engineering should get their facts right before they stick their noses into other Departments." Harry realizes that he can't move straight to the problem in the way he'd planned. So he tries a less direct approach. "You say that your present system is adequate," he says, "and of course I accept that. But any system—however good—can be improved. If you had a free hand to make any improvements you wanted, what would they be?" Bright thinks for a moment. "Well," he replies, "I *would* like a little more accuracy in metering the pigments." Then, fearing he might have conceded too much, he continues, "But it's not a big problem because we calibrate our existing pumps by making trial batches before each main run."

The conversation then moves to other problems. Most of these are minor, and none, in Harry's judgment, has as much potential as the problem of metering exact quantities—which is an area where the Meterflo system is extremely strong. Harry doesn't get the easy agreement he'd hoped for, but when he reviews the call afterward he feels that he's advanced a little toward his objective. "Bright *does* agree that he has a problem with the accuracy of his present system," Harry tells himself, "but he doesn't feel that the problem is severe. It's clear that the objective of my next call must be to convince him that inaccuracies in his system are more serious than he wants to admit." However, this leaves Harry with a difficulty. He isn't an expert on pigments so he doesn't have any way to assess how severe Bright's problems really are.

March 30:   Entry Strategy—
Identifying Probable
Dissatisfaction

Harry calls Flood for advice. Flood tells him, "I know Bright's getting around the problem by making trial batches. But that's costing him plenty. For one thing, he's using unnecessary pigment. On some of the more expensive pigments that could add up to a couple of hundred dollars wasted in each batch. Another undesirable effect of trial batches is downtime. He's forced to hold up the whole line for at least ten minutes every time he makes a change in his mix. I don't know exactly what that costs, but I'd guess that it would be safe to assume it's at least fifty dollars per minute."

April 13:   The Recognition of
Needs Phase

Harry hears that Bright is prepared to meet with him again on the following afternoon. He prepares his selling strategy. "My objective," he tells himself, "is to get Bright to agree that the accuracy problem has some serious implications for the efficiency of the Pigment Department. I know that Bright will be resistant if I try to *tell* him his department's in trouble, so I'll have to ask the kinds of questions which will lead him to that conclusion himself."

April 14:   Recognition of
Needs—Uncovering
Dissatisfaction

The second meeting with Bright takes place. This time Bright has included one of his assistants in the discussion. Although Harry interprets this as a promising sign of interest, he realizes that it's now particularly important not to seem to criticize Bright's handling of the department. So he cautiously asks questions. "I don't understand the economics of your line," he begins, "so I don't know what it's costing you in downtime every time you make a test batch. Do you know the figures?" Bright is obliging. "We have a standard costing system we use to assess our downtime throughout the factory," he tells Harry. "In the case of this line I'm rated at eighty-five dollars per minute." "And a test batch takes about ten minutes?" asks Harry. "Yes," Bright replies. Then, doing a few calculations of his own, Bright adds, "That means 850 dollars per test. We do about nine tests per day, which means that we're using upwards of 7500 dollars in downtime every day. Of course, even if we had automatic computer-controlled calibration on our pumps we wouldn't save *all* that time, because we still have to flush out the system before we change the mix. But if we saved, shall we say, *half* the downtime—that would be 15,000 dollars or more per week." This is music to Harry's ears. A complete Meterflo system would cost about $450,000. From what he is hearing, it could pay for itself in less than 9 months. As the conversation continues, further savings appear. There's a potential in saved pigment costs of about $2500 a week. And there are less obvious savings, too. Waste pigment creates a difficult and expensive disposal problem. An automatically calibrated system could save another $500 a month in hazardous waste disposal costs. By the end of the conversation, both Bright and Harry are agreed that the installation of a $450,000 Meterflo system would probably pay for itself in less than 6 months. Even Bright's assistant gets excited. "This could give us bigger savings than the new synthetic pigment project," he says. Bright agrees. "I think there are some exciting possibilities here."

The meeting ends on a high note. "I'll work out some exact figures here," promises Bright. "Meanwhile, I'd like you to work out some ballpark costs for installing a complete Meterflo system. I don't want a formal proposal at this stage, but some written costs would be helpful."

Harry is taken aback by how fast and how easily things have happened. "Maybe the others are right," he thinks. "Maybe you *can* sell these systems in just two months."

April 15:   Initial Costings

Harry works through some preliminary costings. To his surprise, they turn out to be higher than he expected—just under $540,000. However, he doesn't feel unduly worried because the payback period is so dramatically short. But he decides, in view of these cost increases, that it would be better for him to present the figures personally and not trust them to a letter. Accordingly he makes an appointment to see Bright again on April 22nd.

April 18:   Hot Prospects
Evaporate

In the afternoon there's the monthly meeting of the whole sales team. The mood is less cheerful than it had been a month earlier. Out of a total of 16 promising prospects identified last month for the Meterflo system, seven have been lost. For the nine remaining prospects, each person, in turn, describes where they are in the sale and what their strategy is for the next step. When Harry's turn comes he explains, "This sale is now well into the Recognition of Needs phase. At our last sales team meeting I was still trying to use Jim Flood to help me gain access to people at the focus of dissatisfaction. I've now found those people, and I've got their agreement that the problem is serious and that the cost of a Meterflo system can probably be justified. I'm presenting written costings next week." "Wait until they see the cost," warns a team member whose most promising prospect has just turned him down. "My customer was all excited until people realized what the system would cost; then they turned tail and ran."

Thinking about this comment after the meeting, Harry decides that he shouldn't worry. "What's different," he tells himself, "is that I've tried to build value *before* talking about costs. But some of the others have been presenting costs without first building up the needs. No wonder they've been turned down."

April 22:   Identifying the
Focus of Power

Harry is due to present his costings to Bright. He thinks about his strategy for the call. "I've developed Bright's needs," he decides, "but I may still be at the focus of dissatisfaction. I don't know if Bright has the power to make a half-million-dollar decision. I'd better find that out, because if he can't authorize the decision I'll have to find some way to reach the focus of power." At the meeting Harry explains his costings to Bright, who doesn't seem taken aback that the price has risen by almost $90,000. "I've been working on the potential savings," he explains to Harry, "and they come out at about 870,000 dollars a year. Even with your increased price that's a payback within eight months." Harry is delighted at Bright's positive response.

Remembering that his objective for the call was to find the focus of power, Harry tries to discover whether Bright can authorize a decision this large. Bright is candid. "My authority stops at 100,000 dollars," he says. "A decision this size would have to go all the way to the Head of

Manufacturing, who's two levels above me." Harry immediately attempts to gain access to the decision maker. "Would you like me to
make a presentation to him, showing the savings he'd get from a
Meterflo system?" he asks. Bright appears horrified. "Oh, no," he tells
Harry. "That would be more than my job's worth. He doesn't see
vendors." "Then how will he get the information he needs to make the
decision?" asks Harry. "First I'll present it to my boss," explains Bright,
"then if my boss buys it, we'll go together and present it to the Head of
Manufacturing." "Then perhaps I should at least come with you when
you present it to your boss," suggests Harry. Bright again refuses, but
he agrees to meet Harry on April 25th so that Harry can help him prepare his case.

"This isn't ideal," thinks Harry as he drives home, "especially as it's
got to go through two levels of presentation. But at least I'm helping
him to prepare, so it isn't necessarily a disaster if I can't get face-to-face
with the focus of power."

April 25: Recognition of Needs—Rehearsing the Sponsor

Harry helps Bright prepare his case. With some difficulty Harry re-
sists the temptation to tell Bright what to say. Instead he asks questions which get Bright to explain the benefits of changing to a
computer-controlled pumping system. "Why is it so important to reduce hazardous waste?" he asks. "Cost," Bright replies. "It would
save 500 dollars a month in disposal cost." "Is there any other advantage to reducing hazardous waste?" asks Harry. Bright thinks for a
moment. "I know that the Head of Manufacturing has come under
criticism from other board members for unfavorable publicity about
a toxic waste spill," he says, "so he's under pressure to clean up our
act. Maybe he'd like to see a positive step to reduce hazardous waste.
In fact, that's probably far more important to him than a 500-dollar-
a-month saving." In this way, by asking questions, Harry forces
Bright to think about what he intends to present and helps him to
rehearse his message. The meeting goes well, and, at the end of it,
Harry feels confident that Bright can do a good job on his behalf at
the focus of power.

May 5:   The Recognition of
Needs Phase Ends

Despite his impatience to hear how things are going at Youngs, Harry busies himself with other accounts and does nothing until he hears from Bright. Late in the afternoon, a breathless Bright calls. "I've got approval," he tells Harry. "I've a budget of 550,000 dollars for replacing our old system." Harry is delighted. Several of his colleagues congratulate him as if he's been awarded the contract. "Hold on," warns Harry. "It's not that easy. I've only succeeded in the Recognition of Needs phase of the sale. The really tough work is just about to start. Now that the Evaluation of Options phase is beginning, I imagine that the competition will be knocking on the door at Youngs."

May 16:   Entering the
Evaluation of Options Phase

In his report to the monthly sales meeting, Harry describes what's been happening in his account. "As I suspected," he tells the group, "there's a long way further to go before we get the business at Youngs. After Bright called me on the fifth, he didn't call me again and he didn't return my calls. Then, next thing I knew, I received a Request for Proposal (RFP) from Youngs' Purchasing Department. When I called Purchasing they told me that Youngs is setting up an evaluation committee to look at new pump systems. They wouldn't tell me who the other vendors are, but it's clear that Niagara will be one of them." "That's bad news," says Sally, Harry's manager. "I hear that Niagara is just about to introduce a line of computer-controlled pumps. We could be in for a tough battle."

Harry isn't unduly worried. "At least we've influenced the specification," he reminds her. "That's a good outcome for the Recognition of Needs phase—we've not only persuaded them they want a new pump system, but we've also got them to want features where the Meterflo is strong." Harry reads from the RFP's technical specification. "Listen to this," he says. "'Flow capacity of ninety liters per minute, precision dispensing to within .005 percent of specified volume, stability across temperature range of ten to forty-five degrees centigrade, accuracy unaffected by viscosity changes...' Meterflo is the strongest pump on the market in those terms. I think that our strategy has been good so far."

Sally is more cautious. "The Evaluation of Options phase will be harder," she says. "Niagara is well entrenched at Youngs and they've a lot of friends. The next steps won't be easy, but I'm delighted we've made such a good start. You've certainly handled the Recognition of Needs phase well." Harry is flattered. Sally doesn't offer praise indiscriminately, and he feels pleased that she approves of his strategy so far.

May 17: Bad news—and a Strategic Mistake

Sally's predictions of difficulty come true in an unexpected way. Harry is still congratulating himself on how well things have been going as he makes another attempt to contact Bright. "I'm sorry," the Youngs switchboard operator tells him. "Mr. Bright has left the company." Harry realizes why his calls to Bright haven't been returned. He also realizes that he's made a dangerous, possibly fatal, strategic error. He's relied on one person to be his sponsor. Now that Bright has left Youngs there's nobody—with the possible exception of Bright's assistant, whom Harry's only met once—to give him sponsorship at the focus of dissa isfaction.

Harry's strategy is thrown into uncertainty. "It's bad enough tha Bright has gone," he thinks, "but it's worse that I don't know *why* he's gone. What if he's been dismissed? Nobody will want to take on the sponsorship of a project started by someone who's been fired." He decides to call Flood, his initial contact at the focus of receptivity. As he calls he realizes that he has made another mistake. He last called Flood back in March. If he'd been smarter about it he would have at least kept in contact with him. Now it might appear to Flood that Harry only uses him when it suits him.

Fortunately for Harry, Sally mailed out a technical review of the Meterflo system 3 weeks ago to everybody on her mailing list, including Flood. Initially Flood assumes Harry is calling to find out his reaction to the review. "It's an impressive system," Flood tells him, "and, except for a few questions about reliability, the review really comes out positively. Thank you for sending it." Flood gives Harry some welcome news. "Yes," he says, "Bright's left us. But he's gone to head up manufacturing in a new organization that's part of the Youngs Group. We were all sorry to see him go, but we wish him the best in his promotion." Harry is relieved. "At least nobody's going to be against us just because we were sponsored by Bright," he thinks.

Flood also reveals another piece of good news when he tells Harry about the evaluation committee and who's on it. There are six members, and Flood himself is to be one of them. The committee will have its first meeting on May 23d. Flood agrees to meet Harry on the day after the first committee meeting.

May 24:   Decision Criterion Strategy

Harry spends the morning planning his strategy for the meeting with Flood. "My first strategic objective," he thinks, "is to find out which decision criteria the committee will be using to make its recommendation. Even more important, I should try to find out whether some of these criteria are more crucial than others. Then, if I can, I should try to find out something about who the competition will be."

The meeting with Flood turns out to be less useful than Harry had hoped. "I can certainly give you some of the criteria we discussed," says Flood, "but I can't tell you that any one criterion is more important than others. As far as we are concerned, they are *all* crucial." But, even though Harry can't discover the relative importance of the committee's criteria, he does get an initial idea of the principal factors which Youngs will be taking into account in making the decision. Flood tells him that most of the committee meeting was spent discussing three topics. One, naturally, is *price.* Youngs is under a budget restraint, and there's some pressure to look for a cheaper system if possible. However, in view of the very large savings which the new system should give, Flood doesn't think that price will be a showstopper. "But," he warns, "if we find that your competition is cheaper than you are, then that will certainly influence our thinking."

Another discussion topic, Flood explains, was the importance of good *maintenance support.* Youngs has been in trouble in the past from buying equipment which has performed badly because the vendor failed to provide adequate maintenance. Maintenance support is an area where Harry's competitor, Niagara, is particularly strong. The third factor Flood mentions is *accuracy.* As he explains, it's the lack of accuracy of the old system which is the reason for change. "We'll want concrete proof that the vendor we choose can meet our accuracy specification," warns Flood. Harry's glad to hear this. The Meterflo system is the most accurate available, although the new system from Niagara—with a specification which has not yet been made public—is rumored to be at least equally accurate. But none of the other pump manufacturers has anything which even comes close to Meterflo.

Flood also tells Harry a little about other vendors. "We sent the RFP to twenty-three vendors," he explains, "including you and Niagara.

We'll screen replies and we expect to find six or seven serious ones. By the way, remember that your own reply must reach us by the end of the week."

May 25:   Initial Reply to the RFP

Harry drafts an initial reply to Youngs's RFP. In his reply he focuses on *accuracy*—the area which he knows is important to Youngs and where Meterflo is strongest. His objective is to get through the first screening, so he keeps his submission short, knowing that the committee will probably be reading as many as 20 submissions from other vendors.

May 31:   Success—Surviving the Initial Screening

Harry gets a formal letter from the committee informing him that he's succeeded in the first phase of the evaluation. He will now be one of six vendors invited to make a final bid. If he wishes, the letter says, Harry can talk to a subcommittee of two people who will be available to spend time with each vendor. Almost before he's finished reading the letter, Harry is on the phone setting up an appointment. "I want to get to those two first," he tells himself. "I've got to influence their decision criteria before they start talking to other vendors." A meeting with the subcommittee is set up for June 7th. Harry will be the first vendor to talk with them. Unfortunately, however, Harry doesn't know either of the people. His friend Flood is not on the subcommittee.

June 7:   Uncovering and Influencing Decision Criteria

Harry meets the two subcommittee members. His strategic objective is to uncover and influence their decision criteria. The meeting doesn't begin well. Both the committee members are cold and formal. "This is their first meeting with a vendor," realizes Harry, "and they are being very cautious. Maybe it wasn't such a good idea to get in first." On the spot he revises his objective. "I'll try to influence their criteria now," he thinks to himself, "but I'll also try to set up a second meeting, after they've met some other vendors, so that they'll be more relaxed."

During the discussion, Harry finds that Flood has given him a fairly accurate picture of what's important to Youngs in making this decision. But, possibly as a result of having more time to think about their criteria, the subcommittee is beginning to accept that some criteria will be more important than others. At the top of their list comes *accuracy*. Somewhere beneath it comes *maintenance support* and *price*. They also give Harry a new criterion, *quality*. Harry probes to find how they currently judge the Meterflo system in terms of each criterion.

The two subcommittee members ask Harry some questions about the Meterflo system. In his answers, Harry is careful to show how effectively Meterflo can meet their most crucial criterion of *accuracy*. Whenever possible during the discussion, he reinforces the importance of this criterion because he knows it's an area where he's strong. Harry succeeds in his objective of arranging a second meeting. The meeting will be held the following week with the whole six-person committee, not just the two people he's meeting with now.

June 8:   Decision Criterion Analysis

Back at his office Harry reviews his meeting with the subcommittee. From his understanding of their decision criteria he draws a simple scale, illustrated in Figure 9.1, showing the relative importance of each criterion and—next to it—another scale showing how he thinks Youngs is judging the Meterflo system in terms of each criterion.

This simple decision criterion analysis allows Harry to see some of the strengths and weaknesses of his position. For example, he's strong in terms of *accuracy*, so he was smart to reinforce its importance during yesterday's meeting with the subcommittee. He's also strong in terms of *quality*. However, quality is a "soft" differentiator, and he may have to help the committee get a clearer understanding of what pump quality really means. Turning his attention to areas where he is weak, Harry immediately picks out *maintenance support*. His company, Towtron, has had a mediocre record in this area and—despite some recent improvements—Harry knows that this will be a potentially difficult area as the sale progresses.

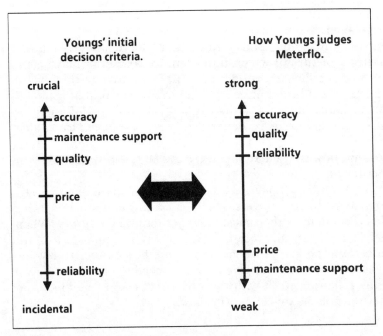

Figure 9-1. Youngs's initial decision criteria.

June 9:   Understanding the Competition

Harry realizes that he needs to know more about his competition in order to discover whether his weaknesses are serious. His weakness in maintenance support, for example, will be a severe disadvantage if his principal competitor turns out to be Niagara, who has a fine record in this area. On the other hand, several other potential competitors have a weaker maintenance support capability than Harry. If they are in the running and not Niagara, Harry needn't be too concerned about his weak maintenance support.

Harry calls Flood in an attempt to find out more information. Flood has both good and bad news. On the plus side, Flood tells him that the six contenders have been reduced to three and that Harry is one of them. On the minus side, Flood reveals that one competitor is Harry's dreaded foe, Niagara. The other is Peterpumps, a Boston-based company that Harry doesn't know much about except that they have a reputation for low prices, although their technology is not particularly advanced. Harry decides that Niagara is the main worry, so he delicately tries to find out how the committee is assessing them. "Their new pump," Flood tells him, "is very similar to yours. Price is one area where Niagara is better than you, although you're both too expensive in my opinion. I know that you've a good reputation for product quality, and that's one of your strongest points with the committee. Personally, I'm not quite sure that the committee knows what it means when it says 'quality is important.' But that's a minor point, because I would guess that Peterpumps and Niagara must be OK in terms of quality, too, or they wouldn't be in business."

Harry realizes that although he's seen to be strong in terms of quality, this may not give him much competitive advantage because quality is a "soft" differentiator. Flood and the others seem unclear about just what they mean by "quality," so Harry wants to try to define it for them in harder and more objective terms. Consequently, he asks Flood to explain what he thinks "quality" means when judging a pump. From the discussion, Harry is able to help Flood define quality more precisely in terms of such factors as impeller durability, bearing wear resistance, and chamber tolerance—all objectively measurable areas where the Meterflo pump is superior.

Before the conversation ends, Harry discovers that the committee is impressed with Niagara's record for maintenance support and that—as he suspected—his own company's record in this area is seen as very weak.

June 10:   A Competitor Is Eliminated

It's another of those good news, bad news days. Harry learns that the third competitor, Peterpumps, has been eliminated. That's good news. But, for Harry, it's not so good to be left with Niagara as his rival—particularly as he's now had a chance to find out the details of Niagara's new pump, which seems to match his own in terms of accuracy. To help him decide on the best competitive strategy for dealing with Niagara, Harry carries out a vulnerability analysis, illustrated in Figure 9.2. To do this he adds another column to the decision criterion analysis he's already carried out, which shows how he thinks Youngs is judging Niagara.

Harry looks at the vulnerability analysis, trying to isolate any areas where he is vulnerable to competition from Niagara. He sees the characteristic V shape which signifies vulnerability in two areas. One is price, where Niagara's new pump—according to Flood—is stronger, that is, cheaper, than Meterflo. Harry isn't too concerned about his price weakness because the new system will pay for itself in less than a

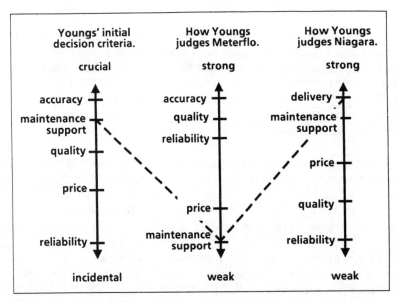

Figure 9-2. Vulnerability analysis.

year and—compared with the potential savings—cost differences between the Meterflo and the Niagara systems aren't great.

Where Harry *is* vulnerable is in the area of maintenance support. He realizes that this will be a crucial area for discussion when he meets with the committee next week, so he plans a strategy for handling this vulnerable area.

June 14: Presenting the Fit to the Committee

Harry meets the full committee. He makes a presentation showing the advantages of the Meterflo system in terms of the objective quality elements he discussed with Flood. He reminds the committee that the small price difference between vendors has to be seen in the context of the enormous savings which the new system will bring. "Because this new system is going to have such a big impact on your whole production process," says Harry, "it's more important to install whichever system is *best* than whichever is cheapest." He's gratified to see that several members nod their heads in agreement.

Then Harry comes to the maintenance support issue, where he knows he's vulnerable. He takes the bull by the horns. "I know you're worried about maintenance support," he begins. "And you're quite right to be worried, because you can't afford to have poor support for a system this important." Looking at the faces of several committee members he realizes that they hadn't expected this frank admission from him. "That means they must feel I'm *really* weak," he thinks. Then he tries to *redefine* maintenance support. "Maintenance support," he suggests, "is another way of saying that you want to be sure that breakdowns happen infrequently and, when they do happen, that they are dealt with quickly so that there's a minimum of downtime." He sees a nod from Flood and continues, "Perhaps, then, when you say that maintenance support is an important factor in your decision, you're really saying that you want a system with as little downtime as possible. Would that be an acceptable way to put it?" "Yes," says a committee member, "because the savings this system is supposed to bring could be completely wiped out if it's always breaking down." "Precisely," replies Harry, "and that's why minimizing downtime is so important. But is maintenance support the only way—or even the most important way—to minimize downtime?" "How else would you do it?" asks a member. "Well," replies Harry, "suppose one system was designed in such a way that it was more *reliable* than the other; then, with the same level of maintenance support, it would break down less often."

Flood immediately sees where Harry is leading and challenges him. "You're going to tell us that your system is more reliable, so it needs less maintenance support," he tells Harry. "I'll need some convincing proof before I buy that." "But," replies Harry, "whether or not I could give you that proof, would you accept the idea that the more reliable the design, the less maintenance support it will need?" "I'll accept that in theory," Flood agrees, "but I still want some convincing evidence before I accept that Meterflo is more reliable than the Niagara system."

Harry takes a deep breath. "It will take me ten minutes," he tells Flood, "but if you can spare that time, I believe I can convince you." "Sure," says a committee member, "this is a very important issue. I'd be more than willing to give you half an hour if you've really got some evidence." "Ten minutes is all I'll need," Harry says confidently. He then crisply and quickly summarizes five ways in which the design of the Meterflo pump will offer superior reliability. It's an impressive performance, especially as it seems unrehearsed. However, what the committee *doesn't* know is that last week—once Harry had identified this as his main vulnerability—he spent several days working on this part of his presentation. He talked with his technical experts and called Towtron's specialists on competitive technology to find all the potential reliability weaknesses of the Niagara system.

During the presentation itself, Harry is careful never to mention

Niagara directly. Whenever he exposes a weakness, it's *generic*. For example, he says, "One of the strongest reliability design factors in the Meterflo system is that the main microprocessors are housed in the control console and not on the pump itself. This reduces vibration. Our tests showed that designs where the microprocessor is integral with the pump have 30 percent more breakdowns due to the unavoidable vibration levels." Niagara, of course, has designed their microprocessors to be integral with the pump. By exposing this generic disadvantage, Harry is able to reduce the committee's confidence in Niagara's reliability without directly knocking the competition.

The meeting ends well. "You did a good job of convincing us that Meterflo is likely to be the most reliable system—and that's a big help in overcoming our concerns about maintenance support," the chairman tells him. Harry feels that his strategy has been effective.

June 16:   Pressure to Negotiate

Flood calls Harry. "We've just had a presentation from Niagara," he tells him. "We let them know that we were leaning toward the Meterflo system, and they suddenly offered us a significant additional discount. I can't tell you how much because they asked us to keep it confidential, but it *is* substantial."

Harry thinks about this new turn of events. He decides to go to his manager. "What can we do?" he asks. "Youngs will be expecting us to cut our price." His manager is cautious. "Let's not overreact," she warns. "I think that Niagara has started to negotiate too soon. It's a sign that they are panicking. We should hold steady at the price we quoted." Harry's not entirely convinced, but he has no choice. Without his manager's approval he has no authority to reduce quoted prices.

June 17:   An Ominous Sign

Harry calls Flood. Flood is in a meeting and doesn't return his call.

June 21:   Danger Signal

Harry calls Flood. Flood is unavailable. Harry realizes that this may be a signal that the sale is entering the Resolution of Concerns phase and that Flood and his colleagues are facing some Consequence issues.

June 22: Hints That
Consequence Issues Exist

Harry comes in early. He knows that Flood gets in half an hour before his staff arrives. He calls him and gets straight through. Flood tells him that the committee is "having some internal discussions" and will be in touch as soon as these are complete. He declines to give further details. Then, without any warning, he asks, "Did your company install one of these Meterflo systems in United Resins?" Sensing danger, Harry replies, "I'm not sure, would you like me to check?" "You should do more than check," says Flood, ominously. Harry's not sure what Flood means but senses that Flood is giving him some kind of warning. After a couple of pleasantries, the conversation ends.

June 23: The Resolution of
Concerns Phase

Harry tracks down the history of the Meterflo installation at United Resins. He finds that this was an early test of the system before its general release. The system ran into severe reliability problems, and, as a result, the design was changed. Since the United Resins test there have been a total of 17 other systems installed, and, so far as Harry can discover, none of them has suffered from the problem experienced by the United Resins prototype. Harry gets some names of satisfied people at United Resins, both production managers and technical staff. He calls several of these people to be sure that they will speak well of Meterflo if asked for a reference.

Late in the day, Harry receives a call from Flood. "The committee feels your price is too high," Flood tells him. "They want to meet you next week for a final price negotiation." Harry agrees to meet the committee on June 29th but arranges a brief lunch meeting with the committee chairman and with Flood on the day before he sees the committee.

Harry sees his manager and explains what's happened. "I don't think that price is the real issue," he tells her. "I'm only guessing, but I bet that Niagara told them horror stories about the installation at United Resins—and now they are worried again about our reliability and maintenance support." "I'm glad to hear that you don't think it's a price issue," she tells him, "because I've just heard from Division that the maximum price discount we can give on this order is five percent." Harry is stunned. "They'll be insulted if I offer only five percent," he tells her. "I was hoping for at least twice that."

Harry returns miserably to his office. Clearly the sale is going Niagara's way, and he now has minimal negotiating leverage. Next week's meetings, he realizes, will be tough.

June 25: Strategic Decisions to Resolve Consequences

Harry spends the weekend thinking about strategy for the following week. He realizes that, during the couple of hours he will have with the committee, he can make or break a sale which has taken him nearly 6 months of hard work.

Harry makes two strategic decisions. First he decides he must uncover any Consequence issues and deal with them. The time to do that will be at his lunch with Flood and the committee chairman. Harry wishes that he'd been able to arrange this meeting to take place a couple of days earlier, but he's hopeful that, even at this late stage, he can use it to resolve the reliability issue.

Harry's second strategic decision is that he will lay out a carefully supported implementation plan at the full committee meeting. Instead of using his 5 percent price reduction as a cash incentive, he uses it to pay for additional training support which he will offer when he presents his plan.

June 28: Handling Consequences

Lunch with Flood and the committee chairman. Harry, knowing he hasn't much time, takes the initiative. "We'll be meeting tomorrow to discuss price," he begins, "but I get a suspicion that price isn't the most important issue on your minds. Something seems to be troubling you." The chairman seems reluctant to talk, but Flood replies, "I hope this system is as reliable as you claim it is." Harry explores this further. "I sense that reliability continues to be a worry to you," he says, "and that nothing I can say will change that. What can I do to help you feel more comfortable?" Flood thinks. "You *say* that it's the most reliable system on the market," he tells Harry, "but we've received information which suggests that your system has some real reliability problems." Harry realizes that he's guessed correctly, that Niagara has been telling tales about the test at United Resins. "What we need," Flood continues, "is some way to find out who's telling the truth here. You say that the Meterflo system is reliable, others say that it isn't. Who do we believe?"

Harry has anticipated this. He takes a paper marked "Towtron Corporation: Confidential" from his briefcase. "On this sheet of paper," he tells Flood, "are the names of our test site and of the other seventeen installations we've made so far. Would it be useful for you to call some of these people to find out their independent experiences with the system?" Flood looks at the list. He sees that United Resins is the first name. "Was this your test site?" he asks. "Yes," Harry explains, "we made a lot of design changes from what we learned at United Resins. To be frank with you, the system we installed there was much less reliable than the others. But perhaps it would be good for you to talk with United Resins anyway. After all, you need to protect yourself against the worst case. United Resins *is* our worst case. Why don't I give you a couple of names of people you can call."

Harry leaves the meeting happy. He knows that the three names he has given will all give a positive report which will undermine Niagara's credibility. As Flood and his colleague prepare to leave, Harry can't resist a direct shot at Niagara. "It's easy," he remarks, "to search out one bad experience and to use it to undermine another vendor. I could do that right now in this sale. But I don't think that's a useful or ethical way to do business."

June 29: The Consequence
Issue Is Resolved

As committee members assemble for the meeting with Harry, Flood leans across the table and tells him, "Those people at United Resins gave a very good report on how your technical folk helped them get the system right. It seems that it's now working even better than they had expected." This, of course, isn't news to Harry. His conversations last week with the United Resins people had confirmed that they would be a good reference.

This meeting is more relaxed than earlier ones, and Harry senses that the reliability issue is finally resolved. The chairman begins, "We're having one final meeting with each vendor. We meet you today and we meet your competitor on Friday. At this meeting we'd like to know what your final price offer will be. Most of our vendors will negotiate price, and we'd like to hear your final discount offer before we make the decision."

Harry takes a risk. "We're not discounting Meterflo any further," he tells them. "In fact, now that it's establishing itself so well in the marketplace, we anticipate that we'll be increasing our prices on future contracts. So let me tell you bluntly that I'm not going to offer you a straight price discount." This is not what the committee had been expecting and there are murmurs of protest. "I've slipped up here," Harry admits to himself. "I should have let them know this was coming. I've let them build up their expectations. They expected a reduction and I'm not giving it."

Before committee members have a chance to voice their reaction, Harry continues, "However, I *do* understand that you're looking for the best possible deal, and I want to offer everything possible to help you. I can't offer you a direct price cut, but I *can* give you the equivalent of one by offering you free support and help in a number of areas which will ensure a smoother implementation." Harry then unveils his implementation plan. Into his plan he's built considerable extra training and technical support. "All this additional support," he tells the committee, "will be at our expense. This is an indirect way to give you a price reduction. Several times during this sale you've expressed real concern about whether the implementation would be well supported. I've taken your concerns to heart. I think you'll agree that the true value to you of all this additional support is many times its cost."

The committee is visibly impressed by Harry's plan, and it's clear that the additional support he's offering has created a very positive impression.

June 30:   More Pressure to Negotiate Price

Harry calls Flood, who confirms that the committee liked Harry's implementation support plan. However, Flood warns him, "You upset them when you said you wouldn't negotiate price. If Niagara offers them a further discount tomorrow, then you're in trouble."

July 1:   The Competitor Responds

Harry spends an anxious day. He knows that Niagara is presenting to the committee, and he fears that it may offer a dramatic price reduction. "But it can't be *too* dramatic," he reminds himself, "because they made a 15 percent cut early on. They haven't much room to play with." Harry hears nothing from Youngs. Today is Friday—and a holiday weekend is coming up. Harry is forced to spend the holiday in suspense and uncertainty.

July 5: Uncertainty in the Negotiation

Flood calls Harry to tell him that Niagara has asked to be given until the end of the week to see if it can come up with a better offer. "They *did* begin negotiating too soon," thinks Harry. "I bet they wish they hadn't offered a full 15 percent last month. They've nothing left." But Harry reminds himself that it's dangerous to make assumptions. It's possible that the delay is because a special deal is being worked out at top levels within Niagara.

July 12: Success at Last

Harry gets a call from the committee chairman. It's the first time he's called, so Harry knows it's important. "Your competitors have come back to us with an improved offer," he begins. Harry's heart sinks. "So Niagara *did* make a special deal," he thinks. Then the chairman continues, "However, it was only a small improvement, and, on balance, we liked your implementation proposals better. Congratulations, the contract is yours."

Harry puts the phone down. For a moment he has that curiously empty feeling that comes when a long hard struggle ends. He goes through the office, and, mysteriously, everybody seems to know what's happened. "Congratulations!" and "Well done, Harry!" they call after him as he disappears into his manager's office.

"You've handled this sale well," his manager tells him. "A few minor errors and miscalculations, but every sale has some of those. Overall you put together a sound strategy. What will you do now?" Harry hadn't been expecting this question. "I feel like taking a long vacation," he tells her, "but now that the Youngs sale is over, I guess what I'll *actually* do is get back to some of the other accounts I've been neglecting during the last few weeks. It will be a big relief to forget Youngs for a while."

His manager smiles. "I was just about to tell you that you'd handled your selling strategy so well that there wasn't any real suggestion I could make for improvement," she says, "but you've just given me one." Harry groans. "Yes," he replies, "I know. Give *more* attention to the customer immediately after the sale." "And remember that the sales cycle doesn't end when the contract's signed," adds his manager. "The next few weeks will be even busier for you at Youngs."

"You're right—the sales effort never ends," says Harry wearily. He returns to his desk and, with a deep sigh, begins writing a thank you letter to the committee chairman. "Selling strategy," he tells himself, "is like any other form of genius—it requires an infinite capacity for taking pains."

Harry's success illustrates the central theme of this book. Effective strategy isn't about grand design, and it isn't about clever tricks. It's about a thorough understanding of your customers and the concerns which they have at each phase of a sale. If, like Harry in our case study, you can use a simple logical understanding of customer behavior to anticipate your customers' concerns and to respond to them effectively, then that's all the strategy you need to be successful in major sales.

INDEX

About the Author

Neil Rackham is President and founder of Huthwaite, Inc. His organization researches, consults, and gives seminars for over 200 leading sales organizations around the world, including Xerox, IBM, AT&T, Kodak, and Citicorp. His academic background is in research psychology. It was at the University of Sheffield, England that he began his research into sales effectiveness that resulted in *Major Account Sales Strategy* and its companion volume, *Spin Selling* (also published by McGraw-Hill). He is the author of over 50 articles and several books which have been translated into a total of 11 languages.

Huthwaite, Inc.
Wheatland Manor
15164 Berlin Turnpike
Purcellville, VA 20132 USA
(540) 882-3212 (telephone)
(540) 822-9004 (fax)